FULL FATHOM FIVE

THE MACMILLAN COMPANY
NEW YORK · BOSTON · CHICAGO · DALLAS
ATLANTA · SAN FRANCISCO

THE "DUNCAN DUNBAR"

FULL FATHOM FIVE

A BOOK OF FAMOUS SHIPWRECKS

BY

FRANK H. SHAW

Author of
Knocking Around, On Great Waters, Haven of Desire, Etc.

Illustrated

NEW YORK
THE MACMILLAN COMPANY
1930

TO

MRS. GEOFFREY MALINS

IN APPRECIATION OF HER HELP

CONTENTS

ILLUSTRATIONS

FULL FATHOM FIVE

CHAPTER I

INTRODUCTORY

THOUGH the magical trend of modern science has ridded the sea of most of its hazards, and tamed its worst rigours, we are reminded every so often—too often alas!—that the ultimate victory remains with the never quite conquered oceans. As it was two thousand years ago when Phœnician traders dared the bitter Atlantic waters in frail craft that were at the mercy of every furious gale that blew; so it is to-day: and all man's ingenuity cannot make his sea-transport invulnerable.

Twenty centuries ago dark-skinned mothers and wives bewailed the non-return of some tin-laden galley from the mysterious Isles of the West: some gallant sea-fighting fabric had sunk, lonely but battling, into the snarling swirls of Biscay's Bay; only yesterday or thereabouts, other women shed tears over those who failed to return from the pitiful *Vestris*. The sea plays with loaded dice, and such as escape its devastating maw might well congratulate themselves on safe faring, rather than deplore the fact that the ship bearing them over almost incredible distances is an hour behind her scheduled time, or that the supply of oysters and caviare has run short of demand. For whether propelled by sail or steam, motor-power or electricity, a ship is nevertheless a ship, and, in consequence, vulnerable.

To walk conqueringly, with thrown-back head and inflated chest, up the easy slope of the *Majestic's* gently-throbbing deck as she thrusts her impetuous, all-conquering bow to the howling west, is good for the body; and good, too, for the soul; the sea from such a vantage-ground is a negligible enemy. To cling to a humming shroud aboard a distressed windjammer, and watch how sea after devastating, merciless sea, roars aboard and tears piece after piece of her solid structure away as if it were paper or pasteboard, is to know humility and awe—and, more than all, a vast and abiding admiration of such as ever picked up the gauntlet thrown down by old Ocean, and built sea-worthy craft to engage in the tireless, unending war. To know a wonder and something more than wonder at the staunch fearlessness of those who dare the sea in search of its secrets; to learn the inwardness of sea-fighters, who realise that they are at odds with an enemy never disposed to show mercy, and never to abide by the ordinary rules of sportsmanship—hitting the beaten foe when down; striking in the dark, treacherous as only the false-fronted sea can be treacherous: that is good tonic for the careless traveller who believes the oceans are bitted and bridled and tamed. The sea never changes; and in its relentless autocracy it mocks the power and ingenuity of man; allowing him, maybe, a little law, a trifle of self-complacent vanity in seeming conquest; and then—striking sharp, devastating hammer-blows to prove to him his inefficiency. The sea is like time—an immutably winning force against which the succeeding generations fret and break themselves in vain protest.

And out of this agelong warfare have inevitably resulted epic battles, the memory of which even to this day sets the blood a-tingle in the veins. With such stately craft as won through to victory this volume has nothing to do; it is its purpose to treat of the vanquished; and consequently the note struck throughout must be a note of tragedy; yet here and there—gloriously often, indeed—the story of disaster is illuminated by chapters of almost inconceivable heroism: not necessarily that spectacular heroism which causes the world to stand in thrilled awe; but the quiet, unassuming gallantry that fights on against inevitable defeat; that holds on when body, soul and sinew are worn and wasted; when only the splendid will to fight endures. The sea is a field of tragedy; but it is also a field marked by unforgettable milestones of daring devotion that the annals of the land can scarcely equal.

In the main these losing fights have been waged in utter loneliness, without the glaring limelight of publicity illumining them. For there is nothing in all the world, I think, quite so lonely and forlorn as a sinking ship. To-day, that stark aloofness is less marked than before the era of wireless telegraphy; to-day, the stricken fabric hurries out her appeal for comradely succour; and if humanly possible, that cry never goes unheeded. Ships—great and wonderful ships, the masterpieces of maritime craftsmanship—die surrounded by eager salvors; in the focussed glare of countless searchlights, with a busy, hasty plying of life-saving boats between doomed hull and triumphant rescuers; and yet, at the last, when everything living has been ferried across the snarling gap, the ship dies lonely and forlorn—but splendid in her very loneliness.

I have been witness to shipwrecks of a different type; when the gallant white-sailed friend of the lazy latitudes has soared wildly to the roaring summit of a Cape Horn sea, and dived—to reappear no more; wiped out of existence as thoroughly and instantly as the writing is wiped from a schoolboy's slate. There was a loneliness unbelievable—at one moment life, courage and the will to fight; at the next—the chilly blackness of death, for ship and man—an obliteration of everything, save, maybe, a mangled fragment of wreckage towards which the questing albatrosses swoop in hope of finding food, only to scorn and ignore: some trivial grating, some mangled plank, a sailor's cap—the pitiful monuments on the boundless graveyard of the sea.

I have with my own eyes been witness to wrecks that can only be considered miraculous. Far south of the gaunt Heads of Sydney Harbour in Australia, the coast-cliffs tower high and unbroken for many a surf-drowned league. For endless distances there range these stark, perpendicular cliffs of ironstone and granite; steep-to, as the saying is: which means that deep water persists to the very foot of the precipices. The ship strik-

[5]

ing such a barrier would touch first with her bowsprit, before her riven keel arrested her headlong rush. On black, stormy nights, when the Southerly Busters are doing their worst, the roar of a tormented surf at the cliffs' foot is thunderous; a note dominating even the crash of the storm itself. At one point in this implacable wall of death is a space of maybe a couple of hundred feet in width: a crevice in immensity, no more. Here is a freakish shelving beach of fair, smooth sand: a little peaceful cove where the angry gods who fashioned the rock-barrier might conceivably have lain to rest and sun themselves when their facetious labours were done.

A hard-driven sailing-ship, bewildered and confused by a series of furious gales, its position lost by reason of drenched skies that had endured for days, was racing uncontrollably before a more than usually furious burst of wind. The night was dark —"black as the hobs of hell" to employ a nautical commonplace. No single thread of lightning wove its way athwart the shrieking sky. Utterly incapable of doing aught to aid his ship, the captain had simply to throw up his hands and let her drive. To heave-to were impossible; there was a dead lee shore somewhere—a shore of death. Nothing to do but drive under bare poles and pray the Lord to have mercy on weary souls. The snarling cry of "Breakers ahead!" from forward bit through the clamour. Breakers were everywhere, ranging to port and starboard hands. Nothing was to be done save close the eyes and await the inevitable crash. She would strike bow-on and crumple her hull into a ghastly concertina.

But she didn't. Hounded by wind and sea she leaped like a scared hind into that almost imperceptible gap of smooth sand; she ran easily ashore, without so much as shaking down her lightest tracery of spars; and held there on an even keel, so that all her recently-hopeless people needed to do was await the break of day and fall of tide, push a ladder overside, and walk to life and safety. Two hundred feet in an immensity of horror—and the ship found it; of her own astonishing volition, according to her master's account; for he did not even know of the existence of this cove. But that is simply one of the sea's many miraculous happenings. Not all craft have such luck as this. When I passed up that way a little while later, with sunny skies and laughing seas to companion me, I saw this craft lying there as sweetly and evenly as if in a dry-dock; and all her top-hamper as snugly in place as if she awaited her critical owner's inspection. But she was a wreck—there for such time as the snarling sea-fangs permitted. Impossible to refloat her; in her final panic-stricken leap she had broken her back and killed herself. Other craft fare more hardly; as such as read the story of the loss of the *Dunbar* will learn. Here were two practically parallel situations—gale-hounded ships driven shoreward in the pitch-blackness of an unspeakable night; but one saved her people, the other lost them all, save that one survivor who was sole survivor of two other catastrophes: apparently a veteran the sea could not destroy.

But of such wrecks traces remain: survivors can narrate the stories of risk and terror; eye witnesses can convey impressions. The coastwise wreck is in itself a terrible disaster; but thanks to the lifeboat service, whose superhuman work is touched on in the later pages of this book, the sea's grim toll of human life has been heroically lessened in the shoal and ragged waters of the shores of the world. It is the deep-sea wreck that is peculiarly tragic by virtue of its unspeakable loneliness; and all such records as exist of such wrecks bear witness to that ineffable aloofness from the living world. Ringed in by remote horizons the good ship dies like the thirst-stricken traveller in the blazing desert, unviewed by other eye than God's. Maybe she is weary of her hopeless battling: maybe she is daring and defiant to the last; but—some crested comber rises and poises and falls; and she that was is not—and another tragedy of white water has been encompassed.

Shipwrecks have affected the history of the world in a peculiar degree. Omitting all allegorical references, that unsailorly shipwreck off the Island of Malta, when Saint Paul was precariously saved, had a very considerable bearing on Christendom; and there is every reason for believing that had Saint Paul perished in that calamity, the Christian doctrine might never have penetrated to the Western world. For a faith, however good, must have earnest prophets to maintain it alive; and Saint Paul was Christ's most ardent advocate. To my mind Saint Paul's shipwreck was one of the world's most important events: of infinitely greater value to the Christian faith than all the Crusades that ever attempted to wrest the Holy Sepulchre from infidel hands. If Saint Paul had not survived the ordeal by sea, there would have been no Crusades; and the world might well have been at present as it was when Rome was its mistress, and paganism was the only common creed.

Again, the wrecking of the Spanish Armada, to take a long stride through the miles of history, was one of the world's epochal events. Notwithstanding the courageous hammerings of Drake and Hawkins and the Elizabethan stalwarts, that Invincible Armada might reasonably have carried its venture to a successful conclusion, but for God's great winds blowing out of outraged Heaven to deliver again the Divine denial: "Thus far shalt thou go and no further!" The human mind indeed staggers under the immensity of the thought: "What would have been the fate of the Western world had not the great storms wrecked that arrogant fleet? What could have become of the pioneer work that caused an Empire's boundaries to be spread to the limits of the world; for a race of slaves would not have embarked on such hazardous excursions as free men risked joyously, for the glory of their country and their queen." Here, then, were a series of epochal wrecks of surpassing interest; but the general story of that shattering cataclysm is so widely known that it shall find no place in these following pages.

Amongst shipwrecks that shocked the country by their suddenness and disastrous loss of life, we have as an outstanding example that of the *Royal George*: whose end came under circumstances that can never be adequately explained. Here was a noble line of battle ship, carrying 100 guns; Kempenfelt's flag-ship, a masterpiece of shipbuilding; strong, graceful and swift; so noble a craft that the navies of the world might have been combed without finding her peer. From the date of her commissioning her record was a golden one; in battle she won out-standing victories. She carried the pennants of admirals whose names ring down the corridors of history like splendid clarion blasts—Anson hoisted his flag at her main; Boscawen, Rodney and Howe trod her snow-white decks in all the pride of success and duty amply done. Her armament was considerable for those days; she was a tall ship in every respect, measuring as she did 66 feet from her keel to her taffrail; and piling her graceful spars high and very high into the air. Coming into Spithead in August of 1782 she moored and made the signal that stores were required and small repairs in need of attention. As she was detailed to rendezvous with the Mediterranean Fleet, her magazines were also in need of replenishment; and amongst other essential matters calling for attention was the question of a new watercock in her bilge to replace an old worn one that kept her people too regularly at the pumps.

It was not worth taking the ship in to the careening slip; this was a task occupying much time and the labours of many men. If she were careened afloat the task of replacing the seacock was comparatively simple; and the order was given to heave her down. This meant that her guns and heavier weights inboard must be shifted to the port or larboard side, lifting up her star-board bilge until the seacock showed above water. On the 29th of August the careening was effected; the port guns being run out to the full extent of their breechings, and those on the other side being transported amidships. Secured strongly by ropes as were these starboard guns, they were not yet secure enough. But the careening brought the water outboard almost level with the sills of the lower deck ports. This was hazardous, since the weather, though fair, was apt to be somewhat squally. Nine o'clock in the morning, and lighters were alongside, together with a small sloop carrying the rum for the crew. Immediate orders being given to unload her rum, they were obeyed; and whether it was the swing of the cranes, the hurrying of men, or the rolling of the rum casks, probably all factors combined, the *Royal George* heeled still more, and water began to lap over the sills of the lower gun-deck ports to port. The ship's carpenter observed the increasing peril, and got himself at speed to the quarterdeck, to entreat the officer of the day to give orders to take the list out of the ship. The officer was a newcomer to the ship, not popular with the men, a bit of a martinet: he returned an answer which might be translated as meaning: "Mind your own d——d business!" The carpenter went away with his tail between his legs; but a sense of duty overcame his awe of the O.D. and back he climbed to the quarterdeck with another appeal.

"She's in danger, sir!" was his plaint. The third lieutenant cursed him in round terms; told him to get back to his job; but apparently a moment's reflection convinced him that the man had right on his side; for he ordered the drummer to the deck, to roll the drum in accepted fashion that the crew might be mustered to right ship and quickly. The men were waiting for this command eagerly—they were alive to the imminent danger; they rushed to stations even before the first drum-roll sounded—too late. For a puff of wind smote the towering spars and the lofty topside; and thrust those opened ports under water. Water rushed in in uncheckable torrents. Already, in a breath, the finest man-of-war in the world was under sentence of death. Full of crimps and peddlers, of harlots and the riff-raff that used to board a ship bound on a long foreign commission, shore-sharks eager to get their hands on the sailors' advances of pay, as she was, she turned over on her side; and everything movable about her—animate and inanimate, tore across to larboard; guns broke loose, women and children were hurled in a struggling mass. Men fought to reach the uppermost ports

—but they failed; there was no satisfactory handhold. The *Royal George* filled herself through those fatal opened ports; and sank—under a blue sky, whilst all about her was peace; and in her sinking she not only robbed England of her noblest ship, but took with her nine hundred souls—victims of the third lieutenant's shortness of temper more than anything else. And this happened under the eyes of a fleet of close on three hundred vessels—line of battle ships, frigates, sloops and store-ships, under Lord Howe's command. And they could do nothing to help—the blow was struck too swiftly, too completely; before a single boat could be lowered the *Royal George,* with Admiral Kempenfelt at work in his state-cabin, unconscious of the menace, went down—and gloom spread over England like a thick and awful cloud.

Another stride through Time and we are face to face with another epochal disaster of the sea: the sinking of the tragic *Titanic.* Here was tragedy at its grimmest: tragedy that froze the pulses of the civilised world, and that turned men's thoughts afresh to that God who declared that limits were set to human achievement. The final word in safety and splendour: a noble vessel designed to defy the worst the seas could do: a very city afloat, lacking nothing known to human ingenuity; the *Titanic* started on her maiden voyage with as certain an assurance of successful completion as any man-wrought fabric ever knew. Laden to capacity with "the proud, the young, the beautiful; the rich, the gay, the fair——" as was related of another good ship doomed to die—she encountered that grim unforeseen contingency with which the sea abounds; and, planing away her bottom plating in wide swathes, she laid herself open to the inrush of devastating water that mocked the efforts of mankind as it chuckled and gurgled its sinister way into her assumedly impregnable bowels. Here was an occurrence to stagger humanity—to remind it of its limitations. The *Titanic* appeared to many as a deliberate gauntlet flung in the face of Providence; and to that many the command of "Thus far and no further" was audible in the echoes that came back to frozen ears.

Witness then the sinking of the *Lusitania:* that cold-blooded murder of a non-combatant ship which definitely swung the scale to the side of the Allied cause in the Great World War. Here again we have an instance of a shipwreck influencing history to an incalculable degree, and altering the face of the earth as it had not been altered since the days of the Cæsars. Maybe the full story of the *Lusitania* tragedy will never be told; maybe it is best, in view of future developments, that it should never be rightly told in all its intricate details; and that a kindly veil of mystery should be drawn over the terrible story—that rumour and counter-rumour should be stilled for ever; but the fact remains that this wreck of a proud ship was one of the decisive events of the world; ranking even before the shattering of the Invincible Armada in its ultimate impression on civilisation and the forward advance of the human race.

The loss of the *Birkenhead* was less an influence on the world's history than any of the previously mentioned wrecks; but it is conceivable that when the end of the *Lusitania* is forgotten, the lesson taught in courage and fortitude to humanity by the men of the *Birkenhead* will persist, and grow brighter. As Rudyard Kipling declares: "To stand an' be still to the *Birken'ead* drill is a damn' tough bullet to chew!" and its very toughness as well as the gallant chewing have set a standard of pluck which must always stand as a bright goal to young daring. For it was not the mad, fevered courage of the battlefield, that sees nothing ahead but the ultimate victory and the reward of valour; it was that cold-drawn early-morning courage which recognises hopelessness and yet persists and as such *Birkenhead* pluck is a definite landmark in the world's history: not merely a national source of pride; but a world-wide lesson.

This work makes no pretence of dealing with shipwrecks of the remote past. In the main the wrecks detailed are of British bottoms; since the records of such are more accessible; and they are tragedies that occurred so recently as still to hold interest to the layman as well as to the men of the sea. The loss of the sailing ship *Garthpool* is described for two reasons: It possesses many features of interest and has a value that is almost satirical; and it marks in a clear-cut way the final page of an era that has endured from the vague and shadowy past until to-day: the spacious era of sail, during which thousands of years the capacity of men to wage victorious war with the devastating sea was tested to the uttermost. The *Garthpool* was the last square-rigged British sailing-ship: the final survivor of all those gallant craft that aided to expand this little England into such an Empire as Cæsar never contemplated in his wildest dreams. To a certain extent her passing puts a definite period to our maritime history; it turns a page on such a chapter of enduring heroism as the world will never read again. She, as all her forerunners, from the clumsy, single-sailed craft that carried fighting parties of Ancient Britons from cove to cove, fought the sea without mechanical aids; was dependent on wind and water alone for her propulsion and her existence. Not all the Atlantic Blue Ribbons can ever count so much in national history as did the countless, indomitable fleets represented by the *Garthpool;* for Cæsar came to England in wind-propelled vessels; Alfred defeated the Danes in sailing ships; Columbus discovered a new world in a windjammer, and Drake circumnavigated that world and gave reality to vague dreams of an expanded Empire in ships that owed nothing to any power but wind and sea.

And the *Garthpool* died in harness: not degraded by a tortured death in an unsentimental shipbreaker's yard. That was as it should be. But her end was tragic, as all ships' ends must be tragic; for every ship, be she stately clipper or fuming tramp-freighter or noble liner, or arrogant, defiant battle ship, for that matter, is more than a mere conglomeration of wood and steel and rope. A ship is more than an edifice erected ashore; and in her building she acquires certain qualities that render her different from the other inanimate creations of men's hands. Consequently, the death of a ship is a vaster and more compelling tragedy than the shattering of an edifice—no matter how noble—ashore; it is more like the end of a living entity—of an actual friend, indeed. A ship of all inanimates had and still has the power to inspire a sentimental attachment in such as have entrusted their fortunes to her. Let such as will declare that ship-captains have remained with their ships through their final plunge to Davy Jones's locker simply because they refused to face the rigour of an enquiry into such ships' loss; I prefer to think that it was a genuine attachment to the almost living, death-stricken thing that held them to their posts so that they passed the portals of death in company. But the greatest stretch of the imagination cannot picture—say—a theatre manager remaining amongst the shattered ruins of his establishment if prospect of safety remains; nor yet the caretaker of a skyscraper continuing at his post for love of the concrete and steel that encase his fortunes! Yes, there is something about a ship, no matter how ugly and utilitarian circumstances may have made her, that differs from any other human fabrication; and it is this quality, known by seamen, faintly appreciated by landsmen, maybe, that makes of a wreck a deep and stunning tragedy.

It is doubtful if any good service would be done by an attempt to arrange the subjects in this volume in anything approaching chronological order. As a matter of fact, since a brief mention will be attempted of the extraordinary work of the life-boats of the world, and particularly of the life-saving craft and crews of the Royal National Lifeboat Institution—that service which all seamen admire and revere—it is necessary to recount the details of one of the earliest wrecks—the *Adventure*—in September, 1789—towards the end of the chronicle; since it was the loss of this ship under the startled and horrified gaze of helpless shore-folk that was the spur to prick human consciousness into that activity which resulted in the genesis of what is to-day the most efficient life-saving service in the world.

Out of countless sea-catastrophes such have been selected as drive home to the full the awful lesson of the price demanded by the sea of such as dare its dangers. Each incident possesses some outstanding characteristic, whether of human daring, or elemental terror, which compels it to stand out in high perspective from the mass of sorrowful scenes. For it is well, in a growingly careless age, when sea-transport threatens to dwindle and become abashed by the increasing conquest of the air, to be reminded of certain elements that permit us, as a race, and even as human beings as a species, to exist and prosper. If there is no country to-day that owes so much to the sea as does Great Britain, similarly there is no such country that has paid such a debt in human life and treasure as its price of Admiralty. Easy enough, having crossed well-arranged and safeguarding stepping-stones, to stride forward stoutly on the farther bank to newer and greater victories; but had the stepping-stones not been there victory must have eluded the pioneer. Similarly, it is by the wrecks of the world that the sea-navigation of the world has been rendered as free from risk as it is at this present time. We who flit from continent to continent without thought, only impatient of delays, might do well to bear in mind that the experience gleaned from the mishaps of the past has rendered secure the vessels of to-day; and whilst admitting that the pioneers did not die in vain, should give them credit for the fact that by their splendid deaths they benefited us to an incalculable degree.

Space prevents a lengthy description of certain sea-tragedies which at the time of their occurrence staggered the world. Wrecks like that of the *Empress of Ireland,* for instance—a magnificent ship, which on the 29th of May, 1914, whilst homeward bound from Quebec, in the River St. Lawrence, was struck down fatally by the Norwegian steam freighter *Storstadt.* Though the weather had been clear, there were patches of fog drifting about; and in one of these, although signalled to give a wide berth, the *Storstadt* charged the C. P. R. liner of 14,191 tons; and gave her her death-blow. Struck between the funnels, the devastating bow tore aft, ripping away the plates completely to the stern; rendering all watertight bulkheads useless. Captain Kendall of the *Empress of Ireland* yelled to the Norwegian captain to keep going ahead with his engines, so that the gap might be plugged; but in the confusion, the *Storstadt* withdrew and the fog closed down. Instantly the big ship listed fiercely, so completely that the boats on either side were unapproachable. The wireless dynamo failed within five minutes of impact; but an S O S was sent out; not proving of much avail; for the ship went down with a rush; so suddenly that many of her passengers were drowned in their very bunks, without a chance to make a fight for life. Within a scant fourteen minutes of colliding, the liner sank in 19 fathoms; her boilers exploding as she went and spreading havoc amongst such as were still on board. Only four boats were launched out of the many; and though 444 people were saved, 1,023 were lost in this ocean cataclysm; amongst them Laurence Irving and his wife; who were not divided in death.

Nor may the loss of the P. & O. *Delhi,* which was driven ashore in thick weather two miles from Cape Spartel, near by Tangier, be more than briefly mentioned. High winds and terrific seas were active; and though a British cruiser hurried to the scene, nothing could immediately be done. Aboard the *Delhi,* in addition to many others, were the Duke of Fife and the Princess Royal, and the Princesses Alexandra and Maude; these were taken off with supreme difficulty in a boat which, on account of the raging surf, sank whilst still some distance from the shore; but as the Royal passengers wore lifebelts, they were rescued; though the Duke of Fife later died as a direct result of this exposure; and a good man was lost to England. Notwithstanding the rigours no British life was lost in this disaster; though three lascars perished and also three French sailors working from a salvage vessel; but the wreck of the *Delhi* created considerable international interest when it occurred in December of 1911, because the story went that the lascar crew panicked abundantly and jeopardised the safety of all on board.

Similarly, a chapter might well be devoted to the recent loss of the *Vestris,* with a regrettable death-roll, under baffling circumstances; and to the wreck of the *Trevessa* and the superhuman boat-voyage made by her people; but there are so many sea-tragedies on record that it is really difficult to make a significant selection.

Whilst we—rightly—erect memorials in stone and bronze to such as perish on the battlefield for the furtherance of national ideals; we may neglect to remember that such as died in the blaze and flurry of war did so under an inspiration of patriotism that merely finds its best expression in the infrequent periods of national danger; though such as died, by tempest, fire or any other of the sea's dire hazards, died just as nobly, without any glittering laurels to reward their immolation. War ashore is intermittent and with wide intervals between any two outbursts; war at sea was—and still is, to such as know—perpetual. Seldom a ship, even to-day, completes a voyage without being required to battle with some shock of storm, or risk some other chance of extermination offered by the sea. Even in stark smooth water, under sleepy skies and passionate stars, across the sleek, evenly breathing deserts of unruffled oceans, grim, evil derelicts lurk —maritime vampires that menace the continued safety of all such proud keels as pulse by. Every fog-wreath holds a threat; even though the world's seas are as competently charted as any road-map of a favourite touring district. And it is only through the incidence of this shipwreck or that that a further weakness is discoverable in ships that appear to be as invulnerable as the ore-beds that gave them birth. Men profit by other men's errors ashore; at sea men profit by lost ships' declared weaknesses —and so a shipwreck holds even more than common human interest in its happening.

There are ship-losses which are known to have occurred and which are yet enveloped in veils of mystery. No attempt has been made to offer surmise as to the root causes of such disasters; since the imagination would be untrammelled by any single fact or scrap of evidence and might roam into exaggerated fields. The *Waratah,* well-found, apparently immune from danger, left her port amid showers of good wishes for safe voyaging; and nothing ever returned or was found to tell of her passing. Here is a wreck which holds in its happening all the accumulated tragedy of deep-water—actuality, mystery, terror, suspense, maybe gallantry inconceivable, conceivably poltroonery that would not bear a second thought. She sailed, she vanished; and her fate is everlastingly unknown.

Let her storm-harassed bones lie untroubled on the shining wastes of undersea sand; above which the tumultuous keels weave an endless pattern of daring and purpose. There are enough sea-tragedies of which all details are known, to occupy attention without straying into the unsatisfying realms of surmise.

On the other hand, the *Waikato* twisted off her propeller down the desert of the Easting, and vanished from human ken for a period of six months; being posted as "missing," then "lost with all hands"; and all the time she was alive; wandering through those ice-flecked solitudes at the whim of every current that beset her keel. Before the useful days of radio, of course; it was impossible for her to announce her predicament or summon aid; for the Easting is so lonely that to sight a passing ship is savouring of a miracle, even when adhering to the traffic lines. But after her wanderings the *Waikato* was seen and plucked into safe harbour, but little the worse for her isolation, save that her passengers were somewhat lean from a diet of sardines and sweet biscuits, which was all they had to subsist on for the latter part of their ordeal. So that the *Waikato* was a lucky wreck— with all the atmosphere and none of the tragedy.

A book devoted to wrecks must of necessity apply one chapter at least to the subject of wreck-remedies; even if only as an antidote to much grim drama. No plague-story would be complete without mention of the physician. To-day the story of gallantry in rescue is a long one, and a noble one. Thanks to the efficiency of wireless telegraphy and the sterling readiness of such as have their business on great waters, it is seldom a ship is allowed to perish without some effort being made to succour her. The heroic tale of the sea shows no abatement of self-sacrifice and sterling effort: our blood is thrilled from time to time with records of dauntless daring as between ship and ship.

Just at a time when we are prone to declare that the fine spirit of the past is moribund, if not actually dead, that steam, internal combustion and electricity have mollycoddled our seamen to such an extent that they do not know the initial elements of seafaring, the newspapers flash to us some record of a deepsea rescue that sets the blood coursing wildly; and that proves the standard of courage to be even higher to-day than in the older times. The captain of a trifling coastwise steamer takes his ship into eddies and rock-cumbered shallows in a manner most daring, and salves the stricken people of a stranded ship, the wind meanwhile blowing a hundred-odd miles an hour, and the sea running to correspond.

The captain of an Atlantic liner hears an S O S call from the misted distance, and hurls his mighty ship through storm and stress with a cool abandon of daring that refuses to admit the possibility of defeat; and after a breathless race arrives in time to launch his boats across a yeasty void and draw the living from the clashing jaws of death. There is no seeming end to the amazing story of the urgent brotherhood of the sea. Nowhere will you read brighter chapters of this stirring epic than in the records of the coastwise lifeboat services.

The Royal National Lifeboat Institution is, without a doubt, the best friend sailors ever had—pleasure-making passengers, too, for that matter. The winter of 1929–30 has been peculiarly fruitful of tempests above the common run; and in consequence the bitter toll of wreckage has been heavier than normal—though normality is heavy enough, Heaven knows.

Writing in *The Times* of January 15th, 1930, Sir Godfrey Baring, Chairman of the R.N.L.I., says:

[19]

" . . . The gales since the beginning of October have, in their frequency and intensity, been unequalled during the present century. . . . Your readers will be interested in a brief summary of the way in which the lifeboat service has met the demands upon it during the same period. I would ask you to allow me to give the salient figures.

"From Oct. 1st up to and including Jan. 13th, there were no fewer than 157 launches of lifeboats. Of these, 67 were in December, and the largest number on one day was 15 on December 7th, the day on which the wind rose to the record speed of 110 miles an hour. During these same 15 weeks the lifeboats rescued 181 lives and saved 16 vessels. That figure of 181 consists of the men actually taken off vessels which were already wrecked or out of control, and of those on board vessels which would have been wrecked had not the lifeboats brought them into safety. It would be considerably larger if there were to be added the crews of 28 vessels to which the lifeboats rendered help in one way or another, or which they 'stood by' until they were out of danger.

"The mere launching of a lifeboat in such unexampled weather at once put the crew in peril of their lives. That is to say, during these 15 weeks, in which 157 lifeboats went out, 1,500 lifeboatmen willingly faced the danger of death in their self-chosen task of going to the help of their fellow-men in peril on the sea. That 181 lives were rescued is the best proof that we could have of the skill of the lifeboat service. That 1,500 men risked their lives is the best proof of its courage and devotion. That not a life has been lost among the gallant crews is the best proof of the quality of the lifeboats and their equipment. May I suggest that a service with such a record at such a time of stress, deserves the admiration and support of the British people?"

To which I, for one, offer a hearty agreement. This letter is a curt summary of the history of the Royal National Lifeboat Institution during the fighting years since its first inception. To read between the lines is to read a story unsurpassable in our maritime annals. It is one thing to fight for one's own life and one's own ship when bound together by what Kipling calls: "The ties of Common Funk"; it is a comparatively simple matter to fight when you know that unless you fight you die—that is the primal instinct of self-preservation. To go in cold blood to fight for others' lives is a different quality of courage; and one in which the coastwise heroes of our lifeboat service excel.

It is fortunate for the land that this short period was marred by no disaster to the gallant men who left security to venture into threat of death. Other periods have been less fortunate; as the recollection of the tragic Rye lifeboat disaster, still fresh—let us hope—in memory proves. There have been others equally tragic, equally costly in loss of valued human life, as witness the combined disasters to the Fleetwood and St. Anne's lifeboats, and to the Caister boat. It may safely be assumed that not one of the 1,500 stalwarts mentioned in Sir Godfrey Baring's letter went to sea in ignorance of the Rye tragedy—it is safe, indeed, to assert, that every individual had the terrible details of that loss vividly in mind when he heard his own particular summons to action. How little the risk weighed is shown in the startling fact that not one man of them all drew back or hesitated when the call went forth. Verily the sea teaches its devotees some toughness not always understanded of the layman.

There are no words sonorous and gallant enough in which to sing the saga of our lifeboat service. The members of that service would be the last to encourage the composition of such a saga, for I have found them shy, retiring, modest to a fault; not prone to speak of great deeds, apt only to make light of the ardours and hazards overcome. They see their duty clear before them, and after the stolid, sturdy fashion of men whose blood is salt with the salt of the sea, they go and do it, uncomplainingly and with a quality of thoroughness which is only comparable to the quality with which Britons the world over saw their duty in the Great War and set forth to do it.

Therefore, when sitting down to breakfast, to eat bread baked of the wheat fetched from far overseas, to drink of tea or coffee fetched from equally remote confines of the earth, it would be as well to remember that but for the ships and the men of this country, our tables would be but sparsely spread; and that for every mouthful swallowed, some hazard of great waters had been encountered and overcome. Through the length and breadth —yes, and the depth—of all the seven seas there floats a ghostly fleet of spectral craft to remind us of all we owe to the wrecked ships in England, whose tormented bones now lie quietly in the gaunt Port of Missing Ships.

CHAPTER II

THE SINKING OF H.M.S. "VICTORIA"

TAKING everything by and large the British nation can bear most surprises and calamities with a stolid equanimity; such quality being, it can only be surmised, an essential feature of the national character. A wreck, indeed a lengthy tale of wrecks, whilst given full value as being the immediate portion of that dire price of Admiralty which a nation whose continued existence lies on the sea, must expect to pay, is taken as a regrettable but unavoidable event. It forms subject matter for newspapers; it is a subject for gossip and regret for a few days; then it is conveniently forgotten, save by such as are intimately connected with that particular disaster; and almost before it is forgotten another wreck is reported to hurry the last into oblivion.

But certain sea-disasters are outstanding, and especially so in regard to the stunning sense of shock which their records conveyed to the minds of men. Of such a quality of catastrophe is the loss of H.M.S. *Victoria,* flagship of the Mediterranean Fleet.

It is thirty-six years ago since the news was flashed through to cast a terrible veil of gloom over the country; and at the time the present recorder was a boy; but even so, I distinctly remember the breathless gasp that informed my immediate vicinity when the news came through.

"The *Victoria*? The *Victoria*! But—the *Victoria*!!! Ridiculous—impossible! Why, she couldn't sink—she's the finest battleship in the world, isn't she?"

But she had sunk; she had disappeared below the surface of the placid Mediterranean. Not during stress of storm—for on

[23]

June 22nd, 1893, the Mediterranean Sea was as placid as the proverbial mill-pond; with hardly a catspaw to mar its smiling serenity. Not by fire—one might have visualised her wreathed in leaping flames and hideous clouds of smoke; not by enemy action, for most part of the world was serenely at peace; but by some mischance that even to this day is more or less obscure. The secret of what led to the *Victoria's* end is locked immutably in the brain of Vice-Admiral Sir George Tryon, and it will never be truly known. Just as the human eye possesses a definite blind-spot which, brought to bear on an object clearly distinct when the light-rays strike at another angle, fails to discern that object; so does the human brain possess its own blind spot which, by certain concatenation of circumstances, renders its normal lucidity overclouded. The reasonable theory to account for this, one of the most deplorable peacetime tragedies of the British Navy, is that Admiral Tryon's blind spot disguised from his normally well-balanced brain the terrible possibilities of his tactical turning evolution until it was too late to undo the harm embarked upon.

H.M.S. *Victoria* was a first-class battleship of twelve thousand tons; carrying a formidable armament. In the light of modern battleship construction which aims at large mobile gun-platforms she was puny; but she was about the latest evolution of naval construction; and ranked to her decade much about as the *Rodney* and *Nelson* rank to ours. Her complement consisted of sixty officers and 600 men. She was the flagship of the Mediterranean Fleet; and so, in addition to the normal battleship complement, carried the extra details of the Admiral's staff. A ship of splendour she was—shining white as to her upper-works, laced with gold by her admiring people—for this was in a day before the dead-level modern Navy-grey was compulsory colouring for all fighting ships—her brasswork glinting in the evening sun like so much solid gold; her snow-white awnings set to a hair, without even the vestige of a wrinkle; for Tryon was a stickler for discipline, and was, above all things, a ship-lover;

THE "DELHI"

H.M.S. "VICTORIA"

with her gaunt guns polished into dazzling brilliancy; and her decks at least as white as the proverbial hound's tooth. She stood for a late descendant of that mighty family of naval ships that had maintained the far-flung British Empire. She was a concrete expression of everything best in the British Navy. Did mutterings of possible war sound on the far horizons, such as heard had but to wave a hand *Victoria*wards and say: "Not with such a ship as that afloat!" to find complete reassurance. See her then, solid as the national constitution; implacable as Gibraltar itself, the stern sentinel of her purposeful beat. See her, a seething hive of care-free humanity—the picked men of the naval service, who hadn't a care in the world; for who would think of to-morrow, except in so far as its possibilities of leave were concerned, with a serene sky above, and a mill-pond-like immensity of sea so far as human eye might observe?

Save for routine duties, work—*qua* work—was over for the day. Her lower deck was alive with joyous men; there was much laughter, not a little hearty singing and the inevitable practical jokers found amongst a congregation of well-cared-for men, were as lively as they could possibly be. Once the anchors were down and the watches set, the final wash-down duties performed and the stately ceremonial of a Navy sunset completed, the ship would be ready for play. Her band was tuning up for its customary concert; and the watches off-duty were busily engaged with supper.

Victoria was chief of eleven good ships; of which *Camperdown* was next in importance. This staunch fleet, which at that time was capable of meeting any other fleet in the world, perhaps, on equal terms, was proceeding in the course of summer manœuvres from Beyrout towards Tripoli on the North African coast, with the intention of anchoring there in the safe and pleasant roadstead. The combined fleet was steaming line abreast—that is to say, each ship maintained a position to port or starboard of the flagship, and preserved a straight line along its formidable front. The sea-castles were proceeding at easy cruising speed in this formation, with navigators preserving distance and dressing with meticulous care by means of angle sextants and range-finders and the many other instruments necessary to maintain an orderliness in big fighting ships' dispositions.

So far all was well. At a speed of eight knots there was not even room for engine-room defects to manifest themselves—the ships were safe as if lying in dry-dock at any one of a hundred ports.

Admiral Tryon, before coming to moorings that evening, decided to put his command through certain tactical manœuvres by way of testing their drill and resiliency as a mobile unit. For on certain occasions a battle-fleet must be capable of acting as one ship, precisely as a battalion of infantry may be required to act as one man, and that man the commanding officer, since his is the brain dictating its movements. In Tryon's skilled hands those eleven ships were merely a fighting-tool. Maybe he was too certain of his proficiency in its handling; maybe some flaw was inevidently present in the tool itself. That is the mystery.

"Signal all ships: Form column of line ahead!" Tryon ordered his flag-captain when the meditated evolution had clearly shaped itself in his mind. Instantly the "bunting-tossers" grew busy—the smartest flag-signallers in the world were aboard *Victoria*. Her signal yards broke out in vari-coloured bunting; her semaphores worked like frenzied and delirious windmills; yet with perfect clearness, for when an admiral gives a signal there is no room for error. The simple evolution was performed without a suggestion of a hitch. Leading ships—*Victoria* and *Camperdown*—quickened revolutions, ships detailed to position in rear of the double column, slowed to allow their forerunners to take position ahead. As an illustration of seamanlike handling of a vast force, it was inimitable; the great ships behaved for all the world like intelligent living entities.

At each ship's signal-yards flaunted the vivid bunting which acknowledged receipt of the various signals; so that their stately beauty was enhanced under the downward slanting sun. The world of the sea smiled approval of smartness.

See them now—two columns of might, the smoke from their many belching funnels forming a deep and widening canopy between the pure blue of the Mediterranean sky and the serene sapphire of the Mediterranean sea. Observing them thus a spectator must have been compelled to quote the stirring lines of an earlier poet:

> "Britannia needs no bulwark,
> No towers along the steep;
> Her march is o'er the mountain waves;
> Her home is on the deep!"

An embodiment of implacable power and might, no less, invulnerable; ships warranted to survive under the heaviest torrents of shot and shell; there they steamed in stately leisureliness, the destinies of them one and all entrusted to a single fallible brain.

The western sky was already reddening; the first vague hint of evening began to brood over that impressive seascape.

Tryon held conference with his staff; put before them his proposal to practise a certain turning manœuvre that was in those days regarded as a masterpiece of naval strategy; but which actually dated back to an earlier era when sea-battles were fought almost broadside to broadside. The naval tactics of the end of the nineteenth century did not differ in any remarkable degree from those employed at the commencement of that era; and started on the assumption of fixed broadsides and a slow rate of fire. Muzzle-loaders were not extinct in the Royal Navy; and the present ranges of gunfire, whereby unseen ships are successfully bombarded whilst behind the horizon, were actually undreamed-of; although it was boasted that the 81-ton gun mounted at Gibraltar was capable of hurling its missiles clear across the Straits of Gibraltar, though without any definite aim being possible. Cutlasses were still cleated overhead in the gun-decks; and the ultimate idea of naval strategists—only thirty-seven years ago, remember—was to lay the ships alongside and carry the enemy by the board, with cold steel as final arbiter.

The two columns proceeded, *Victoria* leading one line, *Camperdown* leading the other—starboard line, which was the more important, since the starboard side has always been prime factor at sea, on account of the steering-board or rudder originally being situated on the right-hand side of a ship when looking forward. Between *Victoria* and *Camperdown*—aboard which latter ship was Admiral Markham, Tryon's second in command—was a space of six cable-lengths—equal to twelve hundred yards; and since the two lines were bar-straight, the same distance separated any two other ships in column.

Tryon now issued a somewhat cryptical order. "Signal all ships," he instructed, "that when fleet passes position already designated for anchorage, course will be reversed. Leading ships will turn inwards, other ships following in the water of leading ships. Speed maintained as before; evolution commences on hauling down of Flag's signal." This meant in lay parlance that the two lines, headed by *Victoria* and *Camperdown,* would, when the final hoist was lowered, by which action a naval signal becomes effective, turn towards each other on an ordinary helm, and, when their heads were exactly reversed—pointing north instead of south—would continue to steam parallel to each other, though at a considerably-lessened distance. The old-fashioned country dance best illustrates the meaning—partners dance towards one another, meet in the middle, link hands and proceed down the centre of the moving lines of dancers. A simple enough bit of work; as ships obey their helms with the sweet docility with which well-trained horses obey the reins.

This setting to partners would reverse the line of progress of the fleet without altering the relative positions of the ships, and the anchorage would be gained in seemly fashion.

What makes the adjective "cryptic" applicable to the order

as transmitted from *Victoria* is the fact that, though the two columns were only twelve hundred yards apart, the smallest turning circles of both *Victoria* and *Camperdown*—twin ships in practically every detail—were no less than six hundred yards. That is, if their helms were jammed over hard a-port or hard a-starboard, with propeller assisting the rudder, the ships could turn a half-circle that would bring them back to the same relative position as before starting the turn of six hundred yards, diameter. That was the emergency turning circle, used only in case of crisis. The normal turning circle, which did not allow for a jammed-over helm, which retards headway and binds the ship to a considerable extent, by affecting the action of her screws, of both ships was eight hundred yards—the double of which is sixteen hundred. Consequently, using emergency helm even, there was not a single fathom by way of a margin of safety when the two ships had completed the inward turn. Tryon's order was that the turn should be performed simultaneously by each pair of ships as they moved into position. Maybe he erred in this matter of simultaneity—it is on the cards that he intended the ships to delay so as to form a picturesque crossing pattern. That will be settled when the sea gives up its dead, and not before. He ordered a simultaneous turn of each two ships; which meant that when the circle was completed one ship would be precisely on top of the other. Allowing for leeway, tidal influence and the wind, as the order stood any two inturning ships' courses were bound to intersect, as common sense shows. If these courses intersected perfectly, one ship was obliged to strike the other.

Tryon's staff recognised the possibility of disaster if the order were persisted in. Three distinct times the admiral's attention was drawn to the impossibility of the situation. Notwithstanding this expert testimony, he persisted in his plotted course. Under his orders the following signal was hoisted:

"Second division alter course in succession sixteen points (i.e. 180 degrees) to starboard, preserving the order of the fleet. First division—his own—alter course in succession 16 points to port, preserving the order of the fleet."

In *Camperdown* Admiral Markham and Captain Johnstone, both sterling tacticians as well as thoroughgoing seamen, were at a loss to interpret this astonishing signal. The first thing imprinted on any ship's navigating personnel is the turning circle, emergency and ordinary, of their ship; since so many factors depend on an accurate knowledge of this factor. Each man well knows that so many degrees of helm affect the ship's course so many points—and the whole thing is reduced to an exact science, provided the water in which the manœuvre takes place, is calm, as was the Mediterranean this tragic night.

"The thing's impossible," was their joint verdict. "Read that signal again." A second reading confirmed the first—a sixteen-point turn inwards, ships preserving fleet-order.

"Signal back: 'Order not understood!'" instructed Markham. In peacetime the order to one in command of a ship is: "Do not unnecessarily endanger your vessel." This can only be overruled by a senior officer on the spot; and a senior officer's instructions must be implicitly obeyed, otherwise in emergency confusion is bound to result. The only possible questioning of such a command as flew from Tryon's signal mast was to say: "Order not understood"; and that conceivably meant an enquiry at a later hour.

Admiral Tryon curtly replied to Markham's official protest: "What are you waiting for?"

It was the senior officer's job. It was not for subordinates to know what processes informed his strategic mind. The beginning of an evolution is not necessarily the end of it. Maybe the senior officer intended to give a practical demonstration of margins of safety. The inward turn could be halted at any stage by another signal; and when two ships are twelve hundred yards apart they appear reasonably distant.

Markham and Johnstone were there to obey orders, not to question them unduly. Discipline dictated that. If trouble resulted the onus would rest on the shoulders of the man at the top who issued the instructions: and if underlings held back, their professional future was unquestionably jeopardised.

"We must do as we are told," was the summing-up of the juniors' discussion. "The Admiral has something out of ordinary up his sleeve. Probably this will be more than commonly interesting." Both men were agreed that Tryon was second to none as an experienced tactician, with every detail of naval evolution at his skilled finger-tips. "Stands to reason," was their verdict, "that he wouldn't imperil any ship under his command." The signal officer was instructed to acknowledge the order forthwith as being clearly understood; and, Tryon's signal being hauled down, the turning commenced.

Not only to the leaders aboard *Camperdown* was that signal obscure. Others of the ships in line saw the danger; and resolved to postpone their share in the evolution until it was seen what happened to the leading ships.

Twice, then, Captain the Hon. Maurice Bourke, of *Victoria,* drew Admiral Tryon's attention to the fact that the two turning ships would be perilously close to one another at the conclusion of the wheel. His experienced eye measured the relative course of these two great sea-castles; and saw in anticipation what would happen. There was a hush around—subordinates saw, too, what impended; but it was not for them to question. Discipline is discipline; and even if men of the services are ordered to death they must go. But it seemed as if the general apprehension conveyed itself to the atmosphere—reddening to the sunset. It is said that the air appeared to grow tense and ominous; almost as if the world were holding its breath in anticipation of a cataclysm. Yet so confident were all concerned in the quality of their Admiral, that not so much as a ripple disturbed their professional calm.

To Captain Bourke's protest Admiral Tryon returned no reply. He may have understood it; he may not. He was silent. The two ships swung nearer to each other with the implacable

[31]

certainty of mighty bodies attracted by a magnetic force to a common focus. Already they were committed irrevocably; under normal helm their courses must intersect. Captain Bourke, understanding—and himself responsible for the individual safety of his ship in case of necessity—ventured the suggestion that the port engines should be put to full speed astern; as this would drag the ship's head round to port in a quicker circle. It was a counsel of desperation.

To his captain's resourceful hint Admiral Tryon returned no reply; it was as if he had never heard it. Captain Bourke repeated his suggestion—again and again. It was ignored. Imagine the emotions of the man who was responsible to his God for the wellbeing of that enormous crew, and to the Admiralty for the continued security of a mighty ship! It was as if his own clear-thinking brain had failed him when everything depended on its clarity. No panic, of course, no indecent protestations, indeed—an outward acceptance of a nonunderstandable phenomenon; but inwardly—emotion chasing confused emotion; the ready brain accepting this possibility and discarding that; the instinct fostered by years of training evolving ideas for safety even thus late along; and, behind it all, a sorting and re-sorting of the ultimate measures possible for the salvation of menaced human life.

There were 660 men looking to him for life; and the inward swing of the two vast ships continued. Apparently nothing could now avert the dreaded impact; and when that came one ship or the other must assuredly be so deeply cut into by the armoured ram of the other, that nothing could prevent her sinking, watertight doors and decks notwithstanding. Bourke repeated his suggestion with increased urgency.

"Very well," was Tryon's curt reply: "Full astern port engines!" That acceptance of a subordinate's counsel was made too late to save; perhaps not too late to minimise the inevitable catastrophe. Time must be lost in bringing such mighty masses of machinery from eight knots ahead to stop and full speed astern and still more time must elapse before the sternward pluck of the reversed propeller took effect on a ship already impetuously committed to a certain course. But the order was instantly transmitted to the engine-room. Meantime, her helm hard over, *Victoria* continued her devastating swing. Not even the swift reversal of both engines could save her now; *Camperdown* appeared to be leaping at her in giant strides, and towering overwhelmingly high.

Markham and Johnstone were alive to the hazard; and as soon as it was realised that Tryon had blundered, *Camperdown's* starboard engines were reversed in effort to twist her more sharply on her heel. But it was too late with *Camperdown* as it was with *Victoria*. The two ships drew remorselessly together on joining courses. Nothing human could avert an impact. Four short minutes from the time of Tryon's signal becoming effective, giant met giant with terrific force. The bows of *Camperdown* struck the broad of *Victoria's* starboard bow like the hammer of doom; and through the stout armour cut a way as a knife slices through cheese. There were 12,000 tons of moving steel behind that blow; and, *Victoria* also moving, what started as a cut ended as a savage tear. The awful, incredible wail and gride of tortured metal sounded; the splintering of timbers; there followed the sleek gurgle of the waiting water's savage inrush. Hit—hard hit! The *Camperdown's* ram had done a task it was never designed to perform. That fearful spur was intended to rive open the scalded bowels of some stout enemy ship; but it did its terrible work equally well on the body of a friend. So great was the impact of collision that, in addition to the ram eating into *Victoria's* vitals—and below the waterline was no armoured protection, so that the spur literally cut down everything in its path—the keen cutwater of *Camperdown* shore into the upperworks of *Victoria,* leaving a ghastly chasm, which widened as the death-agony commenced.

Let us get facts correct and endeavour to draw a living picture of that moment of havoc. Let us remember that the *Victoria* displaced 12,000 tons. Let us remember that she was submerged to a depth of twenty-seven feet; rooted in the non-elastic sea, as it were. As solid as an island, one would think; but the thrust of *Camperdown's* devastating bow drove her bodily sideways for a distance of seventy feet! It was as if a mountain had been pushed aside from its eternal foundations; and as happens when a convulsive force of nature is loosed, so did *Victoria* cringe and stagger before that mighty stroke. She drew clear of the murderous ram. Maybe, had *Camperdown* continued to move ahead, retaining her bow in the breach, *Victoria* would have continued afloat for a longer space of time and the tale of havoc would have been less disastrous. Such a course has been adopted with success in several cases of collision; for it is the initial impact that tears steel apart more than sustained light pressure. The reserve of buoyancy in *Camperdown* may have been great enough to permit her to continue afloat even with *Victoria* hanging to her bow; to continue afloat, at least, until *Victoria's* people were transferred in safety from ship to ship. But *Camperdown* did not continue in the death-gap; and I am of opinion that the impact of collision acted in such a way as to discard the hull of *Victoria* after the biting blow was inflicted. If *Victoria,* almost broadside on, shifted seventy feet as a result of the blow, *Camperdown,* stern on to the sea, must certainly have recoiled; and once having done so it must have been impossible for her to notch her destructive bows into the cavity that was the *Victoria's* death-wound.

Immediately the two vessels drew apart, *Victoria* lurched to starboard; thus giving greater facility of entry to the sea. When the collision showed as inevitable all watertight doors on all decks were closed by the call of a startled bugle. But the guarded decks were riven asunder; not all the watertight doors in the world could have saved *Victoria*. She was marked by the sea-gods for destruction from the moment when she commenced that incredible turn. With solid water racing into her vitals, she began to settle down by the head.

Here, then, was calamity most dire; a nerve-shattering ordeal enough to create panic in the stoutest breasts. To have one's foundations, tested through uncounted stresses, believed in with an ardour of faith not to be understood by a landsman, suddenly torn away; to feel solid foothold melt to nothingness is as disconcerting an experience as human mind can conceive. But mark how the value of iron discipline holds in the face of such disaster even as this. Out of the hundreds of men aboard *Victoria* 359 were doomed to die. Most of all hands believed themselves bound for Davy Jones's locker. It would have been so easy for a panic to arise—nothing is so infectious as fear; it flies like wildfire; and brave men tasting its qualms do things which they repent all their remaining lives.

Aboard *Victoria* the most perfect discipline prevailed from the first moment to the last. Here was no hint of *sauve qui peut*: every man's destiny remained at present in the hands of his superiors. The bugles sounded "Still!" that instant emergency call which locks the ranks into ironlike steadfastness. Men stiffened where they stood until the call of "Collision stations!" sounded hard on the heels of the first. Like rocks they stood. It seemed to be a case of *"Birkenhead* Drill" all over again. There is nothing like taut discipline for easing the full weight of a catastrophe.

"Sick men on deck—prisoners from cells!" came the crisp order. The Admiral's jurisdiction over the ship had automatically ceased when her peril came. Tryon commanded the fleet —as a strategical, tactical unit; but Bourke commanded the ship so far as discipline and safeguarding were concerned. It is gathered that here was no blind-spot; orders came calmly, incisively, and necessarily.

Tryon said nothing of value. Maybe he was staggered by the awful quality of the disaster. Conceivably he stared ahead into a bleak future; no man could expect to survive official censure after committing such an error. What thoughts irked that mind must be left to the imagination: they were never spoken.

The moment it was seen from the other ships of the fleet what had occurred, preparations were made to assist the stricken giant; boat-stations were piped. There were enough available life-saving craft among the remaining vessels to save ten times the men aboard *Victoria;* and there was nothing to deter even a cockboat from leaving its parent craft. Astonishingly, Tryon spoke.

"Signal: 'Annul sending boats!'" he commanded. He was still supreme; his orders must needs be obeyed. In the dead silence prevailing the signal was made; the other ships secured their boats and did nothing. Time was passing, the *Victoria* was sinking terribly fast. Yet the paraded crew remained silent and at attention. It was not for them to reason. They knew a blunder had been made, as did the Light Brigade at Balaclava; what remained for them was to die at their stations if nothing further were said. Magnificent discipline, and—a useless gamble with human life! Flattering to the vanity of disciplinarians, yes; but—futile.

It seems evident that Admiral Tryon intended to steam at full speed to the not-far-distant land and beach his ship; which is an excellent piece of seamanship if it can be carried out. Once a ship touches the sand in fine weather she is safe—for a time. But it was too late for the fulfilment of this manœuvre; *Victoria* was shivering under that pole-axing blow. She was badly down by the head and tilting still more. The decks on which the men paraded slanted evilly; so much so that keeping a footing was difficult.

The order *"Sauve qui peut!"* was given too late. One can but surmise that human mentality was so shocked by the vastness of the mishap that even commonsense precautions were forgotten. Maybe the idea persisted in official minds that the great *Victoria* could not sink—just as the idea persisted in a later tragedy when the *Titanic* was lost in mid-Atlantic. *Victoria* slanted savagely, rearing her stern towards the skies, with the White Ensign flaunting defiantly over the taffrail.

"She's going—jump—save yourselves!" pealed the command. Then discipline was relaxed; the locked ranks broke; men sprang for the side. As they did so—inevitably crowded as those in the front hung back and those behind pressed forward —for after all the claims of life are dominant when the intelligence is freed—*Victoria* slid under that treacherous sea; and, sliding, turned on her own axis as relentlessly as a Juggernaut. Who could have expected that crowning irony of fate? Had she surged down and kept topside uppermost, matters had been better; this deadly twist cost Britain hundreds of gallant men that Mediterranean evening. The ship fell over on the swimmers and on those who dived; and took them down with her to the untroubled sea-floors.

There in the oily swirls a few heads showed; then a few more; a lot; still more. Picture that scene—the big ships standing by without offering a helping hand, still bound by the iron laws of a discipline that was for once mistaken. In the troubled waters, eddying now, uphove, sinister—men dying for want of a helping hand. Dying, yes—and horribly, inconceivably. For *Victoria's* engines were working furiously as she slipped under her final covering; indeed, her entire engine-room staff were at stations down below to the end. The ship was endeavouring to run for shore—and she could not run with stilled engines. The engine-room staff remained resolutely at duty's post—with the water invading and the very foundation of their world parting asunder to the tilt of the drowning bows.

The screws rotated rapidly, I have said. Mark the consequences. The instinct of men in hazard is to climb to the highest point—with an idea of seeing the odds against them. The quarterdeck of *Victoria* was her highest point as she put her bow down—men, released from the ranks, rushed for that quarterdeck. Many gained it; many fell back into the swirling cauldron. Here was no safety for a single minute—that was felt in the shiver and swing of the capsizing hull. All that remained was to leap overboard to swim for life. To leap over-

board—full in among those devilish propellers. To leap and be
hacked to fragments! That was how many of *Victoria's* men
died that fell day. Best draw a veil over such a piteous scene
of horror. Sad enough that so many died; without emphasising
the horror of their death.

The *Victoria* seemed anxious to conceal her shame from the
eyes of men; she hove her vast bulk over her slain; and carried
them down to the deeps with her. The Admiral's staff-com-
mander urged him to save himself, using everything but force
to persuade him to don a proffered lifebelt. Tryon refused the
chance; it was the gesture of a man who recognised his error
and saw no glimmer of hope ahead. He paid for his mistake in
tactics with his life—going down with the ship he had wasted.
De mortuis——

It was not the lowering sun that tinged the Tripoli sea with
crimson that evening; it was wasted human blood.

As *Victoria* tilted farther and farther, she laid her great funnels flat on the sea for a moment or two. It seemed necessary
that horror should be piled on horror that this sea-tragedy might
lose nothing in piteous completeness. For, as the funnels dipped
under, the water, hitherto held in check by bulkheads and pro-
tective decks and so prevented from entering the stokeholds,
poured in torrents into fire-boxes and furnaces, extinguishing
the fires to the accompaniment of a series of snarling explosions
—each one of which shocked some swimmers out of consciousness. Then—as a final curtain—the ship below the water, the
masses of men swimming, struggling—not all could swim—
clinging to the infinitesimal trifles of loose stuff such as buckets
and gratings; and two deep muffled detonations which lifted
sleek mounds of water that broke into roaring foam, precisely
as depth-charges behaved in the War. The great boilers had
burst—underneath the swimmers. How many were lost
through that cause will never be known; but undoubtedly certain strong swimmers—many of them helping their weaker

brethren—died in that fashion. The *Victoria* was down; the troubled waters sleeked themselves and smiled.

The fact of the sinking annulled Tryon's orders to stop the fleet sending its boats; and now began that race for life with every available boat roaring down into the water, with eager men leaping; the thresh of furiously-plied oars and the shouts of encouragement to such as swam. Good work here—three hundred officers and men salved! The one bright glimmer in an otherwise gloomy picture. Three hundred saved; three hundred and fifty lost—in peacetime. Blood being the price of Admiralty, the men of the *Victoria* had proceeded to pay it in full.

A certain young commander of *Victoria* happened to be lying in his cabin, stricken with fever, when the ship was riven asunder. Realising the menace he made shift to gain the deck, shivering though he was; and when the final call to leave an untenable position was given, he went over the side in company with his men, where he was fortunately collected by some one or other of the boats. This cannot be considered anything other than a lucky rescue; for the name of that commander was John Jellicoe—saved by the gods of chance to lead the British Navy into the greatest of all naval engagements twenty-three years later.

Then darkness fell pitifully to wipe out the memory of the greatest naval tragedy for many years; and the fleet, leaving its boats to sweep the sea in hope of succouring some strong swimmer; made for its anchorage—with the sadness that besets brave men who have witnessed men equally brave die unavailingly.

The *Victoria* was no more.

. . . .

On July 17th, 1893, a court-martial was opened at Malta to try Captain the Hon. Maurice Bourke, commander of *Victoria*, on a charge that he did wilfully and by default cast away Her Majesty's Ship, he then being responsible for her safety. The senior surviving officer of a naval disaster must inevitably face this ordeal by trial. No matter how subordinate his position; no matter how impossible for him to have been responsible, the ruling of the service goes that the senior officer surviving goes before the court to exculpate himself if he can.

Admiral Sir Michael Culme-Seymour presided over the court, which sat for ten days, taking evidence of survivors and narratives from eye-witnesses; sifting through the mass with impartial closeness; for a court-martial, if severe, is eminently fair. What puzzles the narrator is why this court should have sat so long. It must be obvious to the most casual observer that full blame for the loss attached itself to Admiral Tryon, the fleet's Commander-in-Chief; who had up to the last persisted in giving orders fatal to the continued safety of his ship, even against the staunch advice and protestations of the experts. Captain Bourke was rewarded, on entering the court, after deliberations lasting an unendurable time, by discovering that the hilt of his sword was turned to him where it lay on the board of green cloth; and that he was honourably acquitted of wilfully casting away his ship! Admiral Tryon's was the error of judgment or the mental lapse that wrapped far-away England in mourning and threw a continuing shadow over the land for many days.

Admiral Markham, as second in command of the fleet, came up for examination. He explained his actions throughout— his signal to Tryon of disciplined protest against what was obviously a false step. The court expressed regret that he had not protested more strongly against the inception of the fatal manœuvre. Well, if Admiral Markham had done so, and there had been no fatality, his protest would assuredly have marked the end of his naval career. But Markham was not censured— there was a realisation that senior officers' orders must be obeyed —otherwise only chaos can result. Markham had obeyed orders; he could have done no more. Not on his soul lies responsibility for the loss of 359 promising young lives.

CHAPTER III

THE WRECK OF THE "DUNCAN DUNBAR"

"Her broad wings swelling to the breeze, she sailed in all her pride
For the shores of Far Australia across the oceans wide;
France on her weather quarter; on her lee our Fatherland;
A gallant crew before the mast; a brave man in command——"

An ancient shellback recited that poem in my ear as my ship towed in past Sydney Heads more years ago than I care to remember. "There," he husked, pointing with a tarry finger, and his voice was tremulous: "there, that's where the *Dunbar* was lost, see ye?" I was young; I was very much impressed by his earnestness.

"Who was the *Dunbar?*" I quavered. Yes; I am certain I quavered. He expectorated solemnly over the rail, and vented a probably natural spleen in helping to get the anchor overboard off the billboard.

"The *Duncan Dunbar,*" he sniffed, "was a ship—an' she was lost over there on them pitiless rocks as ever was—go read yer Bible, young feller, an' learn!"

The record of the *Dunbar's* tragic loss is not found in the Bible, however. My veteran shipmate swore that he was an eyewitness—probably he was, for his tale when he could be persuaded to tell it was circumstantial and gripping enough to have been the straightforward record of one who had seen for himself. But the sailor was a bit of a liar—and if his name had been Johnstone, I fancy he must have given himself an even more intimate association with the piteous disaster even than that of being merely a spectator at the rescue of that seaman Johnstone

[41]

who, the sole survivor of three wrecks, remained the sole survivor of the loss of the *Duncan Dunbar*.

In the recounted loss of H.M.S. *Victoria* reference has been made to a possible "blind spot" in the brain of the Admiral commanding the Mediterranean Fleet being responsible for a world-shattering tragedy. In this respect, and in this respect only, the terrible loss of the *Duncan Dunbar* bears a resemblance to the naval catastrophe; since only by crediting the captain of the ship with a similar aberration can explanation be advanced for his remarkable actions of the night of the wreck. Nothing could be more different from the *Victoria* than the *Dunbar*—the former a powerful steam-propelled battleship, the latter a windjammer, dependent on wind and wave for her movements; unarmed beyond a few carronades for defence against such odd pirates as might be encountered in the further seas. Both died—one in a stark calm, in the sight of horrified thousands; the other in a heavens-hard gale, her end unwitnessed by any human eyes save those of the exhausted sailor who fought ashore and clung to raw rocks until his fingers were stripped to the bone, and his labouring heart failed him.

Owned by the firm of Dunbar of London, the *Duncan Dunbar* was not least among the magnificent white-winged beauties that linked our distant colony of Australia with the Motherland. As a matter of fact, she was one of the finest of that gorgeous fleet of clippers which had won back from America the honour of leading the world in speed, safety and shapeliness. Those were days when men built ships with a vast and honest pride of pure craftsmanship affecting them. They put something of themselves into their workmanship; they aimed at speed and security, and in the result evolved beauty—beauty of a kind which we shall never see again. Here was a fabric meant to conquer the worst the oceans could do—a world-encircling ship, capable of carrying rare freights down the stormy Easting, where the incessant Westerly gales persist, fitted for passengers in a hurry —and people in a hurry in those days were glad to travel by a sailing clipper in preference to the more or less experimental steamers which were dirty, smelly and uncomfortable—and meant to weather the worst furies of stark Cape Horn. She had girdled the world repeatedly, this gallant *Dunbar;* she was a favourite ship, whose arrival in Botany Bay was almost a national event—a source of public rejoicing; and she had cut down vainglorious records for high speed to an incredible degree. So swift a sailor was she that when, on the 31st of May, 1857, her captain, weighing anchor at Plymouth, made the defiant boast: "I'll anchor in Hell or Sydney in sixty days!" people might have protested at the impiety, but in no wise questioned the other element of the challenge to wind and sea. So at least the story goes; and as there is seldom smoke without fire, it appears probably that the *Dunbar's* skipper did say something to this effect as he sheeted home his topsails and notched his clipper's bow on the first lap of the outward trail, whose every frolicking wave he professed to know by sight and name!

You must picture to yourself the beauty, the finished perfection of this tall and lovely ship as she parted from the high blue English land on that sunny May morning so long ago. Give her credit for what she was—a swift shuttle of the Imperial loom; a sure connecting link between the Old and the New. Fourteen hundred tons was her register—and that was a biggish ship for those days, be it noted, when men stowed close and merchants feared to entrust too considerable ventures in one single bottom— the hazards of tempest, fire and pirates being what they were— and her cost, when fitted for sea, was in the neighbourhood of £30,000; which again was a considerable sum to be paid for a ship in 1857. She was ship-rigged—that is, square sails were carried on all her three masts. She was clipper-bowed; and her entry was as clean as the cut of a razor; although stream-lining was unknown by name in those days, she was stream-lined to the ultimate degree—a thing built for the highest speed attainable by wind-driven craft. Down the Easting, where the perpetual Westerlies blow at gale force year in and year out, she was capable of logging her fourteen-fifteen, even her sixteen knots per hour, day after scurrying day.

Her decks shone in the placid English Channel sunshine as the crew threw her rustling white wings to the happy breeze. There was a joyous twinkle of super-polished brasswork along her poop—a long promenade of beauty; ample lounging space for the sixty-three passengers who were accommodated in her cabins. She was a ship run with the perfect precision of a man-of-war; and she carried an ample crew to perform the most intricate manœuvres: a remarkably large crew for her size; since fifty-nine officers and men were signed-on to her articles. I have been required to handle much larger windjammers with less than half that number of hands.

In the broadsheet that was published after her tragic end, the poet responsible for the ballad, makes mention of her richness:

"As rich a cargo in her hold as ever good ship bore;
  Her officers as brave and true as the old seadogs of yore.
  Full-freighted, too, with English hearts her gilded cabins were:
  The brave, the young, the beautiful, the proud, the rich, the fair,
  The parent with his household; and the young and wealthy heir."

Taking her by and large, the *Dunbar* was a rich morsel to offer up as sacrifice on the pitiless altar of the sea. The estimated value of her freight was £72,000; once again, a considerable venture. Her holds were crammed to capacity with clipper-cargo—the exceptional stuff; the peculiar treasures of kings for which a young and growingly wealthy colony was clamouring as a result of the big gold strikes of that picturesque decade.

She moved to open sea with rustling precision; and there was a joyous chuckle of friendly water running at her lee scuppers. She was beautiful as a woman preened and primped for a Court presentation; and she walked the grey Channel waters like a sentient, fine-bred thing. We sailors of an older day held to a theory that a windjammer possessed some sort of a nebulous soul—that she was actually alive, entering into the spirits of such as ruled her. If that were so the *Dunbar* must have thrilled through her every timber, through every copper bolt and every square inch of her sheathing, with determination to fulfil her captain's arrogant defiance to the gods of the deeper seas.

Bustle and excitement in her cabins—not then the palatial staterooms of to-day, the meanest of which is fit to house a Duchess. Simple rooms they were, and the man who bought passage to the Antipodes bought merely space and conveyance: the four walls of his quarters. All furniture and bedding, and all small stores to form a variety in the stark deep-sea menu of pork and peasoup and the like, were provided by the traveller. Shipowners of the middle nineteenth century were autocrats; carrying others than their intimates condescendingly, as a great favour. They did not tout for passengers, well knowing there were four volunteers for every vacant berth.

After a brisk dusting in the Bay of Biscay to sweep away the accumulated dust and cobwebs of tide-water, the *Dunbar* flashed full-sailed into flying-fish weather; and her complement settled down to the reality of a sea-voyage that in those times offered many chances of variety. The halliards-chanties of the crew were the signal for fine weather; and the mellow sound of male voices roaming up among the delicate tracery of the towering rigging was as sweet music as human senses could wish to appreciate. Passengers, able to sit at a steady table again, made contacts, a dozen embryo love-affairs were set in train. Passengers and crew settled down, in the customary fashion, as members of one considerable family; interest was taken in the picturesque life of the ship. At break of day you'd see the men passengers scurrying for'ard for a souse from the wash-deck gang; you'd see the ship's butcher sharpening his knife as he eyed some portentous porker, or weighed the worth of prime pullets. The scrape of the matutinal holystone was the reveille of the ship; for passengers or no passengers, fair weather or foul, that half-religious rite of deck-scouring was persisted in day by day. Once the Trades were fairly entered, the hard-weather

[45]

canvas bent since leaving Plymouth was sent down and replaced by worn canvas that would take no hurt from the flapping and listlessness of the impending Doldrums. The voyagers lent their amateur weight to such tasks; they pulled hard and awkwardly on unfamiliar ropes. Aft on the awninged poop, the women tatted and crocheted and gossiped—comparing patterns of tambour-work; and behaving generally as travelling women are accustomed to do—with a nose-tilt for the insouciant young widow who "attracted so much attention from the gentlemen, my dear!" Great places for mild flirtations, those windjammers, where was no indecent flood-lighting; and where the soft rustling of the piling canvas whispered loverlike hints to bashful swains!

She swept gloriously through phosphorescent seas; she loitered through moon-silvered nights, when the reefpoints on the soft bosoms of the listless sails drummed faintly—as it were a challenge to the distant warfare of the strenuous Easting. Great spacious days, with the infrequent sail of a stranger to provide a mine of interesting chatter and surmise. She overhauled more leisurely ships and by dint of flags conducted long conversations of a complimentary nature as she forged triumphantly ahead of the lumbering freighters. Forward amongst her crew —all of them honest salty fellows, with ropeyarns for hair and Stockholm tar for blood, as the old saying had it—were musical instruments a-plenty; fiddles and fifes and a melodeon; and be sure the services of these specialists were enlisted for moonlight dancing on the poop. Oh, quite *proper* dancing, my dear! For this was an era when even the stately waltz was considered a thought—we—ell, unrestrained. But the polka was very much in vogue, and there were schottisches for the light-minded; and the shadow of an old gavotte for such as had not yet allowed their age to tauten their sinews and stiffen their muscles, although women were definitely elderly at thirty, let it be remembered; and a man of thirty-five was at least middle-aged and thinking of retirement.

[46]

The Line was crossed, we know, in time-honoured fashion. Under a sickle moon and passionate stars, Neptune came aboard to initiate the youngsters who had never crossed south of the Equator; and the passengers were happy to buy freedom of blue water at the price of so much grog. There was sky-larking a-plenty as Neptune was dragged aft on a carronade; and the whispering balmy wind among the towering spars—up there where the skyscrapers fluttered happily—gave no hint of what the future held in store for the man who had vowed to be in one place or the other in sixty days.

So there we have her—almost a fairy-ship questing south across a magic sea. In the infrequent calms she floated as on a mirror, idle as any painted ship and as beautiful. Lord, her gracious loveliness! But few calms were encountered as her master was sea-cunning to a degree. He knew just where to dodge the baffling calms and variables, where to pick up a slant that would carry him down to a blusterous south-east Trade that would swing him widely across the South Atlantic to take a free run to Tristan d'Acunha and a departure for the Easting gallop.

They made the most of these halcyon days. My old-time shipmate who vowed he had sailed shipmates with Seaman Johnstone after the event, was insistent on the quantity of flirting that transpired aboard. "What *he* said was, they hadn't so much as a thought for the day arter to-morrow," was his parrot-like cry. "Flyin' in the face o' Providence, in a manner o' speakin', if you see what I mean." If Providence is apt to get irked by a trifle of flirtation—all ships must arouse Providence's ire; for they're great places for quickening the tenderer emotions. Especially in tropical latitudes, when shore-conventions seem to lose much of their starchiness, thanks to the healing, cleansing balm of the scented winds. And my old shipmate was a great hand with the girls, himself; so he had no room to criticise!

" 'Hell or Sydney in sixty days!' them was his words," he told me, as we stood there surveying the site of disaster. "Fifty-nine days out he sighted them identical Heads; on the sixtieth—Hell took him, accordin' to his vainglorious boast!"

But I think my salty friend was romancing a little there. True, the passage Plymouth—Sydney has been done in sixty days; but it was not in that decade; as it remained for the *Cutty Sark* to scoff at twelve thousand miles of sea to that inspiring tune. Neither do the obtainable facts bear out old Rhys's statement. The *Duncan Dunbar,* as has been said, weighed anchor inside Plymouth breakwater on May 31st. But it was not until August 20th that she raised the land in the vicinity of Botany Bay— as the beautiful harbour of Sydney was called commonly at that time. So that means she had taken eighty-one days on the passage, which seems to point to the fact that the story of the captain's defiance was a myth. But a picturesque one, and a perfectly feasible one; for those old time hearts of oak had so much faith in their ships and so much confidence in themselves as navigators that they would cheerfully gamble a voyage's pay on the result of a race between ship and ship. However, even eighty-one days was not a bad passage for the Easting run. The *Duncan Dunbar* must have been taken pretty far south—well down towards the fringe of the Antarctic ice, indeed, to find winds of sufficient velocity to waft her on her impetuous way in that space of time. Maybe the genial, fatherly skipper— known as well for his social qualities as for his superlative seamanship, wanted to show some of the pretty girls an iceberg!

The *Dunbar* reeled off a brisk and boisterous tale of knots as, with topgallant sails set over single-reefed foresails, she captured the westerlies and scudded down the roaring forties with a piled welter of foam before her impetuous bow; and a fanlike wake like a steamer's reaching astern as far as the misted horizon. She was extraordinarily well-found; her mate was a perfect ship's husband; and it is placed on record that even the testing Easting, which finds out a windjammer's innate weaknesses as does no other stretch of water in all the seven seas, failed to find any feeble joint in her fighting armour. Even minor accidents failed to occur to the galloping, splendid fabric. When the heavier and more ominous squalls roared down her, her crew were handy and ample enough to shorten sail practically instantaneously. When it was deemed inadvisable to run her further, for fear of her broaching-to and running under, she was laid-to under a goosewinged main-topsail, and rode the ravaging combers like any duck. As the squalls lulled and the giant waves eased in their following frenzy; she shook out her white wings afresh, and, picking up her saucy heels, raced eastward like a startled fawn.

So she went on, for day after invigorating day, whilst the flowerlike faces of the dainty women became flushed with the tingling salty breezes of the Indian Ocean. Ended the dances now—the poop was perpetually spray-swept; and the lift and dive of the decks made foothold precarious. But what opportunities for the swains to lend a helping hand to shaky femininity, what chances for reckless gallantry in venturing up the mizen rigging amid cries of warning, to prove to admiring womankind how simple a thing it all was!

By sunset on the 20th of August, the lookout at the masthead, hopeful of winning the customary bottle of grog awarded to him who first sighted land, reported: "Land ho!" It was the high blue bluffs of the Sydney Heads—port was actually in sight. The evening was clear though squally; and the wind—blowing freshly from the east, with only a point of southing in it, was free on the starboard quarter—a port-making breeze if ever there was one. Under such circumstances, with well-trimmed canvas, the *Dunbar* was as manageable as a steamer; and, as the North Head carried a perfectly good light, there was nothing to prevent so capable a seaman as the ship's captain from running between those two frowning heads and finding snug anchorage within the magnificent harbour.

Why this course was not adopted will never, of course, be known. The sole survivor, Johnstone, was a forecastle hand; and even in those days, the forecastle was not admitted into the intimate counsels of the afterguard. Johnstone knew that, astonishingly, with that honest fair gale blowing, with every detail of the land standing out as clearly as if it were high noon, the captain gave orders to shorten sail and head-reach the ship; that is, heave her to without backing her mainyards. To be sure, old-time windjammer men dreaded the proximity of land, which held unnameable terrors for them, since navigation was a chancy science, with chronometers fallible and without wireless time signals to give any useful check. But Sydney Heads are so unmistakable in their imposing profile, that even the veriest amateur could not fail to recognise them, even when coming up from the trackless ocean in the way the *Dunbar* came. Certainly no pilot boat presented itself; but the harbour was familiar to the captain; and he would have known that the pilot-boat was sheltering just inside the Heads, waiting to be picked up and an expert take skilled charge.

"We'll stand off and on till daylight; we won't attempt to run in to-night," was the dictum, according to Johnstone. So the excitedly packed trunks must of necessity be opened again. This last night at sea was celebrated as customary, with a banquet according to the ship's resources. There were wine and music; although the awkward movements of the hove-to ship rendered recreation difficult much piquet was played; and there was a concert embodying all the talent of the cabins.

With the squalls freshening into high gale force, the captain resolved to ease his command, and render her more sea-kindly, since the reports of landing passengers are apt to be favourable or not according to their comforts of the ultimate night at sea. Upper canvas had been handed prior to heaving-to; royals and topgallantsails no longer reared to the hurrying scud above the trucks which swung in giddy arcs across the tempestuous sky.

"All hands shorten sail!" came pealing; and, since all hands were capable of eating the canvas as well as stowing it, each watch took its allotted mast: the port watch forward, the starboard at the main. Four reefs were taken in the big thundering foresail; three in the bigger, more thunderous main course. Hear the hoarse-throated seamen, laying out nimbly on the jolting yards, chantying up the weighty bunts and hauling out the reef-earrings bar-tight.

"Oh, away—ay—ay—oh; and we'll pay Paddy Doyle for his boots!" That was the reefing song; and its thunder roared tunefully up among the gaunt upper spars—the last music that most aboard were ever to hear. Whole water was slopping over the bulwarks; and the harping of the gale in the rigging was like the wailing of frightened souls viewing the horrors of Purgatory. Who cared? More days the more dollars—every twenty-four hours extra meant an increase in the ultimate pay-day, which was always too small to satisfy demands. There was nothing to worry about in the least; shortening sail made the ship kindly; and there was the comforting nearness of land to assure sea-weary travellers that comfort was not very remote. They resolved to hold a concert in the cabin—the cuddy as they used to call the passenger-saloon—and they did it. They sang the songs of the period; and young maidens recited poetry of the "Curfew shall not ring to-night" order. The captain, with an eye to future friendships—for every established settler in the Colony meant a possible house of welcome to the seafarers who'd carried them safely to haven—ordered the stewards to broach his private store of wine. Toasts were given and honoured in Madeira that had thrice made the world tour to give it added quality. Under the poop-deck warmth and light and delirious joy—above, spindrift washed the upper planking; strained eyes were piercing the hurrying sprays to maintain observation on the Sydney Head light! Contrast here—but never a hint of apprehension.

The lively movements of the ship were no worse than many previously experienced during the vivid Easting gallop. When a venturesome man returned from a visit to the deck, a few wisps of spray followed him below before the companion door could be closed; but this was merely cause for riotous laughter—sea-dodging had become a favoured pastime. The elderly gentlemen, their sleek Dundreary whiskers betraying complacence in every hair, expressed portentous sentiments; all of these were directed to the address of the bronzed, bearded captain, who smilingly acknowledged; and probably made a mental calculation of the value of the service of plate that would be presented him as a testimonial and a thankoffering.

The round-shanked stewards shouldered their way about the cuddy, rubbing shoulders along the mahogany and maple panelling; and the swing lamps under the beautiful skylight paralleled the deck-beams above as the ship rioted and danced.

Up on deck, the chief officer—wise seaman, capable navigator—found the evil weight of the squalls increasing; and gave orders to reduce sail still further. The mizen topsail was accordingly stowed—men and boys fighting hard on the jolting yard; especially the boys, for to them was given, as a general thing, the handling of the mizenmast from truck to partners. These sturdy youngsters prided themselves on being at least as good hands aloft as the forecastle men; and they made a businesslike job of stowing this big sail. Then, descending to the streaming deck, where whole water was by now sweeping in chilly cascades, they tackled the spanker brails and soon had that roaring stretch of canvas reduced to orderliness.

"Tell the boatswain of the port watch to make fast the inner jib and maintop mast staysail," ordered the mate when this work was completed to his satisfaction. The two big fore-and-afters were hauled down and gasketed in man-o'-war fashion—men clambered out along the diving bowsprit to make good the work demanded, and stared down at the frothing turmoil of the water parted by the *Dunbar's* bitted bows. The ship was now reduced to almost the easiest sail and perfectly manageable. What canvas still remained set was of the finest quality and split-new, capable of sustaining the attacks of the fiercest typhoon that ever blew. The spars were sound; every inch of rigging likely to suffer from chafe was served with sword-mats and sennet. Not a single weak point was in the whole magnificent fighting-armour.

"Let her go through the water," the mate ordered the helmsman. "Go your course—Nor'east by North."

Able Seaman Johnstone, in giving his verdict, definitely stated that, in his opinion, the ship had been stripped too starkly of her wings. In heavy weather a ship is apt to sag heavily to leeward if she has not got sufficient headway; and only by showing canvas can headway be won. But leeway is a different matter. Every part of the ship exposed to the gale acts against her; spars, hull, even her stripped rigging hold sufficient wind to set her down to leeward. The better speed she makes the less her leeway; and if you point the yards and let her reach up as close as may be into the eye of the wind, she loses her headway automatically and thus gives leeway a chance to get in its work.

But Johnstone's dictum may be accepted with a large grain of salt. He was a much-shaken man when he was required to give his evidence—he had seen unmentionable horrors. Furthermore, the average forecastle sailor of that day knew remarkably little of the art of ship-handling. His ignorance was, as a matter of fact, colossal. He could pull a rope without in the least realising why he pulled it, or its relation to the general behaviour of the ship. He could make a dozen voyages in a ship without discovering the best point of her sailing; he was, in many instances, merely a slow-thinking machine, ready to obey any order unquestioningly; and ready to leave it at that— trusting implicitly to the wisdom of such as were set in authority over him. Maybe he was a bit of a sea-lawyer; but the technique of seamanship was a sealed book to him. It is hardly likely that such an experienced seaman as the mate, acting in close co-operation with the captain, would prejudice the safety of the ship for the sake of adding a little ease to the passengers on their last night aboard.

Let it always be borne in mind how the windjammer sailor of that era had a wholesome dread of the land. I have myself seen a shipmaster, on sighting Australia after a three months' passage, when nothing whatever has been sighted, promptly tack his ship and scud away into the open seas whilst the land was yet no more than a filmy cloud on the horizon, until he hardened his courage sufficiently to tackle the problem of making port. No, the *Dunbar* was not making exceptional leeway that night; of that I am convinced. With her canvas shortened she had ceased to labour; and the seas that had hitherto been deluging her, had lost much of their malignity. It is possible to run from poop-break to forecastle without getting a wetted jacket; and she was handling so comfortably that only one man was at the wheel—this is in itself a proof of her good position. For those old-time windjammers, when fighting furious storms, sometimes took as many as four men to handle their steering— their wheels were double, to permit four pairs of hands to deal with the kick of the jolted rudder and the whimsies of a fabric that, given an inch of rein, would take a cableslength of advantage and swung widely in an attempt to broach-to.

Eight o'clock came—eight bells tinkled aft, to be repeated boomingly by the forecastle bell. The long-drawn hail of the lookouts beat through hum of wind and rasp of wind-stretched canvas: "The lights are bright, sir—all's well!" A note of security there—you always find it in a ship at sea. That "all's well" hail has quietened many tremors of fear—it is a proof that the brains and muscles of the ship's people are combined in a scheme for the safety of such as are entrusted to their care.

The watches mustered under the hang of the high poop; the two boatswains reported: "Watches are aft, sir." The second mate had come up to relieve the mate and the captain was maintaining a watchful supervision from the background.

"Ay, ay; relieve the wheel and lookout. Watch on deck keep aft; watch below keep handy for a call!" That meant the watch going to rest would turn in all-standing, ready for immediate emergency; a common precaution when the ship was in heavy weather or in the vicinity of land. Any sudden manœuvre might be demanded, and if you had to wait until your crew were dressed and oil-skinned, you might lose precious minutes.

The routine was carried out. An A.B. climbed the lee ladder of the poop—it is a deadly sin to approach that stronghold of authority to windward—and rolled aft, stepped behind the helmsman and laid his hands to the spokes.

"Got her, shipmate—all right here."

"Course is Nor'east by North—steerin' like a boat, she is, my hearty! Watch her weather-helm a bit; she's apt to fly up."

"I'll watch the old—— Right, matey, I got her. Tell a boy to prick up them binnacle lamps, will yer?"

The relieved helmsman spat and surrendered the spokes. He shambled forward, tacked up the gangway, and reported to the shrouded watch-officer: "Nor'east by North, sir—all's well." Meticulously the mate repeated the reported course. That was done of set purpose—to eliminate the possibility of a wrong course being passed from man to man. When a sailor is in a hurry to get below, it is a simple thing to say Nor'east by East instead of Nor'east by North, say. By reporting it to the watch-officer whilst the words are still in his mind, he obviates a lot of risk. This unknown helmsman reported correctly; and the mate replied: "Nor'east by North—ay, ay." The relieved lookouts beat their way aft, and at the poop-break loudly reported the fact of their reliefs, naming their successors. The ship settled down to her watchful night routine. The second mate, having the watch, kept a careful eye on the glimmer of the Sydney Head Light; securing its bearing by persistent observations of the compass. A light to leeward in a seaway is a chancy thing.

The captain paced the weather poop; change of watch is always an opportunity for the autocrat to take a few steps of exercise; and the atmosphere below had been stuffy, since the cabin accommodation was more or less battened down; and people were not so insistent on adequate ventilation as to-day they are. He summoned the second mate.

"Take a reef in the fore-course, Mister," he ordered. That looked like heaving-to; at all events, it was a right step to avoid excessive leeway, if excessive leeway there were.

"Hands—reef the foresail!" bellowed the second mate. It was a job for the watch alone—twenty-five men were available. For cooks and stewards took part and lot in the ship's handling then; and often a cook would be as fine a seaman as any before the mast. The second mate went forward to handle the situation; a big fore-course cannot be hauled up like a handful of washing. He saw to the passing of the lazy tack, and the casting adrift of the chain foretack, belayed to the capstan where it had been hove down long before. "Furl the weather and loose the lee" is the windjammer maxim.

"Stand by your weather clew-garnet—man your weather gear!" He eased up the tack as the men took the strain, eased a bit more, let it fly; and with roars and shattering flaps, the great sail was snugged to the yard.

"Lee gear—stand by!" Up went the lee-side. Comparative calm enveloped the *Dunbar,* after the recent riot of shouting men and thunderous canvas.

"Up aloft and reef it!" The second mate led the way; that was his job. The sea idea was, still is: "Come and do it!" not "Go and do it!" The men, beaten flat against the shrouds, clambered aloft, and laid out on the great jolting yard. The reef-cringles were picked up, reef-earrings were passed; the reef band was stretched bar-taut along the jackstays. Nimbly enough the reef-points were knotted; and the work was done.

"Down on deck, and set it!" The lee-sheet was dragged home; the tack was boused down; the reduced sail took the wind and bellied and strained and roared its rare song of striving.

"Aft, the watch!" came through the captain's speaking-trumpet. The men trooped aft, anticipating an issue of grog—the usual reward for extra forced labour of this quality.

"Weather main-brace," ordered the captain; "square the yards." It was his own affair; it was the part of no man to question that decision. The captain of a ship then, as to-day, was lord paramount in regard to her immediate destinies. Conceivably some influential passenger below had fretted at the delay in arrival. Maybe there'd been a word spoken which the captain construed into a reflection on his personal courage and quality of ship-handling. Maybe some pretty girl had coyly entreated him to have his ship at anchors by daybreak; so that she might witness the miracle of a sunrise over lovely Sydney Harbour; than which there are few more beautiful sights in the world. Johnstone was not to know what ran in the captain's mind; and Johnstone had not been down in the saloons to find out what had transpired there. And Johnstone was the only man remaining who could tell anything about those last important hours. Something happened after eight o'clock on the night of August 20th, 1857, down there in the ill-fated *Dunbar's* cabin to change the determination of a sea-wise man. The *Dunbar* was safe from everything except submarine earthquakes; she had a decent offing; and if trepidation had been aroused on that score, it would have been a comparatively simple matter to wear her round on her heel and stand away to the due south on a bowline—the coastline, trending west to the south, could not have embayed her. So it is obvious that a challenge had been issued; and that the captain had accepted it.

"We'll run for the harbour," he said. If the second mate wondered he made no demur; that wasn't his job. He squared the main-yards with meticulous precision and took the watch forward to square the fore; that the ship should be properly balanced.

"Keep her away before the wind!" the captain ordered the

man at the wheel; who immediately complained that the ship was unkindly on her helm under the altered conditions.

"Another hand to the wheel!" The *Dunbar* picked up her heels, welcoming the easing of the stern hand on her bridle; and began to push a noble pile of foam before her eager bow. She was like a dog racing home to its welcoming kennel; every timber creaked with her eagerness; and the roar of the parted water of her impetus was an invigorating sound. Rain slashed down; but through the bursting squalls the Sydney Head Light was clearly visible; and running free the *Dunbar* was as easy to handle as any steamer. The rain-laden wind was aft, not in any way blinding the eyes of the lookouts or the officers aft. But the captain wished to be sure of keen watchfulness.

"Send the third mate for'ard to stiffen the forecastle lookout," was his order. The third mate went forward, to join the two men already there. His instructions were to maintain a close lookout for land; and to report anything out of common. With rain thickening and wind increasing, the captain tasted a keener apprehension.

"Go forward yourself, Mister," he informed the second mate. "And keep your eyes skinned. I'll look out for her aft here." The second mate went forward; and the two officers, one at either cathead, swept the misted seascape with keen glances. A long flurry of rain beat down; shutting out everything but the high and roaring sea. The wind was high; the sea was running in mountains; and the *Dunbar* was wallowing considerably, though the two helmsmen were doing all they could to keep her easy. The captain fretted, moving from lighted binnacle to mizen swifter—staring, thinking, discarding and accepting. Presently he picked up his speaking trumpet and hailed the lookouts.

"Do you see anything of the North Head Light, sir?" he challenged.

"No, sir!" came thinly back from forward. "Nothing in sight, sir!" There was a pause; what time the thunderous diapason of the storm persisted; and then, in a stabbing shriek from the forecastle-head: a cry, rising to panic-tone; a cry pregnant with horror: "Breakers ahead!" The dull white loom of great waters beating themselves to foam at the foot of pitiless cliffs could be seen ahead. There was death; for here was a veritable Devil's Playground of old Ocean.

The captain grasped the portent instantly; he was unshaken. The ship was making greater headway than he had surmised; and the easterly gale was helping the landward-racing currents.

"At the helm there—port! Hard a-port!" he boomed. The wheel went down as fast as two pair of hands could spin the spokes. But you must ready a windjammer if you are going to use her helm to any unusual extent. She ran the risk of being caught aback, of broaching-to, and becoming a helpless victim of wind and sea; likely as not, considering the terrific immensity of the squalls, the masts would be whipped out of her, and she become a sheer hulk. To let go anchors was impossible—the cables would have snapped like pack-thread, even were the water sufficiently shallow to allow the ground tackle to take hold.

"Port fore-braces!" the captain roared. The watch hurried forward; the second mate leaped at a bound from forecastle to deck; and swiftly cast off the starboard braces, so that the yards ran forward with a jolt. Already the crash of the breakers was audible, beating back against the wind; and the *Dunbar* rioted wildly.

"Hard down!" volleyed the captain. "Starboard main braces —let 'em run!"

Too late! It was not the South Head which lay directly ahead, but the North. The action of casting the ship into the wind only brought her into more imminent peril. Her impetus was terrific, hounded by the fury of the gale and the run of the racing seas, as she was. Spilling her sails of wind in no wise checked her. She struck the rocks bow-on, recoiled, crashed forward again; going at something like fourteen knots. Here was no shelving beach to give her kindly harbourage; only stark, precipitous rock welcomed her, with water at its foot deep enough to allow her bowsprit to strike before her keel touched bottom. She roared forward again and crumpling her bowsprit, split herself wide open.

Instantly was shrieking horror. The jarring impact threw those on deck off their feet; a vast wave galloped up, finding the check of the arrested hull, it towered high—higher; then, wind-driven, fell, to make a clean sweep of that tortured deck. Men fought in a welter of furious water on a deck that shivered to nothingness under them. There was no hope anywhere; no prospect of life. There remained no time even to cast loose a single boat-gripe, or to fling a grating overside to which some drowning human might cling for a brief respite. For, recoiling from her second impact, the *Dunbar* dipped her riven bow and in the water swept—as into a tidal cave. She swung her stripped masts in a wild arc, dipped them—further, further, as she slid away from the land that had sentenced her to death; she snarled under; and those in her cabins had not even time to realise what was happening to her. They were trapped by the inrushing water; such as did fight a breathless way to the open deck, were swept off their feet and away by the merciless breakers, whose roar was their death-knell.

The *Dunbar* went down; and the rocks beneath her mangled her out of all semblance to a ship. Her masts crashed as she fell off; but the rigging held them so that they went down with the ship, in deep water. The frothing maelstrom of the breakers beating against the Sydney Head toyed with strong swimmers in their agony, as it toyed with slim, drowned maidens and children who, an hour before, had chucklingly rejoiced in the imminence of dry land and secure foothold.

In that hell-broth nothing could live. In the black darkness and the insistent downfall of the wind-beaten rain, the tragedy was consummated, without spectators. Occasionally a shrill cry fought to be heard above the shriek of wind but there were none to hear it; and nothing human could have availed had the cries been heard; for here was one of the world's worst danger-spots; and modern science had not yet thought out alternatives to destruction.

The captain was thrown down at the first impact; the boarding wave swept him away. Similarly with the officers—such as were on deck. Here, fortunately, were no long-drawn-out horrors of suspenseful waiting for an inevitable end. The sea, in its bitter cruelty, was merciful—it struck and killed without torturing. Very swiftly the creamy breakers roared on without check, as if nothing untoward had occurred. As the unknown poet declared:

"In cavern dark the greedy shark held revel rich and rare,
What food for him, the monster grim, the brave, the rich, the fair!
Britannia needs no bulwark, no towers along the steep;
Her march is o'er the mountain-waves; her home is on the deep!"

For those savage waters that boil at the foot of Sydney Head are the tiger-sharks' playground. The captain of the *Dunbar* had fulfilled his arrogant boast, but Sydney was not the port he made!

The pitiful fate of the *Dunbar* must have gone unknown for some time—although her proximity to the land had been noted during the day before the end came—if it had not been for the able seaman, Johnstone. Miraculously this man, the sport of the breakers, hammered by fragments of wreckage, tangled by loose cordage, was carried clear of the hull when it went under. He was not a strong swimmer—few merchant seamen of that day were; since so many of them obstinately refused to learn, arguing that to swim simply meant to prolong the death-agony. Yet he did not drown. Buffeted by water, stunned by wind, he fought and fought and fought! In his affrighted ears rang the screams of his shipmates whom the sharks snatched ere they died. Presently, almost senseless, a brutal wave picked him up and threw him—trifling flotsam—on to a shelf of rock above the general run of the hounding waves. Here he clung, torn at jealously by those mocking watery fingers; holding on by his eyebrows; his lacerated hands tried almost to the breaking-point. Hour after hour went by, with the gale, as if rejoicing in its ghastly victory, increasing. "Between the hours of ten and two will show what wind and wave can do," ran the maxim; and during this period of purgatory, the sea did its damnedest to snatch Johnstone back. It was like a murderer scared to think that a witness of his crime might incriminatingly remain alive; but Johnstone held on. The shelf was barely wide enough for safety; to the drenched, lacerated man was no comfort of any kind—only, as the quick southern dawn broke, an accumulation of horror. For there within easy eyeshot of him was the wrecked *Dunbar,* jostled among the rocks and hurled up and forward until she was visible; and all around her, washing in the run of the foam, the bodies of those with whom Johnstone had laughed and worked and fed. He covered his eyes with shivering hands and prayed for death to end his torment; and death held aloof.

But the fascination of the horrible caused him to uncover his eyes; and, as the day grew, he saw people—living people, standing at a point on the rocks above the water level. He shouted his loudest—poor human voice against the whip of a gale! He waved his hands, shouted again and again, until his throat lost all power of sound; and they neither saw nor heard him; but disappeared. Johnstone's reason almost deserted him then.

But news of the non-arrival of the ill-fated *Dunbar* was conveyed to Sydney; and, sensing an ominous tragedy, search-parties set out. For long they found nothing; then fragments of wreckage were seen, fragmentary human bodies, too—inaccessible as yet until the rigour of the storm abated. It occurred to some of the searchers that there might be survivors, since the sea is a worker of miracles; and they quested here and quested there amongst those terrible rocks. Ultimately Johnstone was seen, cowered in his trifling shelter. He heard their shouts and waved a feeble hand.

"A living man!" was the word passed round. Impossible to reach him from the sea; and the cliffs were overhanging him to a height of hundreds of feet. But it is not in human nature to allow a fellow-man to die when effort can avail him anything. Many of those searchers carried in their veins the blood of hardy Scots mountaineers—these were men trained to climb, to beat the crags. One man volunteered to descend in the bight of a rope. The attempt was made; it failed; a fresh attempt, another failure. Johnstone lay in an almost inaccessible rock niche. But defeat stirred the rescuers to extra effort; and an attempt was successful; Johnstone was reached, a rope knotted about his limp body; and he was drawn up to the summit—a man more dead than alive, vacant in mind for many a weary day, his soul stunned by the torment he had endured and the horrors he had witnessed. By him, ultimately, the story was told; a story that holds in it as many qualities of mystery as does the story of the ill-fated *Victoria*. In each case the disaster was caused by some failure in the commander's mind; the vulnerable human factor which may never be left out of the reckoning.

Johnstone, miraculously, lived. Shipwrecks were to him a commonplace, apparently. Of three major catastrophes he—an inconspicuous mariner—had been the sole survivor. He stands recorded in history as the man the sea could not destroy.

CHAPTER IV

THE "TITANIC": A SHIPWRECK THAT SHOOK THE WORLD

"So far shalt thou go, and no further!"

MANY wise heads were shaken when the directors of the White Star Line publicly stated their intention to recapture for their company the Blue Ribbon of the Atlantic; if not for speed, at least for size, luxury and perfect maritime security.

"Trifling with Providence—building ships that size," said some. "It's like throwing a glove in the face of the Almighty!" declared others. "A ship nearly a thousand feet long—if she's picked up by two Atlantic waves she'll break her back in the middle—it isn't in seafaring nature to stand that sort of a strain —she's got to break," said still others. By comparison with the meditated liner, the *Lusitania* and *Mauretania,* record-holders for many years of the Atlantic crossing, appeared little better than cockboats. Even for the big-thinking White Star Line, the *Titanic* was a monster; though this go-ahead firm had specialised in big and bigger ships ever since the speed record had been won from them. For, to win success, you must achieve notoriety in one way or another. To build for speed is about the costliest proceeding known to shipbuilding minds; after twenty knots every extra knot achieved costs about as much as the previous twenty. But hopes were entertained that, in addition to being the largest and most luxurious of all the sea-castles, the *Titanic* might prove herself the speediest, though no claims were made on her behalf in this respect; indeed, a hush-hush policy was maintained.

[64]

The public prints dealt exhaustively with the new leviathan's mammoth perfections. Here was the last word in steam hotels —a mechanical vision of a floating city, replete with comfort, abounding in palatial luxury; lacking for nothing that could make for human contentment and enjoyment. There were Turkish baths; there were verandah cafés, there were recreation rooms surpassing the fancy of a Monte Cristo. Details of her provisioning when about to start her maiden voyage filled many columns—so many quarters of beef to be roasted whole in wonderful electric ovens; so many tons of potatoes, so many gallons of ice-cream; so many bunches of grapes—Lucullus might have felt his mouth water at a recital of the gustatory revelations.

There were so many acres of steel plating to be covered with rust-resisting paint; so many acres of deck-planking to be scrubbed white as a hound's tooth every morning. She would carry a crew as big as an old first-rater; she would burn half a thousand tons of coal per day to maintain her speed. The mind reeled to visions of her sheer ponderosity; and, seeing her in course of building, the idea of her size was conveyed to the senses with a suggestion of shock. Afloat, without comparisons of smaller craft to lead the eye to measure her relatively, she seemed nothing like so gigantic as the figures led to believe; so graceful were her lines and so perfect her proportions. She was, in a word, "a lovely ship" as all the smaller ships of her line were lovely: built for beauty of line as well as for safety of voyaging. But we wiseacres still persisted in our theory that she was too big to be trusted in open sea—she couldn't be dexterously handled, we said—not a thing of that size. Why, what would be her turning-circle, for instance; and how would any normal rudder act on that colossal bulk?

Still, her construction went on. We were told and shown how she was being made invulnerable to any hazard of the sea. Here at last was the unsinkable ship: with every contingency provided against. Did fire break out in any part of her magnificent interior, what happened? A small electric tube in a teakwood box on the navigating-bridge changed colour; a buzzer sounded—at once the menaced compartment was indicated. There was not even need to turn the ship's fire-brigade and pumps loose to deal with the outbreak: by the mere act of adjusting a coupling, a small hose-pipe was attached to a copper pipe leading in to the seat of conflagration; and a fire-quenching gas was poured directly in to the danger-zone. Wireless— not then universally carried in ships; but still very commonly used in the bigger liners—was supplied to her; so that she would practically never be out of touch with land. Her very size rendered her inviolate from anything wind or sea could do to her: she was as ponderous as a solid chunk of the land that had created her. No Atlantic storm ever conceived could lave her high promenade decks. Ordinary discomforts of sea-travel were catered for; to minimise her rolling—always a disconcerting problem even in the finest of ships—she was fitted with craftily-planned bilge keels; whilst to make her more sea-kindly, rubber expansion bulkheads were run down through her middle part. To say that all material used in her construction was of super-fine quality is merely to admit that her owners and builders carried out their usual plan in shipbuilding.

The always-possible risk of collision was provided for, similarly the hazard of running ashore. Her double-bottom was practically one ship inside another: it was estimated that did she lose the entire outer skin of her hull from keel to bilge, her tanks would keep her afloat for an indefinite period of time. She had eight steel decks; and, on account of these decks being bulkheaded with watertight walls, each one pierced only by easily workable watertight doors, each deck was an added stronghold against possible inroads of water. To recite a complete list of her manifold mysteries and marvels would be to fill this volume a dozen times over. To-day, we realise that our apprehensions as to her clumsiness and the awkwardness of her vastness were ill-founded; we have ships of infinitely greater size using the Atlantic with the safe regularity of a ferry boat. But in 1912 the Titanic lived up to her name.

Briefly, she was almost nine hundred feet long between the perpendiculars; 883 feet to be precise. Her beam was ninety-two and a half feet; and when in dry-dock, resting on the keel-blocks, she measured 104 feet from keel to upper navigating bridge—as lofty as a ten-storied house, say. Her engines were mechanical masterpieces, capable of developing an almost incredible horse-power: enough to drive this 60,000 ton bulk through the water at a speed of over twenty-two knots. One could hardly visualise the sea that would shake her or the gales that would check her impetuous advance.

We who were privileged to inspect her, as she approached completion, grew amazed and breathless at the perfection of her internal equipment. Her wireless house was like a post office. Her kitchens outdid anything ever inspected ashore. The luxurious splendour of her recreation saloons was indescribable in limited adjectives—baronial halls, oaken panelling, diffused lighting; and in her gymnasium was offered every facility for getting rid of the pangs and woes of overfeeding—the chiefest trouble of the modern seagoer; for most liners' owners believe that complaints seldom issue from a full mouth; and so do their best to ensure that special type of contentment.

Wherever we went were new and breath-stopping marvels. The watertight doors were closable at a touch. Did any specified thing happen, here was the palliative or the antidote. Her navigating appliances were the last word in scientific completeness and complexity—there were fog bells; there were distance-finders, compasses that could not possibly get out of order; her steering engines embodied every mechanical discovery; patent logs and patent sounders—who could specify one-tenth of them all? She carried only twenty lifeboats with a total life-saving accommodation of only one thousand—but we overlooked this discrepancy. Wasn't the *Titanic* guaranteed unsinkable? Those boats, secure in their patent chocks, hanging from their patent quick-release davits, were there merely as a guarantee of good faith—not for actual use. Likely enough they would never be lowered into the water—they were ornamental; put there to satisfy the exactions of a motherly Board of Trade that hadn't moved with the times sufficiently to recognise that a ship could be built that *couldn't* sink.

We envied at the square miles of priceless carpets on saloon floors and alleyways. The liquid refreshment listed for the maiden voyage would have floated a battle-fleet; and the orchestra was credited with an ability to produce such music as would set Egyptian mummies dancing those rag-time dances then in vogue. Then we wondered ourselves ashore, and not a man amongst us all thought for an instant of that unforeseen contingency which always menaces man-made work afloat; the thousandth thing; the unexpected detail which proves Achilles' armour.

No attempt, we were told, when sailing-day drew near, would be made to lower existing transatlantic records; the *Titanic* would run herself in slowly and sweetly; "find herself," in a word. She was making this maiden trip at a time which marked the southernmost drift of the loosened Arctic ice; but who gave a thought to that fact? Not we observers; if we did, we had the proof of our own senses that she was unsinkable. If she rammed an ice-berg head-on she might conceivably shatter the berg; but though her own bows crumpled and shrivelled, her watertight bulkheads would bear her safely through even such a catastrophe, though there existed in that day none of the steady ice-patrols which safeguard the Atlantic routes to-day. Actually, it was what happened to the *Titanic* that gave rise to the formation of to-day's ice-patrol. No, nothing could happen to leviathan. Defiance was flung into the Atlantic's face when she was conceived and launched—and the Atlantic said nothing; it merely bared its teeth in a silent snarl, and—waited. Men had been trying to defy it for centuries; one more or less didn't count. It was the Atlantic, the destroying ocean;

which everlastingly held—and holds—some new surprise up its sleeve.

So, shortly after midday on April 10th, 1912, R.M.S. *Titanic* started from Southampton on her maiden trip to the west. Be sure the ships of all nations then harboured there gave her gay welcome to the noble brotherhood of sea-fighters; be sure every commander of a lesser craft pictured a day when he should achieve the summit of his ambition by commanding such a superb masterpiece as this vast giant whose funnels loomed above the warehouses gigantically; and whose upperworks presented the appearance of a considerable town.

Superstitions are to the superstitious. Who in a material age would give an ear to a growled whisper of evil omen? Out on the blighting prophet! If the giant did set trouble a-curdle in her wake as she proceeded down the docks to open water, what of it?—She was the biggest ship in the world, and her displacements must naturally affect lesser fry! You couldn't have such progress as all this without one or two antiquated shibboleths becoming slightly thrown out of gear. If the suction of her passing so acted on the big *New York*, lying in the tide-dock, as to cause the lesser craft to rear and tear at her moorings until she parted them, what then? If with broken moorings, and the suction still affecting her, the *New York* swung out into the stream as if a mighty magnet had drawn her towards the bigger ship, what of it? Here was imminent risk of a devastating collision, certainly; if those two giant ships so much as touched, the chilled steel plates of which they were built would crumple like eggshells—but a few fenders thrown over would avert that possibility. Too, where were the dock-tugs, anyhow—wasn't it their job to handle this mass of moving majesty? The threat of accident remained a threat, for the *Titanic* was brought up with a round turn; and as her propellers stopped, so did the inordinate suction; thus the *New York* was quickly got under control. But the wiseacres remarked that the great ship had scraped to safety only by the thickness of her paint—which was not a good omen. Neither was the recurrence of trouble lower down the dock; for again that wash from gigantic propellers caused the *Teutonic* to strain and heel and generally misbehave like a frightened colt, even though the *Titanic's* engines were merely turning over their centres to give steerage way. That was the second time. Watchers held their breath, believing the *Teutonic* likely to capsize; but the tension eased; and the leviathan floated slowly—very slowly—towards open water.

"That's twice!" gloomed the prophets of evil. "What about the third time killing the cat?" But beyond these ill-omened oracles, the rest of the world did not heed the portents. Why should they? They saw the new Queen of the Atlantic emerge from dock like a solid chunk of England leaving the parent mass; and the definite impression was there: that no power of wind or sea could affect her to her hurt. Columbus had crossed the Atlantic and discovered the Western world in a ship but little bigger than one of the *Titanic's* twenty lifeboats. Jesters declared that if ships were built much bigger they would no longer be ships but merely bridges. You would embark at the bow and walk to the stern, and so be in America without so much as a vibration!

A maiden voyage is like a theatre play's first night: the world and his wife are anxious to be amongst those present. The initial—and alas, only—passage attempted by the *Titanic* was no exception; amongst her 1,348 passengers she carried some world-renowned people; men and women famous for social rank, for wealth, philanthropy, and for high place in the arts. W. T. Stead was there—a man who had dared public opprobrium for the sake of proving a world-shaking fact. John Jacob Astor was there—a man with a colossal fortune and the ability to employ it wisely.

Amongst eminent people who lost their lives when the great ship went down were Sir Hugh Lane and Jacques Futrelle, the eminent French-English author of thrilling detective stories. Others were there in their numbers: indeed, the *Titanic's* passenger list read like pages of the Social Register. And all were gay and care-free; proud, indeed, to have the opportunity to take part and lot in an historic venture. To care for them, to transport them, to make all things smooth for them, Captain Smith commanded a crew of 860 persons; so that when she left the land, the *Titanic* had aboard her 2,208 human souls; the population of a small town. Some of the passengers boarded at Cherbourg and Queenstown, naturally, since these were scheduled ports of call for the westbound White Star liners.

So, amid screechings of enthusiastic sirens, and tossing of much gay bunting, amid torrential good wishes enough to have despatched a whole Armada safely on its way, R.M.S. *Titanic* steamed stately to open water; and by Thursday evening she had lost sight of land—never again to find its harbourage. She was running satisfactorily in every way: not breaking records, since her commander was naturally averse from pressing her extravagantly at the outset; but everyone aboard was more than pleased with the showing the great new sea-castle made. Fine weather persisted; initial seasickness was overcome— though there was really nothing to cause discomfort even to the most confirmed landlubber—and the full recreational capabilities of this marvel-ship were tested and passed as excellent plus. Here was sea-travel *in excelsis;* gilt-edged and ermine-trimmed —the ultimate word in opulent luxury, ease, safety and gaiety. Brisk, blood-stirring promenades along the slowly throbbing decks, with keen winds administering bracing buffets; the boisterous deck-games—shovel-board, deck-golf, quoits and tennis —real tennis with nets rigged to prevent the balls being lost overboard—the capacity for enjoyment was unlimited. You hadn't so much as a moment in which to be bored. Your latest wish was forestalled and gratified almost before it shaped itself in your mind. Music ringing through the length and breadth of this latest Argosy—and somewhere out there in the Gulf Stream neighbourhood, slinking floe-ice, mostly awash, misted secretively, waiting—waiting! Here was the stealthy assassin of the Atlantic, lightless, soundless; conveying no hint of its presence there in the steam-lanes; and the waters lapping against its edges seemed to chuckle in diabolical expectancy.

Ice was a hazard, they knew aboard the hurrying *Titanic*. But they visualised berg-ice, visible even in mist by reason of that phenomenal ice-blink known to all with experience of the Arctic Circles: a sheen as ghostly as an impression of Vander-decken's fabled galleon; or, audible through its capacity to fling back echoes from a bellowing siren. Berg-ice—nothing to fear, floe-ice—quite a different matter. But who thought of floe-ice aboard the big ship, where the music was exquisite and the fare Lucullan? It was the business of the engine-room to keep the bridge posted as to any sudden drop in the water's temperature which would foretell the imminence of ice; expert lookouts with certified eyesight were posted day and night on forecastle and in crow's nest; with one special lookout officer on constant watch in the latter eyrie. Every known precaution was taken to avoid chance of disaster; because the captain of the world's greatest ship took his duty seriously, and fully realised the almost incredible responsibility that was his. He had an added incentive to vigilance in the fact that a prominent director of the line was listed amongst the passengers; and any old sailor will tell you what a spur to diligence is such an official's presence aboard.

Captain Smith's responsibility was in truth very great. Over two thousand human lives depended on his skill and judgment; sixty-thousand gross tons of a ship lay in control of his finger; there was a freight of colossal value—all measuring its continued existence in terms of Captain Smith's mental capacity and courage.

Nor was the commander of the *Titanic* expected to be merely the diligent seaman tending his ship—countless other duties were laid on his shoulders. Indeed, as is the case with any other liner-captain of these advanced days, commanding the ship appeared to be about the least important of his duties. He was a diplomat, a social light; an arbiter; he was a Governor over

Israel; a good bit of a scientist; a super-policeman, and a swagger hotel manager; plus being a very competent seaman.

Sunday, April 19th—a tragic day in the history of blue water—dawned bright and clear: a fine, sparkling morning of still water, sun-kissed; of near cloudless sky—with only rosy cloudlets floating distantly; and of that crisp coolness which invites the healthy to vigorous exercise. A perfect sea-day, in a word; with no more evil omens attending it than attend an average peaceful Sabbath in a quiet English country village. The cold, though invigorating and apt to kiss roses into sparkling cheeks, presaged ice-berg or floe. It was a presage that the day confirmed: although nothing in the nature of ice was actually sighted from the *Titanic,* wireless messages were received from other ships reporting its presence in positions inimical to the giant's safety. But nothing is to be gained by stopping a ship in mid-ocean; if she avoids running into trouble, she is more vulnerable to trouble running into her. Furthermore, a ship making good speed is more manageable than one crawling; she responds more sweetly to her helm, and can be plucked out of trouble into which a slower and consequently more sluggish ship would blunder disastrously.

In addition to these facts, Captain Smith had a duty to perform; and an honour of which to be worthy. His duty was, if humanly feasible, to keep his command strictly adherent to her schedule; to satisfy the builders, owners and passengers of their rightness in creating and using the *Titanic;* and to please his engineers by giving the hull every advantage conferred on it by the monumental engines. Many known factors worked within the commander's mind; conceivably certain unknown factors were also present. A man can have his own personal pride, as well as pride in his Line; and Captain Smith, capable and trustworthy, was a human being. He was self-confident: otherwise he would not have held the most important mercantile command afloat. He knew the Atlantic: her whims and humours; her tricks, her rages and her subterfuges; he had spent a lifetime studying them, measuring them, adopting means to defeat the worst of Atlantic's rigours. And, what is more, until that tragic Sunday, the presence of loose ice on the sea-lanes had been treated as an ordinary risk of travel; the sea-track was estimated to carry the bottoms free of the southern-most limit of the floating terror. There were no recorded cases of ships of size coming to disaster on ice on that particular thor-oughfare; because what ice travelled so far south was always berg-ice, which towered high into the air and advertised its proximity conspicuously—by day by its outlines, by night by its blink, as aforementioned. And so, it would have been against the common usage of the sea, sanctioned by years of practice, had Captain Smith allowed himself to be shifted from his course by these warnings. You would as soon expect a seaman to be checked in departure from port by rumours of storm a thousand miles and more away!

The White Star Line is absolved from blame of the disaster pending: it was simply a public service, giving an increasingly exacting public what it demanded: speed, comfort and all the rest. The common economic law was considered at the time of the *Titanic's* inception, nothing more; she was never a defiance to the powers of sea and air. If blame belongs—for the actual accident—it attaches to that public whose iterated demand fruited in the *Titanic's* construction. But it is not intended here to apportion blame—merely to record actuality, for that is a tragic task enough for any historian.

What was happening in the Atlantic on that Sunday was this: the *Titanic,* boring a resistless way west, was throwing creamy foam from her bow and spreading it in a great and growing fan to either side and as far astern as the horizon. She walked the waters pridefully—all-conquering; worthy of every excited en-comium that had been lavished upon her, and more. Her circle of the Atlantic was tenanted only by herself. An aerial watcher would have observed that in another horizon-ringed sector of the trouble-breeding sea, a mighty stretch of floe-ice, something like

seventy miles long and twelve miles wide, was remorselessly
bearing down towards the great, unconscious ship—dragged
sinisterly by the sub-surface currents which are always running,
and which act on submerged bodies more than on those which
are shallowly on the surface. The imaginary aerial observer
would have seen that at a certain point the courses of ship and ice
would converge as inevitably as the processes of evolution occur.

On that day the people of the *Titanic* committed no sacri-
legious act. Sunday at sea, before the war especially, was always rather more sedately observed than Sunday ashore: the
old too-familiar service assumes an added seriousness and meaning when recited to the accompaniment of splashing waters and
thunderous engine-beats. Old favourite hymns are—or were
—sung with a fervour almost unimaginable on land: for in
the immensity of ocean wastes, the sheer puniness of dominant
man is hammered home to the consciousness even of affected
disbelievers. To hear "Eternal Father, strong to save" sung with
meaning and with excellent aptness, the audition should be in a
ship, at sea; for that is the proper framing of the fine old hymn;
and "Eternal Father" figured amongst the music of the day—in
the morning at the great general service in the first-class saloon;
in the evening in the combined hymn-singing in the second
cabin.

Night descended on the snoring Atlantic; and the great passionate stars came out to watch—almost, one would think, to
shiver with horror at what impended.

Eight bells—eight o'clock—and the lookouts hailing: "All's
well!"

"Keep a close lookout for ice!" was the watchword. With all
watchful eyes skinned, every guarding faculty on the alert, the
great *Titanic* roared on across those evenly-breathing plains.
The hymn-singing subsided; the pianos were closed; the little
parties that always linger on after normal bedtime—as if hoping
and expecting some impalpable thing to happen—sat around;
lovers in pairs straggled out to the darkened promenades, to read

their fortunes in the distant stars; to hear the songs of their hearts echoed in the thresh and boil and tumult of the foaming wake. Peace afloat—below, the deep, abiding peace of sleep in perfect security; for I doubt if any sense of security can be so great as that existent aboard a great liner snoring on her appointed course over an almost unruffled sea. Four bells—ten o'clock— and the masters-at-arms making their inspectorial rounds—satisfying themselves that no hidden danger lurks; testing the emergency fire appliances, swinging the closing gear of the watertight doors. In the smoke rooms little parties repeating wellwishes; congratulated themselves on work already achieved, hopeful of better work still to come.

"All's well!" from the crow's nest again; its echo from the port and starboard bow lookouts.

"Keep a good lookout for ice, there!"

"Ay, ay, sir!" The final stragglers descend to luxuriously carpeted alley-ways; lingering good nights are spoken to the harping hum of the funnel-guys.

"Another good day to-morrow—isn't this a *crossing?* Goodnight, good-night; pleasant dreams!"

Seven bells—half-past eleven—and the muffled lookouts peering; forcing laggard eyes to stare ahead and on either bow. Officers stamping to and fro on that lofty bridge, their teeth chattering in the bitter chill; but every faculty incredibly alert. "Keep a good lookout for ice!" It is there in the night order book, signed by the captain himself—that is the immediate hazard to be guarded against. A good lookout for ice—for ice that the keenest eyes in the world cannot detect as it slinks along there, so completely awash that not even a splash of the placid sea discloses its imminence.

In the deep stokehold the clang of a dropped shovel sounding up through the roaring ventilators like the beat of a muffled bell; the thud of a closing furnace door, the hissing of quenched ashes. Here is a peaceful efficiency; the entire vast fabric working like a well-oiled bit of clockwork. Security—above all security! Security for such as pass upon the sea on their lawful occasions—here it is, embodied in the evenly moving bulk, whose watchlights glimmer softly on the arrested face of the waters.

One bell—quarter to twelve; time to rouse out the relieving watch. Hints of a stir here and there, a light switched on forward; a port-hole illuminated as an officer answers the quartermaster's call. Clash and trifling tumult of the cleaning fires below; but the snore of the engines not abating a single tone.

"What was that?"

"Queer! Ship seemed to shake herself—like a dog, eh? Can't be anything, of course——"

The invulnerable *Titanic* had given a slight throb that was described by such as noticed it as a jar; a negligible impression of unaccustomed shock; but so extremely trifling as to arouse no immediate comment. As if she had brushed some floating trifle of wreckage, say, she steadied and hurried on, with an impatient shake, and a flirt of her propellers. The greatest and most tragic moments of life seldom give long warning of their imminence; they happen so normally that afterwards men are hard set to say "This thing was." But whilst that little jarring shiver was shaking the towering hull, the *Titanic* had touched with her hastening flank a spur of an ice-floe, slinking under surface; indistinguishable from the marble-like waters in which it hid. And she had torn open her plating from foremast to stern —a gaping rent, unsealable, of many hundred feet in extent. Such of the passengers below as remained awake hardly noticed that tremor; such as noticed it tacked no alarm to its happening. A ship might jar herself as much by negotiating a sudden, unexpected wave.

Up above, down in the engine-room, where the ship's brains worked double-tides, certainty that the unforeseen contingency had happened was born. "Something's wrong!"

"Hst—no alarm! If there is anything wrong and there's a panic——" That was the one thing to be avoided at any cost:

mob-hysteria which washes away the ingrained control of generations, which starts God knows how, and ends God knows where!
Panic in a crowded liner—unthinkable; a frantic mêlée of madness, in which men forget their manhood, and screaming women
ignore the whining babe at the breast! No panic aboard the
Titanic, for Heaven's dear sake!

"What is it?" Murdock, first officer, knew. He had the
bridge-watch; he had taken precautions against the menace
when the crow's nest lookout rang the bell three times to challenge attention.

"Something ahead, sir—can't make it out," telephoned the
lookout officer in a cautious voice; for human voices have an
eerie way of travelling on still nights such as this. "Looks like
ice, sir—starboard bow."

"At the wheel, there—starboard your helm—starboard!"

"Starboard your helm, sir!" The spokes glinting in the
hooded binnacle light as they spun; the whisper of the steering-
gear; a faint rustle of chain and wire. The towering bow began
to swing to port; to gather impetus—to swoop in a vivid arc.
Too late! That ice-fang carved into the *Titanic's* most vulnerable part, below-water, along the bilge, at the very intersection
of the plates of her safeguarding double bottom; and it was of
diamond keenness and determination. It cut through the
chilled steel as a hot knife through butter. Hit—hard hit—!
The whole Atlantic was there outside the rent, but not for long.
Instantly on the blow an inrush of devastating water, as was
inevitable when the barricades devised by puny man collapsed before the assault of the sea and the weapons borne by the sea.

But only those on deck and those at duty below knew this;
all the intimation conveyed to the passengers was the easing
of the engines. Well, they'd eased before, what time a heated
bearing was hosed and thumbed. Queer, though, how oddly
silent the ship felt lacking that stern throb of speed and power!
It almost seemed as if the atmosphere had tautened—with apprehension! Nonsense—the biggest ship in the world, the *Titanic*—

nothing could happen to her. Unsinkable—as soon expect harm to happen to England as to this ship. She is a part of England, solid—solid. But the engines slowed still more—stopped.

"Might be a man overboard—something like that!" But curiosity had small place in such brains as were yet awake. Turn over in these rustling sheets, pull the covers higher under the chins—thank God for safe voyaging! Fine and peaceful now the beat of the engines was hushed—a man might drop off to sleep——

"She's hit something!" This was the thought shaped in Murdoch's mind. "What is it?—we saw nothing."

This ice which had struck the death-blow to the *Titanic* was not even as other ice—as though Fate had decreed that the unforeseen contingency should be absolutely unique. It is believed—it is more than likely to be true—that the ice that hit the *Titanic* was a small berg, and not precisely floe; and that, at the moment of disaster, the frozen island was actually turning over, as all bergs do, when the warm currents under the surface have eaten away the ballasting bulk below. Dry ice is visible—wet ice is so nearly the colour of the sea that, for certain moments, before it has drained itself, it is indistinguishable from the water that bears it.

"She's hit something—yes."

Down below, amongst the unalarmed: "She'll be stopping to see if any harm's been done, eh? That was distinctly a jar we felt——"

Up above, an officer at the engine-room telephone, listening—listening, deafened by his quickening heart-beats. "Water coming in—she's torn herself open!"

"Steady! Steady—no panic! Ring astern on both engines!" If she had struck an obstacle it would naturally be with her bow; and if the hull went astern it would naturally minimise the strain on the watertight bulkheads forward. Let it be borne in mind that, at the outset—and even for long afterwards—the precise quality of the hurt was not known; because it was the thousandth thing that could have happened. A head-on collision with ice, yes. Even a chance of the snarling forefoot striking into the murderous vitals of some sneaking derelict— the ocean jackal—but what of it? Wasn't the ship divided into so many watertight compartments that half of them could be flooded and still the hull retain a reserve of buoyancy sufficient to bear it immune from tragedy? That the entire skin should be ripped, laying bare practically every safeguarding compartment, was unthinkable—it had never happened before; such a contingency had never entered the mind of man.

"Above all, don't let the passengers know that anything's wrong—yet!" Smith—on the bridge like a flash at the first hint of trouble—was prepared to deal with any calamity, no matter how great; but his experience told him that even a minor happening assumes grotesquely magnified proportions when scared passengers are weaving to and fro along the crowding decks.

Dark night outside, the stars still blazing indifferently; the sea still placid and serene, breathing evenly, with little chuckles that might have been reassuring or—devilish. The *Titanic* now throbbing strenuously to the impulse of her reversed engines— shaking from stem to stern, as if quivering with the agony of her gaping wound.

"Close all watertight doors!" Orders issued cautiously—no need for alarm. Remember above everything else, the ship is unsinkable. The order was obeyed; the several compartments were isolated—though the ship's entire bottom was gashed to its death.

"Position to the wireless house—S O S." It wasn't S O S then—it was P D Q; the international signal that meant distress heralding disaster. The ether carried the signal—carried it again and again; a thin blue spark winking at the masthead. Hurry—hurry—hurry!

"See the lifeboats made ready—in case." No real need, of course—reassuring to the non-seafaring passengers, however—

THE "TITANIC"

THE "AMAZON"

who might forget that a 60,000-ton fabric *couldn't* sink, but who would certainly believe that a paltry lifeboat would prove a means of certain security. Over and above everything else, let there be no panic. There were men responsible for the ship and her human cargo who had seen panics before—when men forgot their manhood and fought like rabid tigers for the insufficient boats, trampling women to death in the frenzied rush for paltry life. There must be no repetition of similar scenes aboard the world's most splendid ship: not that any occasion would arise for mob-hysteria but—anyhow, let the officers arm themselves quietly, since prevention is better than cure!

Further news now from the engine-room, which had become the fire-trench under devastating bombardment, and consequently the real scene of interest. Water galloping in—the pumps working valiantly; but how attempt to pump the entire Atlantic Ocean through the *Titanic's* riven hull? Possibility of the water rising and drowning out the fires, thus stopping the pumps for good and all; and if they stopped—what then?

"Muster the passengers on deck—with lifebelts!" ordered Captain Smith. It was done, quite calmly; so circumspectly, indeed, that the passengers refused to believe in any real alarm. It is doubtful if any honest apprehension was present amongst them all—because a sense of danger, *qua* danger, had been so utterly remote from all the people. When conviction is bred in human minds it is anything but easy of displacement. Publicity had done its work, proclaiming the *Titanic* to be ultra-seaworthy. As well doubt the foundations of the British Constitution as the liner's permanent stability!

"Here's a lark—life-saving drill—imitation of the real thing!" was the general impression.

"Have those boats ready for instant lowering," said Smith. And when the passengers saw these preparations they began to lose something of their earlier confidence. Not much; but still a little. Dummy boat-drill was all very well, but not at midnight in mid-Atlantic—that was carrying a joke a little too far.

"Send up another rocket!" said Smith. That whining scream of an upward soaring distress-signal is a sound to turn hot blood chilly. Like the shell-scream of the later war that it so nearly resembled, it affected the mustering passengers to their unrest. "It isn't a joke!" the whisper passed. "We're in trouble—trouble!" Confidence was undermined—fear rippled like a tangible thing along the lines. Here was darkness, here was the impressing of the infinite—that appalling sense of lonely aloofness that characterises all wrecks.

"See the boats manned—women and children first!" came the command. That is a good order: a traditional order, thank God, when the ships of the world are endangered. Men must stand back—the women and children deserve first chance.

Officers moved up and down the tilted decks, calling—confidently, firmly: "Women and children first, please! Take your places in the boats!" And these officers met with difficulty at the outset—the passengers were reluctant to leave a ship that still impressed with a sense of its solid security.

"What—leave this impregnable island and trust to cockleshells like those!" was the common argument. "Trust us—we know when we are well off. This ship isn't sinking—it can't. Who're you—and you—to give us orders like this? Why doesn't the captain say so, if it's true?" There had been no general order delivered from the bridge as yet. "What's the captain doing? If the ship's sinking why doesn't he tell us so?" Later, when the tale was told, certain safely-situated critics administered blame to Captain Smith; since blame is so easy and brings to the blamer a certain amount of limelight. It is not given to us to know precisely what thoughts troubled the captain's mind; but we may be certain that his principal concern was for the greatest good of the greatest number. For that is the way of the sea—which teaches fortitude and self-sacrifice as well as indomitable courage and a spirit that refuses to admit conquest.

Smith acted for the best. He was handicapped by certain knowledge kept from the mass. He knew—who better?—that the *Titanic* was doomed: she'd taken her death-blow; he knew the number of souls in his care; and he knew—terribly he knew —the shortage of lifeboat accommodation. "Then why not have mustered the passengers and explained the situation to them frankly?" the critics demanded. And they had never seen panic run like wildfire through the ranks of people who, normally insouciant and debonair, have capabilities of turning into the similitude of ravening wolves when fear grips at the soul-strings, and desire for life outmasters all the dictates of cold reason. To have spoken of the imminence of disaster to that mixed herd of humanity would have been to precipitate such a frenzy of fear as must have meant an incalculably greater loss than actually took place. Proverbially, the North European in hours of crisis maintains his coolness and his determination to die like a man. Had Captain Smith merely had his cabin passengers to deal with, he would have dealt with them frankly—nothing is to be gained by hiding truth from those qualified to hear truth and face its consequences. But as the North European is capable, so is the South European apt to hysteria when trouble shows its face. Smith had evidence of this—for the bulk of the *Titanic's* passengers hailed from South and South-East Europe: from Italy, Rumania, the Balkans generally; from Poland and from Russia, where, if the conditions of living were hard, the disposition to live—to live at any cost—persisted strongly. No man wilfully stirs up a hornets' nest if he wishes to feel comfortable after the convulsion. Already the steerage passengers had given limited proof of their quality. What time the cabins were refusing to believe in any calamity, the steerage had attempted one mad rush for the boats—and that is not a pretty sight. Smith had sensed his responsibilities—an appeal to the sane—well and good; an appeal to those liable to the frantic insanity of blind fear—impossible!

Captain Smith did what any other wise man would have done—he limited his confidence in humanity that lacked confidence in itself. Turn all hands loose so long as a single hope of outside succour remained? No, never. Wireless had not then become the enormously valuable asset it was later to prove; but there were many ships within touch who must have heard and would be racing at headlong speed to the rescue. Furthermore, the sea was so busy that those up-leaping rockets, bursting intermittently in vivid stars, must have come within eyeshot of some watching eyes on steady ships' bridges. It is human to hope, even when hope has fled; it is wise to hope when despair means disaster of a world-shaking magnitude.

Yes, already there had been a sad exhibition of white feather on the part of the Latins amongst the steerage passengers. Men had shamelessly forgotten their manhood, and fought like wildcats around a boat readied for lowering; screaming devils these cowards were—tearing back the white-faced women with babies in their arms, thrusting forward—forward, yelling that they must have life! So despicable was their behaviour that the officer in charge of the menaced boat found his commands and threats disobeyed; and, to save the people already embarked, he was compelled to fire his pistol in warning. "Next man to rush dies at once!" was his stern dictum. They could have swept him overboard through the gap left by the readied boat; but even raw cowardice recognises manhood and obeys; the Latins fell back—for that pistol-muzzle menaced them all in its relentless swing. The deep-throated baying of the pack sounded all the more dreadful in that it was the baying of cowed men—waiting an opportunity to perpetrate atrocity in the name of safety.

There were so few officers to deal with a concerted rush; and so many to panic! Had Captain Smith shouted a general *sauve qui peut* earlier, pandemonium must have broken loose on the *Titanic's* decks; and mob-madness is perhaps the most uncontrollable force in the world. It is infectious, too—and even stern, strong men, hitherto cool in death's extremity, have been known to weaken and fight and flurry with the worst. But whether Captain Smith were right or wrong in concealing disaster, the situation remained—hopeless.

[84]

The ship was steady in still water; her lights continued to burn brilliantly. She floated lower and lower; but so slow and imperceptible was her inevitable settling that it was not terrifying.

"Get the women and children into the boats—quietly!" pealed the commander's voice, dominating the situation. It stilled fear; it brought the waverers to heel like the crack of a lash. Work went forward smoothly—as if it were merely a practice drill. The men passengers, obeying the sea-call of chivalry, assisted according to their capacity, or, unable to be of aid, stood quietly aside for more expert than themselves to work in the merciful mission. "Women and children first!" As cool as if in dock, officers and men obeyed the summons. They worked efficiently, and the saving grace of humour made their labour seem less heartbreaking than it was. It is in such emergency that the British sailor is seen at his best. He has so grown accustomed to the usages of death that it holds no further terrors for his stout soul. Along the alleys formed by strong men, the frailer members passed—and how may the bitter tragedy of that scene be adequately described? It were kinder, indeed, to draw a close veil rather than harrow the emotions of such as have forgotten.

There were instances of high courage and amazing fortitude. Women entreated to be allowed to remain behind to companion their men on that last threatened journey whose end is the immutable Beyond. Their men, knowing that no sentiment may rightly atone for death, convinced them of their need for life. They took solemn farewells—clinging piteously. One hundredth part of the splendid heroism of the *Titanic* will never be known; for each parting was such a heroism; and there were so many partings. Crying children were held up to look their last on loved fathers' faces. Here is tragedy magnified beyond our limited range of understanding. Young wives were coaxed from the arms of their gallant husbands who had pictured a glowing future in the New World. Brothers and sisters bade adieu in sublime faith of a future meeting when the sea gave up its myriad dead.

Take the case of Mrs. Isidor Straus, on whose course in life Fortune had smiled its most dazzling. She stood by her husband who had made millions—all of which could not have stemmed the tide inflowing by a single drop, or provided a single other seat in a boat—and when officers and quartermasters, yes, and others of her own sex, implored her to take the vacant place in a boat, replied that marriage, for her, was for better or worse; and, having shared the better so splendidly, she was willing to share the worst; which she did, dying with her mate; and, pray God, finding added happiness beyond the veil.

As was she, so were many others. Colonel John Jacob Astor, whose vast fortune would have seemed capable of buying anything, forgot himself. An eye-witness's last view of this very gallant gentleman was when he was seen helping his adorable young wife into a place in a lifeboat and steadfastly refusing for himself a proffered seat. For when such moments of crisis dawn on the world, millionaires and paupers find themselves moulded of the same clay; and the artificial veneers are lifted clean away. Elemental manhood reveals itself in no uncertain fashion; and such as fail to reach the heights of sacrifice and win a continuance of life at the cost of some other one's death gain little in the long run; for to them is the bitterness of having to live with their memories and to cringe before themselves when they venture to face the truth. Death is not the worst punishment Fate has to inflict on its playthings.

Stir and fear and heroism on the boat-decks, then: cool orders, hustle and awe and dread: but in the main an orderly selection of those least fitted to aid themselves, and the stalwarts standing back, preparing their souls for a final judgment; and yet—not altogether convinced that any such need was toward, for still that belief in the ship's rightness persisted. And up in the wireless house—that centre of the troubled brain—the operators: science's newest heroes: faithful at their posts, crashing into the irresponsive ether the repeated call for aid. There they remained, arguing nothing, reasoning nothing; chained to their posts by this intangible thing called duty, which refuses to despair. As they remained above, so the engineers remained below—knee-deep on the swilling plates, waist-deep, breast-deep, forcing the firemen to feed the furnaces and keep those feeble necessary pumps hissing and gurgling and sobbing, with the ash and oil-sleeked water rising blackly whenever they dared to inspect it.

The vast ship was like a town; so that it is not possible to record all the multifarious happenings that occurred aboard her during those fateful minutes. Only cameos are possible. One stands out white and glittering against the prevalent gloom: the ship's orchestra, men not used to the ways of white water, men unimbued by the sea's stern traditions, and yet heroes one and all, coolly collecting the instruments with which they had made the careless ship merry, and, through the clamour of lowering boats and the wails of women and the hard, crisp shouts of men, playing—playing—stimulating music, careless music—and then—when the imminence of death purged their souls of gaiety—coming together in that splendid hymn of appeal: "Nearer, my God, to Thee!" Here is work to thrill even the most callous heart, I declare—the unexpected heroism of the ordinary man: a tale that is gloriously true through all the ages of sea-voyaging. Trained seamen are bred to accept the possibility of death as a matter of course; as one of the things for which they are paid; but the musicians of the *Titanic* were not trained seamen; yet they gave as excellent an example of *Birkenhead* drill as if they had been born with salt in their veins and the roar of savage winds in their brains.

The work went on. Rising water in stokeholds and engine-room forced those below to quit their posts reluctantly: to remain were futile, else they would certainly have remained. The boats were filled and lowered—not all of them filled to capacity yet, because Captain Smith and his officers had no wish to subject delicately nurtured women to the unsheltered rigours of an Atlantic night unnecessarily. An April night off the Flemish Cap can be so bitterly frigid that the heart refuses duty; and at the low level of a boat's thwart, the cold is intensified out of all belief. Better then for as many as possible to stay high on the sheltered decks—let the lifeboats stand by handily, to receive their added human freight when the stagger and heave presaging the last dread plunge were felt.

There would be lots of warning for all before the ultimate dive, was the opinion in the minds of all responsible. And it must be rememered that Captain Smith and his officers were not reliant entirely on their own judgments; aboard the *Titanic* were master-minds, theorists and practical men a many. There were quick, clear-thoughted conferences up there on the high bridge; for the problem was too colossal for one brain to tackle unaided. It was the cold and exposure that threatened the worst hostility to the people—and human nature is always disposed to postpone the ultimate test.

Not all the boats were lowered in safety, either. The distance from the boat-deck, where those twenty insufficient lifeboats were griped, was over seventy feet—a great height to lower a weighty structure, supported only by its two ends. One boat was reported to have broken its back in the tackles. Another, laden full, was lowered too quickly after its predecessor—one boat crashed into another striving to thrust off from the sheer side, and brought common destruction on both—the wails of drowning women rose eerily. There was so little that could be done. Men swarmed down hastily-flung ropes to succour the perishing; some succeeded, many failed; for the inevitable eddies around the arrested hull swept the strugglers away into the black obscurity that was death's ante-room. Reports differ as to the precise amount of damage done in this way; it must be remembered that the reporters of the tragedy were not dispassionate onlookers, holding none other than academic interest in the event; all who had a story to tell had been actors in their stories—and their own observations and emotions were prone to colour the full narrative. So that one man, seeing a hint of panic, related that general panic ensued; another, impressed by the heroic calm that was everywhere in his vicinity, stoutly refuted such a scandal, vowing—in all sincerity—that not a single suggestion of panic was evident.

Of course there was a panic—that was unavoidable. But equally, of course, it was controlled before it resulted in that mad *sauve qui peut* which resembles the thoughtless rush of the Gadarene swine. Out of disorder a form of order was created. Even when the final plunge to the Atlantic floors was imminent, that order persisted. It was realised that many of the boats which had been lowered half-full had pulled away from the stark sides in fear of the vortex resultant on the swift downward plunge, and were lost to view in the star-spangled dark, yet order was maintained. Every possible precaution for saving as many as could be saved was taken—and if the individual boat-commander erred the general scheme was good. And even the boat-commanders' errors were pardonable, since their interest was to save such as were entrusted to their charge. The gravest error of all was that which allowed the *Titanic* to proceed to sea with an insufficiency of lifeboats and rafts. Lifebelts will support a drowning person for a certain time, provided those belts are properly applied; but frequently they are not properly applied, as was shown regrettably in the tragic Rye lifeboat disaster (q.v.); and for deep-water ships lifebelts can never be considered adequate substitutes for boats. Most of those who perished with the *Titanic* died from the cold rather than by drowning as drowning.

There were unquestionably misunderstandings. The *Titanic* was close on a thousand feet long; her various departments were widely separated; orders were passed from mouth to mouth—and naturally distorted. If a man at one end of a village street told another man a certain thing and invited him to pass it on man by man to the other end, the story at the end would be grotesquely different from the original narration. An intention for the boats to close in on the sinking hull and take off such as made a last-minute leap, or were actually immersed, failed somehow—that is not denied. Considering the limited number of qualified deck-officers, expert in boat-management, available for such boats as there were—six officers at the outside—the remarkable fact to my mind is that as many were saved as were. For several boats were in charge of quartermasters and even deckhands, men accustomed to obey, not to command; and these would naturally obey the insistence of such of the passengers as wished to be remote from the final disaster when that disaster came.

Such as had found precarious safety in the boats were awe-struck at the spectacle revealed to them when they turned to look back at what had been their splendid ship. Worst wounded forward, the *Titanic* had taken a forward tilt; her vast stern was lifted almost out of the water. She blazed with electric light from stem to stern—in addition to ordinary deck-lamps, mushroom clusters were shining like miniature suns. These myriad glows were reflected from a sea-surface black as ink, smooth as polished marble. Even at this juncture it appeared impossible the giant craft could disappear; her suggestion of solidity persisted.

Meantime, help was hurrying towards her from the hidden distance. Her wireless appeals had been heard and, after the fashion of the sea, answered. To receive that piteous summons of distress is to act, in the brotherhood of deep water; seldom is the call made in vain. All business must be suspended, all faculties concentrated on that humane mission of saving life. Many ships had got the signal. The nearest of this fleet was the Cunard *Carpathia*: a biggish ship of the intermediate type, with a maximum steaming speed of fifteen knots. She was distant fifty-eight miles from the *Titanic* when the wireless operator picked up the summons, before midnight. Instantly the *Carpathia's* course was altered for the scene of havoc. Her stokehold watches were doubled, and steam—and steam—was called for. News of emergency acting as a spur to her firemen, as to all others aboard, the Cunarder proceeded to show what she could do when human lives were at stake. She covered the distance of fifty-eight miles in three hours and a half—not bad, considering how difficult those extra knots of speed are to win. Eighteen knots and more from fifteen-knots engines, is good, as any engineer will admit. Let it be borne in mind that the S O S transmitted mentioned the reason for the catastrophe as being ice—dread of all navigators—and it will be seen that pluck of a superlative kind characterised the complement of the *Carpathia* in taking their ship through ice-littered water at a higher speed than they had ever before compassed. One, having experience, may understand the heart-stopping suspense of that wild race against time and the inrushing Atlantic—when every ripple noticed under the stars might be translated into a threat of ice. But the Cunarder roared on triumphantly, heeding no hazards, intent only on its glorious mission of mercy. Let praise be given where praise is due—that midnight rush of the *Carpathia* is one of the best pages in the stirring history of the sea.

On the other side of the ledger is the regrettable fact of the *Californian,* which was distant only twenty miles from the zone of death when the signal was made. In those days an unbroken wireless watch was not insisted upon; and few ships carried a sufficiency of operators to warrant a steady wakeful relief at the earphones. The wireless operator of the *Californian* had gone off duty prior to midnight that night, and so failed to secure the message. Such rockets sent up from the *Titanic* as were dimly seen by the *Californian's* watch, were deemed simply to be signal lights put up by fishermen on the Banks. Who would have thought that on a calm, clear night such as this, any rockets would be sent up for the purpose of intimating distress? Consequently the *Californian* pursued her lawful occasions untroubled. Had the story been different the loss of life in the

Titanic must have been negligible; for she remained afloat long enough after the hurt to allow the *Californian* to come clean alongside, had she turned at the moment the signal was sent.

Back aboard the *Titanic* the end was realised to be inevitable. Those remaining aboard were praying, hoping, despairing, according to their calibre. Efforts were being made to rig rafts, anything floatable, out of the scanty means at hand. A modern liner is surprisingly lacking in buoyant materials apart from her buoyant hull; and there was little material at the people's disposal. Certain of those remaining aboard decided to die in a delirium of drink—a veil shall be drawn over such pitiable details. We, who have never been required, maybe, to face such a hopeless fate, may not venture to criticise; for no man knows his real quality until the testing time approaches; and such as are heroic in a thousand emergencies might fail in one; just as a coward might rise to incredible heights of gallantry if the circumstances are favourable.

The spectators in the boats found pains afflict their hearts as they watched the leviathan, still reluctant to die; still defiant of the pitiless element she had been designed to conquer. They saw the long rows of deck-lights and gleaming portholes tilt more and more—and the stern climbed higher and higher against the starry background. The foremost lights seemed to reach to kiss the water; they burnt still as they slid beneath the surface. Higher and higher the stern climbed in the void.

Two o'clock in the morning—calm still, serene and majestic. The lines of brilliancy tilting more and more; and the expanse lessening—lessening, as the reluctant bow crept under the idly lapping sea! Eager eyes on the slanted upper bridge still staring, straining themselves in hope of spying a succouring signal. A conviction of hopelessness growing—growing. Men compelled to cling to handrails and stanchions now in order to maintain that upright footing which shall denote defiance when the ultimate plunge shall come! A slow, dreadful rattle and crash as loose objects took charge and sped down the sloped floors and decks—vast weights crashing through bulkheads; splintering wood, tormented steel screeching to the regardless heavens. And the water lapping up the foredeck hungrily! Similarly men have stood in torture dungeons of the Inquisition and watched the walls close remorselessly in upon them, inch by inch, unable to retard the inevitable by so much as a second of time or a nail of distance.

Two-fifteen; and the death-knell was struck. Two-fifteen, and the *Titanic's* bows dipping slowly, so terribly slowly!—and her stern lifting higher and ever higher; until the line of the stricken hull approached the vertical. So she remained revealed whilst watchers might draw a dozen deep, frightened breaths.

"She's going! Oh, my God!"

A sob as much as a cry; and working faces hidden in tremulous hands. It is ever a tragedy to see a good ship die, even when it is known no single living thing remains aboard; to witness this death, knowing how many hundreds of precious lives were intermingled with it, spells tragedy of the grimmest kind.

Two-sixteen—and of a sudden the serried lights were quenched, instantly; as if a mighty hand had touched a master-switch.

"She's gone!"

"No—see—oh, see!" As if her last defiance were visible, the full blaze of lights returned—for an instant only. A message of farewell, of hope, maybe, to such as had won clear. Darkness again—and a silence! Only the moans of women and the enraged cries of men to mingle with the light plash of oars and the gurgling eddies of the disturbed, indignant water. Let her die in peace!

No! What's this? A sudden grating, roaring din—hideous, like the triumphant outcries of all the fiends of the deeper waters. The reversing of the hull tore loose vast masses of machinery, which crashed downwards, treating all obstacles as if they had been wet paper. The entire inner economy of the greatest ship on earth tore loose, and rumbled and screeched and rasped towards the submerged bow. That might have been the death-call of leviathan—a sound that cannot be adequately described; and when it ceased, the silence was trebly profound. Blackness everywhere now, save for the faint starry twinkles from the infrequent boat-lamps.

Black against that blackness the upreared hull of the *Titanic,* standing fairly on end, her bows aimed for the bottom which was ready to receive her. An inward sough of incredible breath—"Now—she's gone!"—and the world's miracle-ship tiredly slid to her eternal rest. A moment of hushed silence; then a new torrent of sound—the screams and stern cries of hundreds and hundreds of human beings struggling desperately in the icy waters; people who had remained aboard—*faute de mieux*—until the last moment; and then had leaped; many, alas! to eternity. A medley of calls and death-cries—shouted defiances, piteous wailings—humanity vocal in its last dire extremity. Two-seventeen; and still an hour to go before the *Carpathia* could arrive—an hour of freezing water; of a death-chilled air. The first wild chorus thinning, as voice after voice was quietened by death's chill grip for ever. Cries cut short midway—coming in dreadful echoes over the implacable water. The boats hesitating—advancing to the appalling zone, checking, lest unnumbered hands should grip their gunwales and swamp them by sheer weight of numbers, so that even those precarious few must perish with the rest. The strong cry of a gallant swimmer—the gurgle as hands reached him selfishly and bore him under in a struggle where reason and mercifulness could not prevail!

Humanity does not die easily; and those plunged into torment from the *Titanic* fought hard for that precious, tantalising boon of life. If their sufferings were agonised, what of those who must listen inactively—knowing that their own safety depended upon the hardness of their hearts? The instinct of such as commanded the boats was to return; their duty was to lie off —to treasure what had been retrieved from the merciless sea.

So they waited, and the dreadful chorus thinned and waned and ultimately was silent in the frozen silence of death.

It is doubtful if many of the survivors were earwitness to those last unmentionable moments; for cold and shock had stunned their brains mercifully to a dull apathy. They crouched there, teeth chattering, limbs a-quiver, staring out of sightless eyes upon a world that seemed to hold no vestige of hope. Let the veil be drawn!

At three-fifteen, the *Carpathia* arrived; and her searchlights flooded the area. Dead men were everywhere; but they were dead; and they were left to the sea to inter. Remained, then, the living; and to these the Cunarder turned her attention. In her safe, well-warmed cabins was activity—blankets were being baked, hot refreshments provided, stoking of fires was eager. Everything that could be done was done. Boats were lowered to effect touch with the numbed survivors; and the sorrowful boatloads were towed to the Cunarder's sides; where many willing hands were ready to receive them with all the sympathy the situation could demand.

Their bodies were frozen; that was with the cold; their senses were frozen with the horror of the thing they had seen. For the most part they were incoherent, unable to distinguish between this life newly granted and the death they had so narrowly escaped. Once satisfied that all living survivors were salved, the captain of the *Carpathia* turned his ship about and headed back to New York as the nearest port of refuge.

There the bitter roll-call was taken; and the full magnitude of the casualty became known. Eight hundred and fifteen passengers, and six hundred and eighty-eight of the crew had perished: a total of fifteen hundred and three human souls. Five hundred and four passengers and two hundred and one of the crew survived. The percentage of the crew was too high: it was their duty to remain behind and give place to those who had trusted themselves to professional keeping; but there the facts remain. Fifteen hundred people had died—unnecessarily, judged by the circumstances. It was, as has been said, the fault of the shortage of boats; and, further, the fact that the boats that were had to be lowered down a seventy-foot cliff in the darkness. The world shook to its core when the tale was told. Fifteen hundred people swallowed up in one fell disaster! The sense of shock, as I remember it, was overwhelming, for in 1912 the world was not hardened to such wholesale slaughter; 1914 still held its horror piled on horror in time's womb. The sea, considered conquered finally, remained the same dread monster, exacting its toll of the daring who trusted to its merciless mercy. There were recriminations, bitternesses—there were relieving features—unexpected reunions; slowly-told tales of incredible gallantry.

True to the traditions of the sea, Captain Smith and the majority of his officers stayed at their posts to the end, and died with their lovely ship. Maybe it had been better had they lived; for no shadow of blame attaches itself to them—they attempted the impossible, and they did the utmost in their human power. Until the truth was made known, rumours followed hard on the heels of panic. The most exaggerated statements ran like wildfire over the world. It was said that, immediately the possibility of disaster was realised, Captain Smith had committed suicide on the bridge; and that this had resulted in an incredible, unspeakable orgy of fear. Rumour-mongers licked their greedy lips and magnified misstatements out of all proportion. They said there had been so much white feather that innocent babies had been torn from the boats to make place for strong men; that women's hands had been hacked off as they clung to the gunwales; in short, that atrocities had been perpetrated. Then came the truth to refute these lies—a tale of quiet gallantry and manhood in face of vast disaster and almost-hopelessness; of women and children being given pride of place; of men whose lives were nearing their end standing back to allow to youth, vigorous and full of unknown promise, the chance of life in their stead.

Yet, with it all, the loss of the *Titanic* stands out as probably the most shattering disaster the annals of deep water record. The inevitability of the tragedy in surroundings and circumstances that make tragedy appear ludicrous, is the most striking feature of the happening—the helplessness of those whose every urge was to help and help and help again. The grim irony of these combined circumstances shook the world. But to some good effect; for out of all evil a little good must come. So indignant was public opinion when the truth about the inadequacy of the boats was shewn, that agitation succeeded in altering the Merchant Shipping Laws. The court of inquiry that was summoned to hear evidence and return a verdict, presided over by the late Lord Mersey, made a recommendation that stands good to-day, and will stand good for as long as there is sea. No passenger-carrying ship may leave a British port to-day without sufficient boats to hold all hands, and even then allow an ample margin for emergency. How necessary and how valuable this safeguard was, the not-far-distant World War, with its inhuman sinkings, was to show. So, maybe, the *Titanic* did not die in vain.

CHAPTER V

THE "BIRKENHEAD"

When it comes to a crisis, physical or mental, in human affairs, the quality of courage is that which is most admired and admirable. There are varying qualities of courage, as history discloses; as every man knows from his own intimate experience. The finest form of courage is that which, recognising danger, faces it indomitably in cold blood, and refuses to be shaken by any concatenation of influences, no matter how terrifying or grimly grotesque. Consequently the phrase: "*Birkenhead* Drill" has passed into the language as a sort of Victoria Cross of stout-souled endurance in face of the inevitable; and as such it promises to endure so long as the English tongue is spoken.

Unquestionably, of every form of this human attribute of courage, that two-o'clock-in-the-morning brand best answers the tests; and it is the form that every man would prefer to display if the emergency happened to him. To go forward to storm an enemy trench, with hot-hearted companionship on either hand, is an act of bravery. To endure for days and weeks, indeed, a furious hostile shelling; to stand fast in the face of hideous poison gas; to hold on to a definitely hopeless position against wave after wave of a relentless attack: these are all splendid in their way; just as it is splendid when a nurse or a surgeon sucks away the virus from a diphtheric throat to save an innocent life. But in all these shapes of devotion and gallantry there exists a hope—a belief that the best will eventuate —the poison-gas will fail in its effect; the protagonist will cross the shell-torn waste unscathed; the surgeon will escape the deadly germs. The men who established the standard of *Bir-*

kenhead courage did so in the face of the completest hopelessness human beings can ever know—for they saw before them a sea teeming with man-eating sharks; and I doubt if the most spectacular hero of the most chivalrous war ever fought could reconcile himself without a shudder to the possibility of being torn limb from limb by these foul monsters of the deep.

The stoutest swimmer amongst them all understood that his prowess could avail him nothing. But at the command they all stood locked in the ranks, and refused to be daunted by the fast and terrible approach of death. We who are of their race may justly pride ourselves on the high standard of courage it was permitted to these Britons to establish without any consciousness of writing a never-to-be-forgotten page in the history of our land; which is a volume abounding in daring acts and heart-stirring sacrifices. In more recent years perhaps, the most outstanding example of human beings approaching the *Birkenhead* standard is that of gallant Captain Scott and his party steadfastly awaiting the destroyer in the lonely Antarctic wastes.

Death must always, in its anticipation, bring a sense of fear to the thoughtful as well as to the thoughtless. This anticipation works differently in different entities. It lessens in its fearful rigour when to accompany the dread there is a sense of satisfaction in that the sacrifice is aiding others or doing good to the world in general and the country in particular. If you ask any acknowledged hero if he feared destruction during his exploit he will generally admit that he did; but went on in despite of that dread. Observe, he went on—he did not stand inactive; and the mere fact of action stifled his natural apprehensions. So long as one can do something—however trifling—to give the imaginative mind employment, the brushing of the Terror's dark wing loses something of its soul-quelling quality. Because there was nothing to be done, the staunchness of the men who died with the *Birkenhead* stands out head and shoulders above the common run of heroism as known to-day.

The details of the story are almost a commonplace; but in

view of the countless criticisms levelled at manhood of to-day as being effete and lacking in the firm fibre that characterised their forebears, a repetition may not be out of place, as it might conceivably sound a trumpet-call of devotion and endurance to those of a malleable age and mentality. No hero dies in vain if but one man takes example by his sacrifice and resolves that when his time comes he shall not be found wanting in those essential qualities which stamp a man as a man. Not that I sympathise with this outcry against ineffectiveness and effeteness: that cry dominated the world before 1914; and the ensuing years most splendidly disproved its worth. None the less, the story of the *Birkenhead* carries such unusual quality that it should drive home a lesson for every day: the triumph of will over human frailty; and the faith that enables a man to hold on indomitably when, as Rudyard Kipling says: "There is nothing in him; except the will that says to him: Hold on!"

The *Birkenhead* was originally conceived as a fighting ship pure and simple: being designed by Mr. Laird, of the famous Birkenhead shipbuilding firm, as a paddle-wheel frigate; and was built of soft iron in a day when men were sceptical of the possibility of iron ever floating and deemed this building of metal vessels a direct and definite trifling with Providence. Ship-propulsion by steam was in its infancy; the possibilities of the screw propeller had hardly been estimated; but when the *Birkenhead,* taking her name from her birthplace, left the launching ways, not a man present at that imposing ceremony had the vaguest idea in his mind that before seven years were past, that name, mentioned prettily as the wine-bottle shattered on her bows, would echo round the world in an entirely new connexion; and that her ending would establish a glorious code: a standard of conduct to be aimed at by succeeding generations of all such as use the sea. For it cannot be denied that the magnificent and inevitable call following on any sea-catastrophe, of "Women and children first!" had its real origin in the deplorable disaster that overtook H.M.S. *Birkenhead* on February 26th, 1852.

Conceived as a fighting frigate, her value as a transport quickly became evident; and it was whilst serving in this capacity that she was lost off Danger Point, fifty miles or thereabouts from Simon's Bay, South Africa. Acting as a transport she earned for herself golden encomiums—she possessed all the advantages of this class of ship, and few, if any, of the disadvantages. Old-time trooping was not the gilt-edged affair of to-day; men stowed close, and endured discomfort; and the lot of the rank and file was only a degree removed, if the truth were known, from that of the felons convicted to transportation to Botany Bay in the *Birkenhead's* generation. But the men aboard the *Birkenhead* tasted security if they lacked ameliorations; and the ship was indeed considered on all sides as the finest troopship borne on the Admiralty's books.

After a series of useful and uneventful voyages, she was ordered to Cork to embark reinforcements and replacements for the British forces in South Africa, at that time under the general command of Sir Harry Smith. At Cork she took on board drafts from ten different British regiments, to the total number of 491 officers, non-commissioned officers and men; together with three surgeons to minister to them on the passage out. But in addition to fighting troops and departmental details, she carried 25 women and 31 children, wives and relatives of her military complement; and her ship's company of 130 brought the total of her human complement to 680 persons. Not many, perhaps, judged by the thousands which the modern trooper is capable of carrying; but quite a number when the comparatively small size of the *Birkenhead* is borne in mind. She was barely of size sufficient to serve as tender to a trooper of these days; and so the close stowage aboard her accommodation may well be imagined.

Commanded by Captain Robert Salmond, with senior officer commanding military details, Colonel Seton, of the 74th Highlanders, she left Cork on January 2nd, 1852, with Cape Town and

Algoa Bay as her ports of call. It should be borne in mind that amongst her crew—not her passengers—she carried a file of the Royal Marines—members of a corps which, known variously as Leathernecks and Beetlecrushers, has contrived one way and another to cover itself with quiet distinction both before and since its staunch loyalty to the Crown during the mutiny at the Nore in 1797; since which period the Marines have invariably been berthed aft of amidships, in such a position as to form a human bulkhead between the seamen of a warship and the officers.

Nothing in any way exceptional occurred during her outward passage to Simon's Bay, beyond heat and cramped quarters. She went along leisurely as judged by modern standards; her old-fashioned walking beam engines giving her a top speed of about eight knots, which then was considered phenomenal, since it persisted all the time, and was not dependent on the whims and whimsies of the wind. Arrived at Simon's Bay, most of the women and children, together with certain sick details, were conveyed ashore; and their places were taken, since ship-space was precious in a day when overland travel was arduous and hazardous, by some civilian passengers and certain military details for Algoa Bay; which was then being utilised as overseas base of operations against the rebellious Kaffirs. Her total muster now numbered 638, included in which were thirty women and children.

Held up by waiting for important despatches at Simon's Bay, the *Birkenhead* was able to resume her voyage on the 25th February, under urgent orders from the naval C-in-C at Cape Town to proceed to Port Elizabeth and East London. On account of war casualties and wastage by sickness—since campaigning of that day was more onerous than in later times—the reinforcing details were sorely needed at the front; consequently full speed was ordered; and in order to make short what would otherwise have been a lengthy and tedious passage, the course was set to hug the coast as closely as might with safety be.

So active and keen were her engine-room staff that the ship made a level eight knots speed; and this was excellent in a day when steam was in its infancy and a ship's boilers working under a twenty-five pound steam pressure, even if so much were attained. Fine weather persisted; and the crowded complement were allowed on deck as much as possible. The daylight hours were occupied in arduous physical drills and "soldiering" equipment; since the more men are employed in close confines, the less time have they for appreciating and enlarging upon their own woes. Drill, however, was a cramped matter—more like wooden soldiers going through the stiff movements; but how efficacious that drill was the future was to prove spectacularly.

It is doubtful if any apprehensions were felt by the navigation staff. Although the much iron of the ship's construction naturally affected her compasses, already some progress had been made in the science which pins down magnetic deviations; and the compasses were under perfect control. What navigational difficulties were likely to arise would be encountered when the Agulhas Channel was reached; for here the currents of the Indian Ocean combine together to make hideous maelstroms, which are apt to play havoc with even big vessels' equanimity.

It seemed perfectly safe to keep the *Birkenhead* within the two-mile limit. Deep water persisted almost to the shore-line; and the trooper was not a deep-draft ship. Good navigation demands three factors: lead, log, lookout—and the *Birkenhead* was in the hands of expert navigators; consequently speed was recorded regularly, and the sounding lead was constantly being hove. Every conceivable precaution was being taken. Below decks the numerous human freight slumbered serenely; for the coolness of the sea tempered the normal heat of the summery latitudes.

At one-fifty in the middle watch, the leadsman suddenly and surprisingly called: "Deep twelve, sir!" reporting a mere twelve fathoms water, when a considerably greater depth was anticipated.

"Ay, ay—what's that?" came from the watch-officer. "Twelve? Heave again!"

The leadsman coiled up his line; and began to swing the blue pigeon in accepted fashion; forward—aft—clean swing round —throw. Before the plummet touched the surface the *Birkenhead* piled herself on to a submerged and totally uncharted reef of rocks just off Danger Point. A mass of iron driven at eight knots possesses colossal force; and the bottom of the ship was immediately holed by an upjutting fang. Instantly a cascade began to pour into the hull just abaft the foremast. It was such a devastating inundation that the men asleep in hammocks in the lower troop deck were drowned where they lay—the torrential water floating the hammocks up against the deck-beams above and giving no opportunity for escape. It was swift death striking there in the overcrowded orlop; and the darkness around was impenetrable. Such as survived that first devastating rush of water swam, struggled, scrambled up the indifferent ladders to the deck, under the impression that the ship was already foundered.

Captain Salmond took instant control of the situation. The record of his immediate actions proves his qualities to hold his appointment. There was no panic, no cursing, an accomplished fact. He realised that he had close on seven hundred persons looking to him for life.

"Stop her!" he commanded; and the giant paddle-wheels stilled their revolutions for the last time. "Let go the second bower!" It was done. Obviously his intention was that the tug of the tautened bower-cable should prevent the stricken ship from slipping off her rock into deep water where she must immediately have sunk. "Lower out the emergency sea-boats!" was the next order. In past days, before men were taught by bitter experience, a ship's boats were carried anyhow—upside down, stowed closely inboard, oftener than not used as repositories for livestock and ship's gear—spare ropes, spars, anything that had not its appointed store. In a ship carrying an abundance

of passengers at least one sea-boat was kept handy for quick
lowering, in the event of a man falling overboard; and in the
Birkenhead, thanks to the capable quality of her commander,
more than one boat was so readied. These hanging in the cranes
aft on the quarterdeck were got out, lowered, and brought alongside the smitten hull.

"Good—cast loose and lower the galleys!" was the next instruc-
tion. These bigger boats were carried more securely on the
sponsons of the paddle-boxes, being heavily lashed and protected with canvas covers. Their purpose was to serve as tenders
between ship and shore when in harbour, rather than as life-
savers. To lower them out was not easy; and whilst this operation was in progress Colonel Seton, aroused at the first hint of
trouble, and out on deck from his stateroom almost simultaneously with his arousing, took swift counsel with all the other
military officers, who, following usual custom, had mustered at
a previously named rallying-point. Such a contingency as this
had been foreseen; for no one deemed the *Birkenhead* unsinkable.

"There must be no panic!" declared Colonel Seton. "Im-
press on the troops the need for perfect silence and iron discipline. We are passengers; and the people of the ship must not
be interfered with in any detail." He knew his job, and he
knew those responsible for the ship knew theirs, else they had
not been there. It is something to be self-confident, for it teaches
confidence in others.

"You, Captain Wright—you will form liaison between the
commander and the passengers. See that any orders are immediately conveyed and executed." This was Wright of the
91st Regiment, not least amongst the worthies. Wright sa-
luted and immediately took post; and Colonel Seton, after
issuing other curt commands, drew his sword and stationed himself at the gangway, whence would come any disorderly rush
of frightened men. His intention was to run through any
coward, by way of encouraging the others; but even he did not

know the quality of the men in his charge. That sword was not required, either as a threat or a tool.

"Fall in in drill stations!" was the order to the troops; and the men obeyed it without question, without hesitation. Something had happened; something out of ordinary was still happening. These men had heard the death-cries of drowning comrades; and had escaped from that violent inrush of water; but they obeyed the snap of command instinctively. That is what discipline is intended for—to steel a man when his own heart and reasoning power are gone by the board. In the velvety darkness, with the scoop and rush and grind of water against an arrested hull to create formless terrors in their minds, they fell in, dressing as precisely in the starlight as if on noontime parade. When it is remembered that a large proportion of these troops were recruits fresh from the barracks at their depots; men who, only a few months before, had trailed at the stilts of a plough or toiled in the close heat of a factory, their docility and stoutness of heart appear all the more remarkable. Seasoned veterans of many years, arduous service might have been forgiven a qualm, even with long-known officers commanding them. These rough drafts were under new officers, not their own, men whose qualities they had not yet had opportunity to test and appreciate on a stricken field. There is no dissentient statement regarding that *Birkenhead* discipline—it approached perfection.

Fallen in, it was possible to make dispositions. Men standing erect at attention would not help a ship in her agony. By parties of fifty the troops were told off to man the pumps on the lower after deck. Fifty pumped, fifty marched at attention to relieve them; the rest stood still. This relieving, mustering, numbering, continued throughout until the ship went down. Marvellous —human beings, with feelings and emotions, faced with the prospect of death, moving with the precision of Robots through the stealthy minutes of the lowering hours!

Almost before the first shock of striking had trembled away,

Captain Salmond ordered the engines to be reversed, with an idea of backing off the rock-spur which had impaled the troop-ship. Tactically this was wrong. Had he left the engines alone, or, for preference, kept them moving slowly ahead, the ship would have remained steady, if helpless; and probably her sinking would have been delayed. But the error of judgment may be pardoned, surely. The natural instinct on striking anything is to recoil, if only to ponder over the mischance. There is, of course, the chance of over-running a rock if the engines are kept moving, in which case the ship would either slip over into deep water and sink, or otherwise break her back, and the two parted ends sink with disastrous suddenness. But the general practice of to-day in the event of calamity of the nature afflicting the *Birkenhead,* is to move the engines slowly ahead and maintain pressure against the cause of the trouble. Steam, however, was so young a servant in the year 1852, that Captain Salmond may be excused for not recognising its possibilities. What happened was that, rearing back to the impulse of reversed engines, the troopship released herself only enough to strike again—the water in her lowering her draft; and she was immediately holed in the neighbourhood of her engine-room. A fresh torrent of water spouted in through this second gap; and nothing could alter the fact that the *Birkenhead* was a doomed ship.

Here, as in the later case of the *Titanic,* we have a wreck of formidable proportions occurring when all the circumstances seemed in favour of a safe survival—fine weather, calm seas, and competent discipline. But the most tragic sea-catastrophes are not necessarily those which take place on a stormy stage; a ship lost in hard weather usually ends swiftly, and the sufferings of the victims are short. It is the long-drawn suspense and the slow fading of hope which are the paramount features of these fine-weather disasters; when there is so little fighting to be done by which men may work off their apprehensions and give surcease to their imaginations. To know death is near, to watch its slow, stealthy approach, to taste the futility of effort—these are the factors that undermine courage and breed poltroonery. In these conditions, the men of the *Birkenhead* stood as firm as the Rock of Gibraltar. Whilst the troops moved to the pumps, the officers on the bridge released distress-rockets, in hope of a passing ship seeing them and sending assistance; but such signals were not seen as the sea in that neighbourhood was much lonelier than it is to-day; and there were no means of effecting communication with the settlements. The wan, ghostly glare of blue-lights haloed the doomed craft around; shining ghastly on the immobile faces of the paraded troops; by dint of peering the two-mile distant shore was observable; but that tract of country was wild and practically uninhabited; and such rare scattered settlements as there were were too remote to be aroused by the signals of distress.

None the less, the immediate situation hardly gave cause for acute anxiety. It was precarious, disastrous, even, but the ship was still afloat, and she had, if not a sufficiency of boats, yet some boats. But it usually needs a catastrophe of the first magnitude to discover the latent weaknesses in any organisation. That is the customary cause of all major tragedies—the neglected defect; the infinitesimal flaw in the armour of proof. Only three of the *Birkenhead's* boats, as the event proved, were capable of being employed—three boats for close on seven hundred threatened souls! The ship's pinnace—a big, roomy craft capable of holding close on a hundred people with a reasonable amount of safety, was carried, as was customary, upside down and lashed on the midship deck. Davits as we understand them to-day were practically unknown; and the idea of carrying boats along the rails handy for speedy launching was scoffed at, because it was assumed—often rightly—that boats so carried were extra-vulnerable to the attacks of boarding seas, which were liable to smash them into matchwood.

And something had happened to the great pinnace. The shock of impact had caused wreckage to fall; a mast to drop heavily; a funnel to be torn from its seating, maybe—details are not clear in any account. Something had happened, however, and the pinnace—the strongest hope the ship possessed—was a wreck. It requires very little to put a boat out of action; and that habit of housing boats bottom-up was resultant of much damage, since the vulnerable bilge was the most exposed portion of the craft.

The pinnace was out of action; but there were the cutters and gigs and the whalers—a whole flotilla of handy craft. Men laboured arduously to get out these others—rigging tackles from the yardarms to further the effort, since, as has been said, davits were more or less unknown. They got the port boat up over the rail and pendant over the sullen, surging sea; when the fall of the tackle carried away with a sinister snap. The boat crashed down on the rail instantly, bilged itself out of further action; and in so doing killed and injured several of the seamen engaged in hoisting it out. The work being carried on in close darkness naturally rendered it hazardous; and boat-drill was one of the rarest exercises practised in that day's ships, whether naval or mercantile. Gun-drill was a more frequent custom, indeed; and the seamen of the *Birkenhead* were expert gunners. Once again a ship was up against the unforeseen contingency, of course. There are several remarkable parallels between the end of the *Birkenhead* and the *Titanic,* when the narratives come to be analysed. The last thing expected aboard either was that the boats were to be requisitioned; and that was what happened in both cases—the boats were required in haste, and were not altogether available.

Abandoning the broken boat, then, an attempt was made to get out the starboard boat. Here again trouble was encountered. Neglect of the lowering gear resulted in crane-pins and sheave-pins being hopelessly rusted. Normally these comparatively trifling pins should be scraped free of rust and smeared with a mixture of tallow and black-lead, which is both preservative and lubricant; had this precaution been taken the blocks would have run smoothly, without so much as a creak. Thanks to the conditions, the tackles jammed. The evidence, from a seaman's point of view, seems to show that the old trouble of big ropes and small blocks was in evidence—anyhow, the tackle-falls jammed hopelessly, and as the *Birkenhead* was now giving unmistakable signs of breaking up and foundering, it was impossible in the remaining time to get this starboard boat over into the water.

Hurry followed. "Get out the gig!" was ordered, when the havoc amongst the bigger boats was realised. The gig was handled, put into position under the lowering gear; got over the side, and, containing several men to sheer her off from the side, was lowered. Only part way, unfortunately—a fall parted; the tackle unrove; and the gig's after part remained suspended whilst her bow crashed into the sea, spilling out the human contents disastrously. A broken wave snarled up and licked such as clung to the thwarts out and made a clean job of it. Better fortune attended the launching of a cutter; it was put into the water without mishap, and brought close alongside. Into this boat the women and children were swiftly placed—the women shivering and afraid; the children crying bitterly.

"Women and children first—women and children first!" was the gallant cry. It was left to the men to display the material of which they were made; women were weak and protected; the children would be the men of to-morrow; of more value to posterity than men whose life-work was already partly done.

There was an increase in the hurry—the ship was breaking up. Iron had not the tenacious elasticity of wood; the fretting on the rocks was cracking the mild metal wholesale. Although the sea was normally calm, there was the inevitable long-barrelled swell, which broke over the reef whereon the *Birkenhead* was impaled, and created a considerable surge; enough to lift the hull a little before it was crunchingly set back. Fate's greedy jaws were grinding what had been a notable ship piecemeal.

There was something very suggestive of a ravening monster in the action of the combers amongst the rocks and wreckage.

So those thirty helpless ones were embarked; the cutter pushed off; and the men aboard carried on. It takes long in the telling, but events were happening in swift and sensational succession. Let it be realised that less than a quarter of an hour elapsed between the ship first striking ground, and the breaking off of her forepart. Less than fifteen minutes of life, with so terribly much to be done!

The men aboard carried on; in that lies the glory of the record. Not so much in the mere fact of remaining—that was practically compulsory; but in their going about their duties so unmovedly—the troops parading in silent fortitude fulfilling their duties, manning the pumps, retiring, replacing themselves in the orderly ranks. Under their feet they felt the ship crumbling; occasional lurches of the broken hull cast them out of perpendicular; they steadied, without outcry, and remained—intelligent men, as full of human emotions as their brethren on land—erect and unafraid.

"We must give the horses a chance," Colonel Seton decided. "Let the troopers tend their mounts—give them a chance for life!" The men of the 12th Lancers were dismissed to stables; they came on deck leading their chargers; and the snorting, affrighted animals, not understanding, were thrust out of the opened gangways into the sea. Every four-legged animal swims instinctively. Instantly they started swimming—as instantly they became targets for the shoals of voracious sharks drawn to the spot by a calamity; as sharks invariably are; being the vultures of the sea. The death-scream of a horse is one of the most agonising, terrible sounds in the whole gamut of noise. It dominates all other outcries; it expresses such pain as can hardly be conceived. These appalling screamings beat at the brains of the paraded men remaining aboard the *Birkenhead,* informative of what that mouthing sea under their feet held for them in the way of suffering. Time and again that piteous outburst of affright beat down the fret of foam and the gride of splitting metal and the thud-thud of the labouring pumps. Men swallowed thickly, men shivered, but they faced their front indomitably and held their tightly-collared heads defiantly. Gradually the terrible clamour eased, as some of the struggling horses died and were devoured, and the others swam clear of the menace and gained the two-mile distant shore.

It was just now that the fore-part broke away from the main hull with a sickening shriek of metal and a splintering of timbers. The fore-part seemed, say eye-witnesses, literally to leap bodily into the air before it crashed and disappeared; the bowsprit flying like one of the assegais these heroes were never fated to face. Down crashed a funnel, adding confusion to the dark threats. It fell to starboard and wrought havoc; for on the starboard paddlebox were many men still wrestling with refractory lowering-gear in attempt to get away the boat housed there. The funnel fell, crushed and swept away the boat, mangled the workers; and rolled suddenly with a clang, like the knell of a passing bell to inform the remaining men how scant their hopes of ultimate salvation must be.

It would need the pencil of a Doré adequately to illustrate the scene at this moment—the frenzied horses beating the water to foam overside, their nostrils agape with panic, their hoofs threshing; their crests upreared, until one by one they disappeared, dragged down by the sea-monsters; the havoc existing on deck where the funnel had crashed; the mangled men moaning where they fell; the ship breaking up—and there safely in the near distance that little ark of safety, the cutter, in which the fainting women and whimpering children crouched, not knowing what dire fate threatened them; whilst, there on the afterdeck, rock-like in their steadiness, the British soldiers stood paraded and defiant. It is a good picture—a picture we might do well to treasure in our memories in an age when we are told on all hands, by ourselves as well as by strangers, that we are effete and played-out, if ever we had any stamina worth the mentioning. The men of the *Birkenhead* were British; although no epic film has been made to translate their valour into terms understanded of the people.

There are some who will say, desirous of belittling this illustration of valour, that the men were yokels, lacking imagination and in consequence, the ability to know fear. They will say these protagonists of a magnificent drama did not know what it meant to be shipwrecked; and that sheer ignorance stiffened them. If any man, even the most phlegmatic of them all, failed to learn the horrid lesson of those tortured horses' shrieks enough to apprise him of his own imminent fate, he must have lacked even instinct as well as brains. The men of the *Birkenhead* knew well enough what they were doing, make no mistake on that score. They knew that though the shore was only two miles distant—little more than a pleasure-swim away, actually, considering the circumstances of calm water and warm weather—those two miles were a happy hunting ground for about the world's cruellest sharks; and that even if they reached land, it seemed reasonably certain that they would not be able to set foot on it, because of the deadly kelp-weed that fringed it; weed that would strangle the efforts of the finest swimmer, and drag him down to choking death.

And knowing it all, they endured, steadfast! They endured through the dull distant pounding of the dreadful backwash on that beach they would never reach alive. The shore at this point was steep-to; and even though no wind blew, the ocean-long swell pounded incessantly, and the scooping backwash would never allow anything living to stand on its feet. Let this fact be well borne in mind, in view of the supreme act of self-sacrifice that marked the end. Every man among them all, whilst realising the worst, naturally believed that, at a pinch, he would be given a chance to take it fighting. These paraded soldiers were not numbed with cold and lashed into impassivity by the fierce pounding of many seas: they were clear-minded, able to understand values. Any man's natural egotism enables him to count himself stronger than death in an equal struggle. Given a fair chance a man will welcome a fight for life. If it be contended by the sceptic that these men had little to look forward to beyond drastic campaigning in an arid country, against an enemy that knew little of chivalry or mercy: campaigning that meant much thirst and marching under broiling suns, many deprivations and vicissitudes; with at least a fifty per cent chance of meeting mangled death under the Kaffir spears; and that, having so little to hope for, death in company was preferable; I say that such a sceptic lies. The men were not ignorant of the conditions of active service; they had never been used to much comfort or consideration; life ashore offered many opportunities of adventure and even of distinction.

With men still active at the pumps, with men still working like heroes to get away more boats—two more were launched in the event—the ship drew near her death. Her stern tilted high in air, with the midships part breaking in two near the engine-room. There came again that horrid grind of metal on water-washed rock. Hope of salvation died in that moment. Captain Salmond funnelled his hands and shouted: "All men who can swim leap overboard and swim for the boats!"

And the officers—soldiers—saw the grim danger the captain —a sailor—had overlooked. They saw it in a flash: three boats only; one of these loaded to its full capacity with women and children. On the *Birkenhead's* slanted deck were several hundred men; and if they jumped and swam and fought a way to the puny craft, it was inevitable that those who were already in precarious safety would die. For with struggling men gripping the lowered gunwales by the hundred at a time the boats would be swamped or capsized, and those within washed out.

Colonel Seton, Captain Wright and Lieutenant Girandot had an instant's counsel among themselves. "The men will stand fast," said Seton. Forthwith these three went forward and tersely explained the full measure of hazard.

"We must stay steady and give those others a chance," was

the burden of the plea that was in effect a command. "Understand, we have to die, but those others will live. Stand fast, men!"

Three men's nerve gave way out of all those many; these three ran to the side and leaped. For the rest, they stiffened to an increased attention; their proud heads went further back. The officers moved up and down the long lines, steadily, encouraging, commending; as if in the commencement of an action; setting an excellent example of indifference to death. So they waited—waited; the ship crumbling under them. They stood there, whilst queer shivers shook the mangled hull. The waves snarled, beat up and broke in spray, they recoiled, baffled. Then with a grate and a roar, the *Birkenhead* broke again in two, fairly amidships; and her stern-part, sliding backwards off the holding rocks, instantly sank. In an instant she was—she was not; in place of the solid decks were only a medley of men swept off their feet and struggling for bare life in the terror-haunted waters. Released from parade they were at liberty to effect independent action. Of many the sharks took savage toll; the night air was rent by the screams of tortured men. Others struggled desperately against an utter ignorance of swimming; others—able to maintain themselves afloat, swam seaward, incapable of locating themselves, and, swimming to exhaustion's point, gave up the struggle and drowned. Others again found the path to the shore and succeeded in avoiding sharp rocks and sharper teeth; and, disdaining to appeal for aid to the boats, contrived to reach land.

But a harbourage offered to others. When the stern-part went down it rested on a rock-ledge in such a fashion that the maintopmast, which had not carried away, remained above the surface. To this about a half-hundred men clung, after reaching it; and climbing the rigging, or lashing themselves to the spars, waited for help to come; though not all were able to wait, exhaustion weakening them to such an extent that they fell into the sea and were devoured; whilst the sea-tigers' daring snatched down others who had not succeeded in climbing to a sufficient height.

The *Birkenhead* had gone down; her passing marking one of the proudest pages of our history. Here is a story to resound through the ages as a perfect example of two-o'clock-in-the-morning courage—cold-blooded endurance in the face of incalculable odds. No chance to hit back, no chance to avert the end; only an opportunity to display unparalleled fortitude was theirs; and how noble that exhibition was will surely be remembered through the uncounted centuries.

Dawn came hurrying over the curve of the world to throw light on the pitiful scene. It revealed mangled corpses afloat in the red-tinged swirls; it revealed fragments of twisted, tortured wreckage washing the hell-broth about the rocks. It brought to view the yet standing topmast, with some few of those to gain its harbourage still desperately clinging. It showed the draggled boats aimlessly drifting this way and that, unable to effect a landing on the close-by shore because of the surf and the kelp; and it showed—apart from the still bodies still swaying in the kelp's strangle-grip—the sails of a schooner shot with fire in the offing.

This schooner, the *Lioness,* standing along the coast, sighted the boats and the wreckage and realised forthwith that a major tragedy had occurred during the hours of darkness. She stood cautiously down to the scene, and lowered away her boat. Cheery voices reached the deafened ears of such as clung to the topmast-rigging; hearty hands reached out to salve them. Here was radiant life born out of the dark womb of death! The *Lioness* cruised this way and that, eagerly searching; succouring all she could. She stood down to the aimless boats and collected their people—tended the women and children in the cutter and gave them harbourage and all such rough comfort as was possible aboard a vessel of her quality.

The *Birkenhead's* gig, however, had taken a line of her own;

dropping away from the larger boats, she had managed to pull steadily along the shore outside the fringe of kelp and surf; and succeeded in reaching Port D'Urban; a tiny enough settlement, but an accessible place, with a landing. Here the exhausted people scrambled ashore; and raised the alarm. So far as Port D'Urban was concerned, there was nothing to be done save succour these afflicted castaways. One of the gig's people, however, neglecting his own unease and sense of tragedy, realised the need for a wider measure of help; and securing a horse, without a pause for rest, he rode a full hundred miles to Cape Town, bearing to that port the first news of the terrible event. This gallant man's name deserves mention in such a record of this: he was Dr. Culhane; one of the surgeons attached to the trooper for her outward voyage. Riding through bleak, inhospitable country he reached Cape Town in good time, and informed the authorities of what had occurred.

Immediately the *Rhadamanthus* was despatched to the calamitous scene. Making her best speed, she arrived there in time to assist the *Lioness* in bringing the survivors to port; since the small schooner was overcrowded to a degree approaching the danger-point. The ships returned in company to Cape Town and made it a place of deep mourning; yet, through the woe there ran a thrill of admiration when the story of that *Birkenhead* discipline was made clear. Here was something to arouse abiding pride and admiration. The occasion had produced the men; and our island records had no need to be ashamed of this latest page.

The toll taken by the sea was heavy indeed. Including five officers, sixty-eight men contrived to run the gauntlet of sharks, surf and seaweed, and reach the shore by swimming. Others were picked up from the topmast; and those in the boats were saved—all the women and children without loss reaching security—thanks to the self-denial of the men. If any people still live—very old men and women—who were numbered amongst the huddled company in the cutter, they must realise quite clearly that had not *Birkenhead* drill endured, they must have perished ignominiously on that tragic night.

Four hundred and forty-five men were lost. These included the leading officers: Colonel Seton, Captain Salmond and the rest. One hundred and ninety-three were saved in the various ways enumerated; and these included the women and children. When the news reached England, in a day when news travelled almost as slowly as ever it had done, the Motherland was plunged into proud mourning. But the story of the *Birkenhead* as its magnificent detail filtered through, was acclaimed as an epic of sturdy heroism; and as such it bids fair to endure for ever. It set a standard—it created a noble precedent. No matter what disaster befalls a British ship to-day or to-morrow, it is a safe assertion that the first order will be: "Women and children first!"

At Home, once the flush of pride had lessened, the critics began to give tongue. Someone had blundered, someone must be condemned. Captain Salmond, as senior officer, came under review, his death at duty's post not serving to exonerate him from the tongues of the wiseacres who knew nothing of the inward circumstances. He was censured for hugging the shore so closely in order to get the reinforcements to their destination a little earlier; but in my opinion such censure was altogether unjust. When an experienced ship-commander is instructed to make haste in a voyage, he obeys orders; and it had been impressed on Salmond, after the wait at Simon's Bay for the delayed despatches, how urgent was the need for speed. He took a perfectly justifiable risk in keeping close in to shore, thus avoiding adverse currents, and cutting corners which must otherwise have prolonged his passage; and the blame attaches itself to the insufficient cartographers who neglected to make a note of that hidden reef off Danger Point on which the *Birkenhead* ran that idle, summer night. If a seaman observes a charted danger, he gives its vicinity a wide berth. Even the most regu-

lar and painstaking soundings cannot always guard against a
sharply shelving reef of rocks; for between two casts of the lead
the water might easily shoal to the danger-point from perfect
safety. Captain Salmond did his duty; as did every man aboard
the ill-fated trooper. England admitted it when she gave her
attention to it; and the *Birkenhead* lives in memory not as a
record of one man's failure but as a high-water mark of many
men's devotion to duty, steadiness and heroic self-sacrifice.

In the colonnade of Chelsea Hospital, where walk and dream
many who have notably written stirring words in England's
history, there is a marble memorial: not ornate or overpowering,
but simple, with the simplicity of greatness. It was placed there
by command of the late Queen Victoria, to record for all time
the worth of the men of the *Birkenhead*. Even so unimaginative
a monarch as the then King of Prussia was so impressed by their
heroism that he ordered its record to be orated at the head of
his all splendid regiments of men—as a lesson in unhesitating,
unquestioning duty. And none may deny that he did right.

CHAPTER VI

WHEN THE "AMAZON" TOOK FIRE

STRESS of storm, hazard of reefs, stealthy treachery of floating ice, risk of collision: these are all casual hazards in the lives of such as use the sea, and are accepted as a matter of course. Speaking from personal experience, the most awe-inspiring and nerve-shattering calamity that can befall any ship on any sea, is fire—the merciless destroyer. Fire anywhere is bad; fire at sea is worse than in most other places; for the area is so limited that it is all affected by the danger; and the outlets of escape are so limited that if the weather be bad, the entire personnel of a blazing ship is liable to be engulfed in the common cataclysm. True, it is possible to fight fire; often enough to overcome its ravages, and bring the burnt ship safely to some port of refuge, for her main structure may not be overly weakened even if her interior be charred and gutted pitiably. But many old seamen of my close acquaintance have confided to me that they would cheerfully face any peril of deep water time and time again rather than once find themselves aboard a burning ship. Aboard a steel vessel, divided into fireproof compartments and equipped with all the latest fire-fighting gadgets, it is bad enough to cause the hair to rise on the scalp. Aboard a wooden ship, which the years have rendered tinder-dry, the ominous quality of an outbreak of fire can almost better be imagined than told in insufficient words.

Certain years of past sea-history stand out as peculiarly tragic in so far as the number of major calamities to ships and people is concerned. Often enough, two, three, sometimes four decades will pass without the world being shaken by any bitter recital of havoc on deep waters; ships pursue the even tenor of their way, go about their occasions undramatically, make safe landfalls, carry vast numbers of people to and fro between the world's most widely separated ports; and all this, as the sea-saying goes, "without starting a ropeyarn". Then again half a dozen disasters of magnitude are crowded into a remarkably short space of time. The period that witnessed the loss of the *Titanic* marked also the burning of the *Volturno,* the loss of the *Berlin,* and the tragic disaster to the *Empress of Ireland.* The middle of the nineteenth century was astonishingly fertile in sea-mishaps; whether because this era marked the gradual change from sail to steam and from wood to iron and steel or not, it is not possible to state. These alterations may conceivably have been contributory factors. The introduction of steam and steel created such an upheaval in accepted methods of navigation that unquestionably certain tragedies may be directly traced to the change. A mariner's compass is a tricky enough instrument under any circumstances; when situated in a steel ship—in itself nothing other than an enormous composite magnet which alters its effect on the compasses with every alteration in the direction of its bow —a compass can become a thing to make strong men's brains turn dizzy. And a faulty compass means accident sooner or later; since by the compass the mariner makes his way across the oceans of the world. The older school of shipmasters relied more on their compasses than on their quadrants or astrolabes or any other of the quaint devices used to solve the mysteries of the heavens. So long as you headed in a certain direction as indicated by compass, you got somewhere—and having sighted land, you made such dispositions as the individual circumstances rendered necessary.

Machinery, too, with its attendant fires, was a fruitful source of trouble. Men were not familiar enough with the limitations of fire to treat it scornfully; and occasionally they exaggerated their precautions to a ludicrous extent, until sheer over-caution rendered them careless, and then swift-running disaster hurled

itself upon them. In the early days of steam the hose for quench-
ing sporadic outbreaks was more in requisition than the revolu-
tion-counter; and old-timers have left on record how they never
doffed their clothing so long as the steam rumbled in the boilers.
A sudden lurch might throw open a furnace door, flaming
embers might cascade; sparks be whirled up to dry wood; and—
there was the element of ruin and horror immediately at hand!

The year 1852 comes into the category of direful years almost
as no other year does. It was the year that marked that disastrous
wreck of the *Birkenhead,* but when the world shook at the narration of that imperishable story, it was barely recovered from the
anguished throes of another calamity, even more dreadful in
certain aspects than the loss of the historic troopship. For it
was in 1852 that the *Amazon* was lost by fire; and the incidents
attaching to this tragedy of the sea are in many cases so grim as
to curdle the blood.

There are certain parallels to be drawn between the loss of the
Amazon and the end of the *Titanic.* Both stood for the high-
water mark of size—of their generations—of luxury and of safeguarding equipment. Both perished miserably though from
different causes on their maiden voyages, before the astonishment
at their perfections had abated. But as compared with the vast
White Star liner the Royal Mail Steam Packet Company's
Amazon was little more than a cockboat, capable of being carried entire on the *Titanic's* promenade deck without seriously
embarrassing the giant; though, for her era, the *Amazon* was a
biggish ship.

She was reputed, at the time of her building, to be the biggest
timber-fashioned steam-ship sailing out of a British port. Not
by any means the biggest ship—for many sailing-craft were
bigger, and so were many iron-built steamers—but she was in the
category of big, luxury ships. Her dimensions for such as find
interest in figures, were as follows: Length between perpendiculars, 300 feet; greatest beam, 41 feet; her tonnage—gross burden
—2,256 tons. Her engines were estimated to produce 80 horse-

power; not much to drive all that bulk along; almost negligible, one would say; but the engines of ships of that era were to a large extent auxiliary, utilised to supplement stick and string in calms and head-winds; and not taken very seriously. Indeed, marine-engineers of the period had very little rank; and came more into the category of under-deck workers than officers—they were mechanics, and subject to derision from the deck crowd; although worthy men enough in every respect; and, as they proved, no less heroic than their brethren of the upper air.

Being the crack ship of a crack service—and there was no mercantile service in a position to beat the R.M.S.P. of the middle nineteenth century, it stands to reason that the *Amazon* was commanded by a man world-renowned for his skill, experience and hard-boiled courage. Captain Symons knew his job from A to Z; as a man trained in the West Indies run, where hurricanes happen with disastrous frequency, might be expected to know it. His resourcefulness was acknowledged on every hand; and the sea and the skies held no terrors for him.

Being an able man he picked able men to assist him; and his crew was selected from the best sea-blood of all England.

With every confidence in his ship, his men and himself, Captain Symons sailed in the *Amazon,* from Southampton on Friday, January 2nd, 1852, carrying not only the mails for the West Indies and a most valuable cargo, but also, in addition to his crew of 110 officers and men, 50 passengers, most of them of considerable distinction. Perhaps the most distinguished of these was Major Eliot Warburton, author of *The Crescent and the Cross* and other books of widely-read popularity. She was a novelty of a ship—a wooden steamer. Immediately the novelty had worn off, certain of her more timorous passengers began to taste apprehension. Although the hurricane season was over, and fine weather might be expected once the ship had crossed the dreaded Bay of Biscay, these new engines were cause for timidity. From the outset a strong head-wind was blowing; and since mail ships may not waste time, Captain Symons was not content to beat a tiresome way to the west under sail. Instead, he took in his canvas, sharpened his yards on to the backstays, and as he would himself have expressed it: "Wound up the coffee mill for a good fair breeze!" But the eighty h.p. engines found it a difficult task to push two thousand-odd tons along through the smother of sea, and against the wind resistance of the masts, upperworks and spars; and, being new, they seized frequently, and grew hot. Heated bearings became a commonplace, and the cooling hoses were never idle. Inevitably news of such unpleasantnesses reached the passengers in their opulent quarters—the stench of hot metal would alone be enough to give them qualms of fear—and the news also penetrated to the forecastles. Gossipy firemen, resting after a strenuous four hours below, told the deckhands that things weren't working smoothly below the waterline; and the deckhands—stick and string men naturally enough, magnified these stories into alarmist rumours.

When you come to consider it these alarmists had much on their side. Steam was so new, so novel, so full of surprises. Steam needed fire for its generation; fire in a wooden casing was an abiding threat. Fire in a confined space might not be considered with equanimity; and the *Amazon,* like the other ships of her period, was insufficiently supplied with life-saving appliances.

The engineers below did their best; but heated bearings have a way of their own; and only a stoppage will permit them sufficiently to cool to warrant another start. Each new stoppage aroused fresh apprehensions amongst the timorous; and deputations waited on the captain to advocate an immediate return before what would be a fair wind, to Southampton and safety. These deputations spoke their mind freely—there was no gainsaying the fact that a general spirit of alarm was prevalent. The protests of the crew were easily dealt with—they would be derided as mutinous dogs and conceivably threatened with the gratings and the cat; but the wealthy passengers were a different matter; to be listened to deferentially.

"The ship's as safe as a house," Symons stoutly asserted. "What's a hot bit of a bearing here or there? No more than a snap of the fingers!" He would snap his fingers, one assumes, with a sturdy defiance to fate. Turn back for a trifle of discomfort like this? Not likely! He was a man who had defied the worst of the West Indian hurricanes; who had fought successive ships through the sea at its worst into triumphant harbourage; and a bit of heated metal—pshaw! You can see his whole stout figure dilate with indignation, and his sea-bronzed face grow purple under its gold-scuppered cap. But his stout assertions failed to carry proper weight amongst his hearers; and repeated entreaties were made to him to put the ship about and head for a port of refuge.

"She's going forward," was Symons' stubborn rejoinder to the craven-hearted; and she went forward sluggishly and timidly, as if scenting her fore-ordained doom. She went forward for a period of thirty-six hours; by which time she was entering the stormy Bay, where a violent head-wind was blowing; and a biggish sea running up, white-crested and formless, but menacing enough. In that seaway the *Amazon* threw herself about like a giddy cork; and one realises that most of the passengers and possibly many of the crew were violently ill.

Night enwrapped the labouring ship; water sluiced wholeheartedly over her dipping sponsons, and crashed torrentially over her decks. Driven difficultly by those insufficient engines, she pushed her nose stolidly into the run of the seas, piling them over her forecastle, slashing them aft in broken spindrift that rattled like grapeshot in the tough face of Mr. Trewecke, the mailboat's second officer; and drove him to the aftermost part of the long, exposed bridge between the paddle-boxes. Ships' officers of that day were granted scant protection from the elements; they had been trained on windjammers' exposed poops to maintain a lookout through everything that came without seeking shelter. Mr. Trewecke merely stepped aft of the bridge for a moment's breathing-space after incessant assaults of spray;

and there he saw the thing he saw—the thing that caused his heart to quicken its beat, and a lump to rise awkwardly in his gulping throat. There were flames evident, issuing from the upper structure in the neighbourhood of the much-criticised engine-room. Outside the gale was raging; inside the fire-devil was stealing sinisterly. The lookout for the *Amazon* was distressing enough.

The stout Cornishman summoned his crankhatchman—the person told off to pass orders from bridge to engine-room, in supplement to the jangling bells which were the forerunners of to-day's efficient telegraphs—and instructed him to inform the captain, and not to make a fuss about it. But the passengers got wind of what was toward; their worst fears were realised; and an immediate alarm spread from one end of the ship to the other. The outward indications of the fire were staggering enough; for it had broken out, so far as was ascertainable, in the oil and tallow store—the most inflammable quarter of the entire ship! Not only was there abundance of flames; but a foul choking smoke immediately penetrated to all corners of the ship, spreading awe and dismay.

Not that the people of the ship were inclined to take this calamity lying down. Almost as the first detection was made, Stone, the fourth engineer, made a desperate effort to get below and stop the engines; but in this effort he was foiled by the torrential, unbreathable smoke. Anyone who has smelt and experienced the foulness of flaming tallow and machine oil will readily realise the engineer's feelings. The atmosphere below was as if the foulest kind of poison gas had been released.

"Fire stations!" ordered the captain, as he reached the bridge; and the men were already hurrying thither; dragging hoses along the deck below the promenade; but already the atmosphere below was unbreathable; and the fire fighters had no recourse save to abandon their hoses and seek breathable air on the upper deck.

"Keep those passengers below!" was Symons' order; and the

saloon doors were secured forthwith. From her upper deck
the *Amazon* already presented a weird and awe-inspiring sight.
She was shouldering through storm and the night was as black
as pitch. The upleaping flames from that doomed oil-store
flickered a baleful light on pouring water leaping hungrily over
the lurching rails; and brought the roaring wave-crests into
vivid relief. Threat without, menace within! Here was the
worst conceivable tragedy of the sea in process of fulfilment.
Hope of conquering the devouring flames quickly fled; the ship
was simply a chunk of tinder; and the strong wind blowing
fanned the fire into roaring fury. We, accustomed to the ships
of to-day, may hardly imagine the potentiality of horror presented by the conflagration. There were no isolating bulkheads—all was wood, safe against sea, of no avail against fire.
Oil-barrels, bursting in the heat, caused their contents to flow
widely; and sinister flame-tongues licked along these trains
and seized hold of everything inflammable within reach. The
roar of fire underran the roar of the exultant wind; and strong
men gazed blankly, powerlessly, at the havoc being wrought.

The heat penetrated to the saloons as was inevitable; the
surge of flame increased in loudness; and the huddled passengers, as yet only half-aware of the magnitude of the disaster,
grew desperate. To face death in the open is one thing; to cower
helpless in a confined space, growing steadily hotter; to smell
scorching paint in every breath that is drawn; to feel the deck-
planking heat underfoot—these are to incite such horror as ordinary human mentality refuses to compass. The passengers
crowded to the fastened doors, and, regardless of the remon-
strances of the half-dressed stewards, burst their way out of their
immediate prison and swarmed in streaming torrents on to the
ravaged deck. It was then they took in the full magnitude of
what menaced them. The ship was well alight—as firemen put
it—that is to say, the flames had won such a fervent hold that
human power was impotent to overcome them. Down below
in engine-room and stokehold the position was untenable—the

black squad broke for the open deck, braving the roaring flames that burst like fury into their quarters. Not all of them came through the zone of fire—many were scorched and licked away from the ladders, to drop writhing into the growing furnace; where they died with wild screams of agony. Such as won clear to the open met the alarmed passengers as they emerged from the saloons; and a frantic panic instantly ensued. Here was no well-disciplined *Birkenhead!* As the flames leaped and ran without control, so did fear leap and run, making gibbering maniacs of once-brave men. There were scenes that had better not be described. The frenzied crowd milled wildly; women fell on their knees to pray to an apparently indifferent God. They were jostled to the bulwarks and crushed and trampled; heavy blows were struck as that maniacal horror of fear gnawed into men's souls. Here were wild beasts, changed from the semblance of their manhood—furies that might have been spewed up from the Pit. Through the welter of confused struggle the roar of the growing flames sounded a sinister note of hopelessness.

The fire gained fresh hold; rapidly it extended across the entire deck. Only inflammable wood stood as a barrier to its advance. Outside the gale-lashed sea roared and bellowed, licking its snarling crests in spindrift across the wall of flame, and clouds of steam beat down scaldingly on the miserable people. Anon—almost in a breath, for though long in the telling, in the happening it was almost instantaneous—a sheer wall of fire reached clean across the main deck as high as the summits of the paddle-boxes. The crew were on one side of that barrier, the officers, who should have controlled them, on the other; and no man might pass the barrier and live. Many of the crew, regrettably, made for hiding in the forecastles, like rats imbued with terror. The calls of the afterguard failed to stir them from their apathy of despair.

Only one hope of salvation now remained—the boats. But these were aft; and the men who should have handled them were forward—there were the tools lacking the expert hands to employ them. Tragedy magnified itself. Some of the men, stouter of heart than the others, attempted to crawl through the forbidden and deadly zone of fire, but they were driven back —some of them. Others simply collapsed and shrivelled to the breath of destruction; their death-screams vying with the clamour of the incandescent furnace. Confusion grew as the knowledge of hopelessness spread. The officers banded themselves together with the utmost gallantry and endeavoured to fight fire; coupling hoses to the stand-pipes, attempting to lug them into position where the nozzle could play to some effect on the raging destroyer. The heat of the decks charred the canvas pipes and caused them to leak and burst; and the resultant trickles were unavailing. As men toiled closer to the flame-wall they were beaten back by unimaginable heat, but they persisted. Drawbuckets were brought into use—it was like sprinkling the holocaust with teaspoonfuls of water. We who have watched firefighters employing up-to-date appliances cannot conceive the handicaps under which the afterguard of the *Amazon* laboured. They were attempting miracles with worn-out tools, that was all. The courage and the will were there but the means were absent.

And all around and about this mobile furnace was the blusterous sea, snarling and leaping hungrily; so that it was easy to regard it as a merciless devil licking greedy lips in anticipation of a ghoulish feast. Fire ashore is bad—but there are loopholes of escape; fire at sea is appalling, especially in a storm, for the isolated unit of a ship affords no outlet, save the questionable alternative of drowning.

"No use—nothing to be gained by it—quit!" ordered the captain. "Do something useful!" The charred hoses were relinquished; the paltry drawbuckets cast aside. "Get her before the wind—keep the fire pinned forward," decided the one man in whose charge all these lives were. And the horrid screams of tortured animals ran an echo to his words. He was obeyed;

the helm was put over; and the *Amazon,* lurching to the run of
the combers, staggered away before the gale rolling her rails
under; galloping now like a frightened hind, unable to escape its
fate.

With the wind aft the flames leaped higher and roared forward. Such animals as were there died quickly; the confusion
of cries subsided. But those on the after-decks were momentarily relieved; the choking smoke blew over the bow; the
after advance of the fire seemed to be checked—so far as the
deck above was concerned. That it ate its way aft owing to
eddies and draughts, was only natural. It ate its way to the
boiler-rooms and engine-room; bulk-heads crackled to dust
before its progress. The decks blazed, chasms appeared in the
planking; a hundred horrors developed all at once. Incredible
things happened; but the most incredible of all was still to come.

Even by dint of stretching the imagination to its tautest it is
not possible to conceive the grotesque irony of the new situation. Picture first of all the fire-riddled ship: parts of her
actually incandescent; the wooden hull a mere shell, and the
leaping water turned to scalding steam as it reached the decks.
I have seen a great ship burn herself to a hollow carcase in an
hour or so; I have seen her sides white-hot above the waterline, and the cascading steam hissing everywhere; but that was in
a still and tranquil harbour; and even with a remembrance of
that raging furnace I cannot yet adequately envisage the appallingly incredible condition of the doomed *Amazon.*

She carried a complement of nine boats. Four of these were
lifeboats of the then accepted type; boats fitted with air-chambers
to warrant buoyancy; though naturally enough unsheltered.
They would float, but they were, of course, not self-righting.
There was, likely enough, room for all the *Amazon's* people in
these craft. And those nine boats were of little value to those
who needed them most, simply because they could not be got
clear of the parent ship. The action of turning the steamer's
stern to wind and sea caused her to become a windjammer, in

the respect that the gale laid hold of her sparring and upper-works, and blew her along at a headlong pace; but this was not all. Her engines were still working furiously—and no man could get below to close the throttles. Her paddles roared and threshed; the ship shook to the urge of those clumsy engines —and she raced before the wind, in a high, breaking sea, at a hopeless speed of thirteen knots. To drop a boat overside in such circumstances was to invite the worst. Very seldom indeed, even to-day, are boats lowered out from a ship unless her course is arrested; for, apart from the hazard of tearing her apart and breaking her back, there is a big risk of the boat spinning wildly on her central axis like a magnified teetotum.

It only requires that one tackle shall be prematurely let go to forecast a tragedy. If the after tackle is relinquished, the boat spins—at such a speed; if the forward tackle be cast loose, the boat simply goes mad, and smashes herself to matchwood against the hull. There are certain dynamic laws which work irrevocably; and boats and ships are as liable as any other constructions.

Nine boats and no means to lower them in safety! Outside the sea, inside the volcano! And somewhere about a hundred and fifty human beings still imprisoned in the furiously racing, furiously blazing death-trap!

"Wait—she'll stop of her own accord when she's emptied her boilers," said the captain. He knew little enough of steam: the engine-room was not his province; and in those days a working knowledge of the new driving force was not esteemed a necessary qualification for a master-mariner to possess. That was a job for the engineers—they drove, the captain piloted. That the boilers could burst when depleted of water, never entered the captain's mind. Not that that new horror was imminent. It stood to reason that sooner or later the boilers would be empty. And the engineer who, dreading an explosion, had turned on the tap that allowed the tanks to keep the boilers replenished, had perished in the initial stages of the conflagration. There would be no lack of steam, however; the captain was buoying himself up with hopes that were false. And so long as there was steam, so long would the *Amazon* race; so long would the boats remain unworkable.

"Hold fast those boats," the captain commanded. The after-decks were packed by now with the affrighted passengers. So sudden had been the alarm; so hideous was the sense of panic aboard a wooden steamship, that few of the voyagers had taken time to clothe themselves; they crowded up in night attire; and the wind was freezing; the falling sprays were icy. The heat of the fire scorched one part of them, the elements froze another —they were paralysed by the awful aspect of that devouring wall of flame across the deck. And the fire inevitably ate its way back against the wind; running under-deck to gain fresh hold, bursting through, enveloping everything in its fiery breath. The whole picture now presented an impression such as a mad-man might form of the seventh hell.

At last, in desperation, seeing the swift gain of the flames, after all witnesses had died a dozen deaths in anticipation, Captain Symons issued orders to lower the forward boats; and even as he gave the command he realised its futility, for the indicated lifeboats were themselves on fire and blazing furiously. At once it meant that a certain percentage of the people were hopelessly destined to die—and to die in unspeakable torment. All the boats would probably hold all the survivors; half the boats could not possibly do so. Knowledge of this spread to the clustered passengers; and with this knowledge grown, the last remnants of decency and order fled. There was lacking a master mind. Here was present no Colonel Seton to lock the affrighted mass into a semblance of composure, that certain at least might stand a fighting chance for life. Judged by the evidence, discipline aboard the *Amazon,* weak from the initial alarm, went all to pieces when the drastic truth became known. Mob-panic arose, and spread with even greater swiftness than did the devouring flames.

There were disorderly rushes for the remaining boats. No one appeared to regulate these unskilled efforts; so that each boat became the focus of a mob of screaming, desperate maniacs, clamorous for life—for life! Weaklings were ruthlessly torn back and thrown down and trampled; stronger ones gained the objective and failed to utilise their strategic victory. The encroaching flames mocked them as they tore futilely at the gripes and fastenings of the boats. Men broke their hands and cursed; women writhed into shelter and screamed unavailing prayers. White feather—the most dreadful thing that can happen in any emergency—was there, obvious, rampant!

The decks became a horrid shambles. People, thrown down in the struggle, lying helpless on the dripping planking, were cast, by the pitch and 'scend of the rabid hull, fairly into the roaring holocaust of flame.

A so-called improvement had been instituted aboard the *Amazon,* in order to minimise a not unusual risk. Lifeboats in a ship of low freeboard are very vulnerable to the attacks of the seas; a swinging comber might easily bilge the planking and render the craft of no avail. Further, boats suspended in cranes or davits, on account of the ship's plunges, are liable to take charge and break their tackles; after which they are of no more use. To guard against contingency of this nature, the *Amazon's* boats were secured in iron cradles, as well as being suspended in the clumsy davits of that period. To get them clear required the attentions of skilled men; and the skilled men—the deckhands—being isolated forward, were lacking. The fact of these gripes or cradles being there was not grasped by the maddened mobs who fought about the lifeboats. Consequently yet further tragedy was piled on tragedy. The boats were filled with people, who scrambled up and over the gunwales without standing on the order of their going; and as a boat was crammed to capacity, the tackles were loosened to lower it overside into the snarling cauldron of the hurrying white water. Inevitably overbalancing, the boats capsized outboard, spilling their human freight to death. Recognising the immensity of this fresh

[133]

tragedy, Captain Symons and Mr. Roberts charged into the thick of the fray, and made wild attempts to reduce order from chaos; though without much success.

Yet somehow, human nature being defiant of death, five boats were manhandled clear of their gripes, and, filled with people indiscriminately, were got over the side. That they were not instantly capsized seems to the narrator to be miraculous. There could have been little skill employed in their launching; it was a case of trusting entirely to luck. Yet five boats were set clear—out of the fire-zone into the storm-zone. It was a case of Hobson's Choice, undoubtedly! You simply chose the threatened fashion of your death without hope of being permitted to live: either you drowned or you roasted. But the five boats were got away; and then—there being nothing else remaining—Captain Symons, a desperate man, sickened to death by what he had seen, went aft to the quarter-deck; took the wheel from the steersman's hands and said: "Save yourself, lad; I stand by the ship!"

There, for all evidence to the contrary, the captain died—a lonely man at the post of duty. *De mortuis nil nisi bonum.* We who even to-day do not know the full intricacies of this deplorable disaster, cannot venture to condemn. It is not enough to make amendment for error by dying—it is better to live to profit by error; but it is very apparent that the captain of the *Amazon* preferred to die rather than face an earthly court of enquiry. We must leave him at his post, staring bleakly at the wall of advancing flame, under his feet the heaving timbers of the finest wooden ship of her day; and outside the raging waters sprinkled with the corpses of those who had died so dreadfully. Symons was never seen again.

Five boats got away—into what? Further peril, naturally. Not so great peril as those remaining aboard the menaced *Amazon* faced, maybe; but still nearly as great. Those left aboard perished unconditionally; they *had* to perish. Some of those in the boats saw the furiously blazing ship surging along before the gale for a considerable time; saw the flames leap triumphantly higher and higher; then they saw a sudden upward shoot of livid fire, and the dull muffled explosion of the magazine rumbled to their ears through the wind. The *Amazon* was naturally armed; for in 1852 the high seas were not entirely clear of pirates and she would carry certain carronades and powder enough to blow out her bottom. With the explosion the ship's funnels leaped high above the volcanic mass and then shot over side; and, her agony ended, the *Amazon* slid under water and disappeared from view for ever.

Turn now to the boats and the people in them. They were afloat, and that is all that can be said for them. Mr. Neilson was instrumental in getting the starboard lifeboat away first of them all; he and fifteen other souls took refuge in the craft. Hardly was the bigger boat in the water when the small dinghy was got over; but she took water clumsily; and, as the lifeboat blundered down on her, hailed her, with a shrill cry that the smaller craft was filling and sinking. A midshipman, Vincent, and four other people were in the dinghy; and after some clumsy manœuvring—with only the glow of the burning *Amazon* to direct them, those in the lifeboat contrived to get alongside the dinghy, and succour her people, bringing themselves into hazard while doing it; but securing this little group of castaways. It entered the bemused mind of Neilson that even a swamped dinghy might be better than nothing, considering how many still remained aboard the scudding *Amazon;* consequently he took the little scow in tow, and made to sail after the parent ship. The *Amazon's* speed was now reducing; the boilers had at last given out; and she was simply being driven before the wind and sea; and the lifeboat, being handier, would be able to hang astern of the battered hulk, in case anyone leaped overboard. It had been better if Mr. Neilson had abandoned the dinghy; for it was lighter than the lifeboat and ran ahead of its towline; it rammed the bigger boat, tore away its rudder and stove in its stern-planking. All hands that could find utensils were turned-to to bale for dear life; and, as the gale still continued, though with promising signs of abatement, the only thing to be done to safeguard the twenty-one people was to lie-to head to wind; otherwise she must have been unconditionally swamped; and although she might have kept afloat in the strict sense of the word, those aboard her would have been washed out to death. Consequently, the oars and mast were lashed together to form a primitive sea-anchor; and without oil to lessen the furious run of the short, steep sea, the lifeboat clumsily rode out the continuing flurry. As the *Amazon* had not yet come to her end, the lifeboat's people were able to watch it—impotently. They took spells at baling and huddled down, staring death in the face with every succeeding minute. They saw the tall masts crash down one by one; fresh sparks and torrents of flame upleaping against the sullen gloom of the thunderous sky; and they could only lift helpless hands to high, unheeding heaven in protest against the tragedy.

They had cause to protest against an even greater inhumanity before the *Amazon* went down. That seamen could witness that appalling devastation without bearing a hand to aid, appears incredible, when one remembers how far-flung the chivalry of deep water is to-day. But a barque, under short canvas, outward-bound and making bad weather of it, passed within four hundred yards or so of the boat. The long-drawn hails of those within reached the ears of the sailors who replied by burning flares— but there their sympathy ended. No effort was made to approach the *Amazon;* nothing was done to get in touch with the lifeboat; the barque sailed on into the void and was lost to view. It may be that her commander feared to jeopardise his own safety; but it seems to have been a deliberate act of cowardice. Only everything was such a medley of horror that the sailing craft's neglect of ordinary decency may have been magnified by the survivors, who were prone to see things as through a glass, darkly.

With the foundering of the *Amazon,* as if it had completed its

fell work, the gale abated; and it was now possible for the lifeboat
to attempt some headway.   Enough wind remained to allow sail
to be set; and she was clumsily got under control, and headed
for the coast of France, as being the nearest possibility of safe
havenage.   Oars helped the rag of canvas; and the people took
shift by shift at the sweeps, labouring valiantly; as much for the
sake of warmth as with any hope of ultimate succour; for the
iron of bitter suffering had eaten into their souls.   Daylight
came and found them toiling; the hours crept wearily by.   All
around was a heaving sea, white-capped, deep in the trough;
and the boat laboured woundily; there was no ease anywhere;
water constantly intruded; and it was necessary to rid the people
of part of their clothing in order to caulk the leaks in the stern-
planking, which were too heavy for the balers.

Three hours after daybreak those in the lifeboat sighted a sail
dead to leeward; and made for it.   The sighted ship could do
little to aid, even if it saw them—a lifeboat can be curiously
insignificant in a waste of water—but the strenuous efforts were
rewarded; after two hours of bitter battling they overhauled
the stranger, which proved to be the brig *Marsden*.

Immediately they were succoured; the brig hove to, and got
the lifeboat alongside; lifted out the people, numbed and perished as they were; and tucked them away below with blankets
and hot rum and soup, and all such matters as could be devised
for their comfort.   Their worst sufferings were over.   By midnight on the Tuesday, January 6th, they were put ashore at
Plymouth; after a bare four days afloat; and into those four
days were crowded such a wealth of harrowing suffering as
has seldom fallen to the lot of man.

So much for the lifeboat and dinghy: two boats out of five.
The next boat to be lowered from the doomed *Amazon* was the
pinnace; no lifeboat; but a moderately roomy craft none the less.
She took 16 people aboard; and there was but little equipment in
her; no canvas to set.   But there were desperate and ingenious
people aboard.   Though the *Amazon* had given them nothing

but horror, they kept company with her—as much with a desire to be picked up by some craft attracted by the racing, blazing fabric as for companionship; but to keep such company a sail had to be improvised; and this was done out of a woman's shawl, lashed to an upended oar. Survivors in this boat, by keeping nearer, had a better view of the parent ship; by the time they had contrived to rig and set a sail—twenty-five minutes or thereabouts from dropping into the water—the *Amazon* was ablaze from one end to the other; and with a great gaping hole in her side, apparently caused by the bursting of her boilers. So far as these castaways could tell the ship contained only a few living folks; obviously such as were still aboard must have been incinerated by the rushing flames. Once the *Amazon* sank from view after that ultimate explosion, the pinnace followed the lifeboat's example and turned her bow towards France. Not until noon did they raise anything to inspire hope; and then they saw the low canvas of a distant ship. Promptly the shawl-sail was lowered and the oars got out; they rowed like maniacs, spelling each other at the sculls when effort ended in fatigue. But it was a long, dreary pull before they came up with the craft—not until six o'clock did they reach her—a Dutch galliot; a clumsy vessel in a seaway; but in her roomy beam offering comfort, offering life. The pinnace's people were welcomed aboard and treated with every consideration.

Not content with giving harbourage, the honest Dutchman decided to head up for Brest; that being the nearest port; and on the way thither maintained a constant close lookout for possible other survivors of that tragic voyage. Through the night nothing was seen, but at daybreak another boat from the lost *Amazon* was sighted and salved; this held eight castaways only; one of them a woman.

The people of these three boats, then—the lifeboat, the pinnace and the last-mentioned—returned ultimately in safety to England. Their bodies were undoubtedly safe, but their minds were badly shaken. They made a total of forty-two survivors;

some having perished of exposure; and it was assumed that this meagre handful represented the total of saved from the stunning catastrophe. But after a lapse of days: on January 15th, to be precise; England was shaken by hearing that the after port life-boat had succeeded in winning clear of the ship, and, after hazardous voyaging had been picked up by another Dutch galliot, and its thirteen occupants landed safely in Plymouth.

This final surviving boat had endured heavy suffering and hazard. In the rush she had come under command of a Royal Navy officer—Lieut. Grylls; he had been travelling aboard the *Amazon* as a passenger. With naval efficiency he had handled the boat surprisingly well; although all the odds were against survival, as the boat had suffered considerable damage. Pounding seas had breached her bow-planking; and clumsy lowering had increased the opening; so that she must have foundered disastrously had not the only possible means been resorted to—people stripping off their clothing and cramming it into the gap. The bow of a boat being peculiarly vulnerable, the mere fact of this improvised plug being in position was not sufficient, and it was necessary for three men at a time to rest their weight on it to ensure its safety. The men took spells at this task; and that was much about all they had to do. Of food there was practically none; neither was there water; and the sufferings of all aboard were intense.

To huddle in a leaky boat, up to the middle in sluicing water, in the Bay of Biscay in January month, is not an enviable experience; the marvel is that these miserable castaways survived at all. They had made strenuous efforts to live; but often and often despair assailed them. Once a barque passed them at comparatively close quarters; but utterly failed to notice their frantic signals; it sailed on into the blue and left them desperate and forlorn. Again on the Sunday they sighted a sail, and hope was renewed; they applied themselves to the oars and pulled with might and main towards it; but as they believed themselves to be gaining, the ship, outward bound and making a traverse, tacked and stood indifferently away from them. They set out in chase; and as galliots are notoriously slow sailers they were able, by dint of Herculean efforts, to come up with her by a little time after sunset; and their worst troubles were over.

One hundred and sixty-two souls set sail in the *Amazon* on that disastrous voyage; one hundred and four perished, either by the action of fire or the power of wind and sea. A sorry showing enough—in all truth.

CHAPTER VII

THE "LUSITANIA": THE SHIP THAT WON A WAR

OLD enmities are being forgotten, wisely; old errors are being condoned, and the general trend of national feeling runs in the direction of peace. The old-time, foolish war-idea is being more tightly scotched with every passing year: the arbitration of brute force and scientific killing is being rightly condemned. As the human race improves in intelligence, so must it realise the futility of insensate slaughter as a means to bring about the millennium. For centuries the whole world was writhed in the grip of a chosen few who deemed war and its attendant horrors a suitable calling for the gallant and the free; and who cheerfully sacrificed that world's best and bravest for the fulfilment of an idea wrong in essence, bitterly wrong in effect. War is Hell, we have the authority of many wise, experienced men to prove; that it will be an increasing Hell in future, if permitted to endure, goes without saying. If the expert war makers, the strategists, the propagandists and the tacticians, were together required to put their theories into practical effect in their own persons, it is likely there would be no more war; but the theorists are those who are farthest removed from the battle-zones; and only the dismal echoes of their wanton achievements reach their wisely deafened ears.

Of all the limitless horrors actually associated with the Great War of 1914–18 or resultant from that world-calamity, it is doubtful if any one struck such a paralysing note of amazement and disgust as the wilful sinking of the R.M.S. *Lusitania* in 1915. Into the merits and demerits of that insensate act of slaughter it is not advisable to enter with any too close detail. That the

Germans, by making this callous gesture to the world, brought about their own undoing cannot be denied; for a great and wealthy country, aghast at the loss of its neutral nationals, was in honour bound ultimately to throw its weight into the scales against the adversaries and so wring victory out of the very jaws of promised defeat. Without America's aid, the Allies might have done no more than bring about a calamitous peace; without the sinking of the *Lusitania* it is conceivable that the United States of America would have held aloof; consequently the assertion that the lost Cunarder was instrumental in winning the war is not too absurd to bear merit.

Controversy has raged, is raging, and presumably will continue to rage about this drastic wartime action. On the one hand it is claimed that the torpedoing of a merchant ship, bearing many women and children amongst its non-combatant complement, was a wanton massacre, unjustifiable by any known code of morals; on the other hand it is as freely stated that the sinking of the *Lusitania* was eminently justifiable: that the great fast ship carried a full freight of munitions of war; that her holds were crammed with engines of destruction meant for the mortification of the Central Empires; and that ordinary rules of war completely covered her case. Precisely what the *Lusitania* carried below will obviously never be known; she lies in deep water, inaccessible to divers; and the record of her manifests is sealed in certain minds that will never divulge the truth. Lying there on the pallid sands off the Old Head of Kinsale, the ill-fated ship guards her secrets inviolate; but the agonised spirits of those who died with her in that awful hour may still be heard, sailors will tell you, in protest against their murder, with every wind that blows.

Broad details of this ocean tragedy are doubtless still vivid in many minds; but for a generation to which the war is merely a vague and unpleasant memory, a curt recapitulation may be considered advisable.

R.M.S. *Lusitania* was a lovely ship: sharing with her sister, the *Mauretania,* the record of the Atlantic blue ribbon for speed; and second to none in beauty and opulent spaciousness. She was a veritable queen of the seas; a ship of which Britain, as a seafaring nation, was almost inordinately proud. What her quality was, her sister ship the *Mauretania* has proved through many stormy, conquering years; for the *Mauretania* until recently retained her claim to the Atlantic honour; and even when it was taken from her by a ship specially contrived by the very country that had destroyed her sister, made an unparalleled attempt to regain the blue ribbon, exceeding all expectations in the magnificence of her performance. As is the *Mauretania,* so was the *Lusitania*—a glorious vessel, and, so far as cause for pride and satisfaction are concerned, almost as national a possession as any warship afloat under the meteor flag.

R.M.S. *Lusitania* was built in 1907—a State-subsidized ship—as was the *Mauretania,* for the purpose of regaining the Atlantic record, held for long by the *Lucania* and the *Campania,* but wrested from these two stalwarts by Germany a little while before. To remain successful a shipowning concern must show advancement; and though crack liners are customarily expensive luxuries, running for the most part at a loss, where national repute is concerned, no effort can be too great or costly to retain or restore it. The firm of John Brown & Co., of Clydebank, accepted the challenge issued by Germany, and drew out plans for a conquering ship; and so the *Lusitania* was born, to the Cunard Line's specifications.

She was a big ship; though much smaller than the *Titanic* was to be. A big ship for 1907, however; when men's minds had not grasped the possibilities the future years were to reveal. Compared with the present Cunard giant, the *Berengaria*—erstwhile a German ship—the *Lusitania* was almost a pigmy; being only 755 feet long, with a greatest beam of 88 feet, and a total depth of 60 feet 4 inches; yet quite a sizeable craft; and beautiful in outline as a gracious woman—a picture amongst ships by reason of her perfect lines. I saw her when she started on her maiden trip, and was struck with the clean run of her hull; her excellent entry, and her general aspect of slim power and determination. Her total tonnage was 30,395 gross tons; nett tonnage 12,611. To explain this extremely wide difference between gross and nett tonnage would call for a lengthy technical chapter which would be out of place in a volume of this character; but briefly gross tonnage is the total capacity of a ship and nett tonnage is that capacity less certain deductions for unprofitable spaces, such as engine-rooms and the like.

Being built at a time when the safeguarding of sea-going people occupied a prominent and humane place in all thinking minds, she conformed to Board of Trade requirements in every respect. With a total man-capacity of 3,000—including passengers and crew—she had lifeboats ranged along her towering boat-decks capable of holding 2,605 people without undue crowding: 48 boats in all; of which 22 were of the ordinary rigid type, seaworthy craft up to the most exacting specifications; 26 of the collapsible pattern, equally efficacious when rightly handled. Her other life-saving equipment comprised some 2,400 lifejackets of late pattern—125 of these being specially sized and adapted for children; and 35 lifebuoys; although her equipment did not include life-saving rafts or other details that could be utilised in emergency. Had these useful aids to safety been included it seems pretty obvious that when her time of travail approached the tragic loss of life would not have been so great; for although boats and belts are excellent things, there arise emergencies when there is scant time to lower a boat, and a belt becomes more of a nuisance and a menace than a help. A raft can be easily thrown overboard, calls for no complicated handling, and is buoyant enough to support a considerable number of people. But the *Lusitania* had none.

As regards her commander: Captain Turner; no praise can be too high for his qualities. I knew him personally; indeed, it was my fortune to sail shipmates with him in a more peaceful period; and I know that he was a very Bertrand du Guesclin of the Atlantic; a fearless knight, widely versed in the problems of the sea, and especially the treacherous Atlantic; and never one to lose his head in any emergency, however dire. The ill-fated Cunarder could not have been commanded by a better man. She was engaged at normal times in the most difficult and hazardous trade in the world; and with enemy warships, both surface-craft and submarines, on the lookout for her, her risks increased from the outbreak of war; but to sum up the quality of her commander it can be said he was worthy of his beautiful ship.

In order that the brain of the captain might not be overtaxed by the countless additional problems arising out of war-time running, she carried an additional staff-captain: Anderson by name; not personally known to me, but by repute a worthy lieutenant to Turner; more than which cannot be said. The remainder of her officers, on deck and below, came in every respect up to Cunard standard; which, as everyone who knows the sea is aware, is a very high standard indeed. So far as her crew are concerned, the evidence goes to show that all hands behaved promptly and courageously and strenuously when the awful moments of trial arrived. There were 702 men included in the crew-lists; and the larger proportions of these would naturally be stokers and stewards; since the deck department of a modern crack liner is comparatively trifling; up-to-date machinery replacing man-power.

So far as her internal economy was concerned, the *Lusitania* was a perfect ship. She was built primarily for speed and strength; but as is often the case when these desiderata are aimed at, beauty grew out of the combination; and the interior was fitted to compare with the graceful exterior. She was the final word in maritime opulence; her saloon resembled palace-apartments; her staterooms were duchesses boudoirs; and the miraculous quality of her catering departments staggers the imagination. There was actually nothing known to seafaring science left out of her construction; and her enormous turbine engines had proved themselves through gallant years capable of developing a colossal horse-power and driving the hull through the water at a rate of twenty-four knots and more. In bursts, her 68,000 horse-power engines had picked her up to the 25-knot mark; and had she been driven to full capacity she would probably have exceeded this speed.

There, then, is the ship herself—proved by years of Atlantic voyaging to be all that was foretold of her, and more; a vigorous matron, no longer a fretful child, embarking timidly into the Unknown; but a ship that had long ago found herself, and shaken herself down into that supple suavity which laughs defiance at the worst the sea can do.

She was torpedoed and sunk off the Old Head of Kinsale on May 7th, 1915; her assailant being the submarine U-20, in command of Kapitan-Leutenant Schweiger—I wish him joy of his job!—and in the sinking 1,198 precious human lives were lost; very many of them belonging to helpless women and still more helpless children. Amongst those who perished were 124 citizens of the United States of America, then holding neutral from the raging conflict in Europe, although sorely tried by circumstances, and obviously challenged by the Central Powers, so that these belligerents might claim to be at war with all Christendom.

Before the *Lusitania* left New York on her final, tragic voyage, warnings were issued on behalf of the German Government to certain of her intending passengers, that the ship would be treated in all respects as a combatant ship. The fact of this warning is disputed; its truth is certain. It was known beforehand by the experts that on this journey an attempt would be made to destroy the proud ship, hitherto deemed invulnerable on account of her speed. Certain intending passengers profited by the warning enough to cancel their berths. It was bruited about that the *Lusitania* carried munitions, that she carried commissioned officers of King George V; that she flew a belligerent flag—the Blue Ensign; that she was armed. Naturally enough those responsible for her killing would wish to make as clean a case for themselves as possible. This was before the "sinking without trace" period of hostilities dawned; but there had been innumerable cases of pacific ships being challenged and sunk almost without a shadow of warning; and though the then enemy pleaded that the end justified the means, and actually struck medals in the event to commemorate this dastardly murder, public opinion still holds to the belief that sinking the *Lusitania* was a cowardly, treacherous and entirely unjustifiable act.

Shortly before the ship sailed from America, the New York papers contained an advertisement as follows:

"Travellers intending to embark for an Atlantic voyage are reminded that a state of war exists between Germany and her Allies and Great Britain and her Allies; that the zone of war includes the waters adjacent to the British Isles, that in accordance with the formal notice given by the Imperial German Government, vessels flying the flag of Great Britain or any of her Allies are liable to destruction in those waters; and that travellers sailing in the war-zone in ships of Great Britain and/or any of her Allies do so at their own risk.

"Imperial German Embassy,
"Washington, D.C. April 22nd."

This was sufficient warning of the enemy's intentions; it was directed immediately against the *Lusitania,* without a shadow of doubt. But issuing a warning does not justify a crime. If a man shoots another man in cold blood, it may not be argued in his defence that he gave him a fair idea of what he intended to do: the fact of murder remains. And the sinking of the *Lusitania* was as foul a murder as any perpetrated in the name of war.

Her total passenger-list contained 1,257 names; and many citizens of the United States were numbered there. There were Canadians, too; but these were belligerents. There were many women, many little children; for in a remote country aloof from hostilities it is difficult to accept the fact of war; and, too, such atrocious methods of waging war were new to Christian minds. Ostensibly the ship's cargo was general—comprising a little of everything. Her manifest was openly listed as including five thousand cases of cartridges; but this parcel comprised the whole of her explosives, according to report; and though the German Government declared stoutly that she carried masked guns and was in effect a covert cruiser; that she was packed from stem to stern with devices for destruction, that she employed trained gunners, and carried special ammunition—that would be depth-charges and the like for dealing with undersea craft—and that she was engaged in transporting troops, and was consequently a fair target; these claims have been refuted strenuously.

In addition to the aforementioned official warning published under the seal of the German Embassy in the newspapers of New York and many other cities, the officials of the Cunard Line in New York and all the passengers booked to sail on this momentous voyage had received indirect notice from the German Ambassador at Washington that the *Lusitania* was in danger of destruction by torpedo; and these warnings may be placed to the credit of the Central Powers. If the *Lusitania* had been torpedoed and only torpedoed, no blame could have attached to the perpetrators, except that it is always a crime to destroy a beautiful ship; but the *Lusitania* was torpedoed without challenge or warning; stabbed in the back, regardless of the menace to innocent human life; and therein lies the assassin's blame. To hold up a ship, to order her people to save themselves, to sink the empty shell, is justifiable under any code; but U-20 did not do that; so the onus of crime must rest with those responsible for the attack. The sinking of the *Lusitania* was a less justifiable action than the bombardment of the English coast-towns in the winter of 1914.

The German Ambassador at Washington, Count Bernstorff, when asked by newspaper men to enlarge upon the published warnings—which were, to say the least, extraordinary—merely replied: "We did it to ease our consciences, lest harm should befall persons who were not informed." This was purely Jesuitical: the end, apparently, justifying the means. The intending killer explained to his victim beforehand precisely how he would destroy him by way of alleviating his crime! But in an ordinary court it is doubtful if such a plea would carry much weight with a well-balanced jury. At all events, it aroused vast indignation in America; and the public Press let itself go ardently in condemnation—as America can when its temper is unsettled.

Notwithstanding the portents, however, the *Lusitania* was scheduled to sail; and although certain who had booked passage were deterred by the suggestion of menace, the majority adhered to their original plan; and when they boarded the ship, these were handed telegrams, signed with faked names, repeating the previous warnings that they would risk death for their temerity in making passage aboard this foredoomed ship. Maybe these adventurous souls decided that the alarms were "hokum" or "ballyhoo" in their own picturesque *argot;* or else that they were, to use a phrase very common in the war period: simply "hot air!" At all events, so far as the records show, not a single intending voyager who had disregarded the earlier warning cancelled passage on account of these later messages. Mr. Alfred Vanderbilt was one man to ignore the suggestion; and Mr. D. A. Thomas, later Lord Rhondda, and his daughter, the present Lady Rhondda, were others. Before the *Lusitania* cast off her moorings—for the last time, as the event was to prove—from the Cunard Pier in the river, further warnings were conveyed. Odd voices from the massed throngs on the boardwalk were lifted, shouting advice not to take the risk; and it was marked at the time that these croakings were all made with an evident German accent. But doubtless many who heard and noted the warnings took them as casual jokes—since the German accent is far from unknown in the common speech of New York. The Germans thus claimed that everything human was done to ward off evil consequences. These cooing voices from the stringpiece possessed no magnetic appeal; no intending voyager was deterred from making the trip, even when the last tug boat blew its farewell and the pilot dropped into his skiff and went ashore. You can picture the passengers as being somewhat elated, a little vainglorious, indeed, in evoking so much public attention. See them striding masterfully along the shining expanses of the holystoned promenades; bowing to the vigorous breeze already created by the great ship's movement through the air; walking briskly, because although summer had come to New York the sea-chill set the blood a-tingle in their veins; discussing the worth of these warnings, wondering whether during the passage they would actually see anything of that war which even in its immensity was little other than an echo on the western seaboards of the Atlantic.

Veterans of the ship noticed that she did not whip up to full speed; the tenacious, powerful throb of her decks was diminished on this First of May; and they were told that ever since November, 1914, the *Lusitania* had not been run "all-out"—as economy, in fuel and manpower, had required the closing down of six out of her twenty-five boilers. The Cunard Line selected men of the Naval Reserve for their pre-war crews in so far as it was possible so to do; and these Reservists were naturally called up on August 4th, 1914. Furthermore, stokehold hands as a rule were drawn from the ranks of discharged soldiers; and these had joined the colours with a rush at the first outbreak of war. So, as manpower was limited, and as the securing of fuel was less easy than it had been, and, further, as nothing was to be gained by overhaste, the *Lusitania* was slowed down for the war-years. Her maximum speed with the steam available was in consequence eased to twenty-one knots; and even so, she continued to be the swiftest vessel using the noisy Atlantic Ferry.

There was little of interest transpired during the early days of the run. It was more or less assumed that the German High Seas Fleet was securely bottled up in the Helgoland Bight, under the watchful eyes of Jellicoe and Beatty; and since submarines were more or less limited in their range of action, the

The S.S. "PARIS" ashore near Lowland's Point, The Lizard, show

[*Photo by Gibson & Sons, Penzance*

"MOHEGAN" on the Manacles (on the horizon to the right)

Atlantic, for most part of its width, was immune from danger. Jutland had still to be fought; but the Dogger Bank battle was over; and apparently Germany had no wish again to taste the quality of the Allied fleets. Aboard the *Lusitania* an extra lookout was kept; and her people naturally tasted varying apprehensions. Matters were not looking well for the Allies on land: recent attempted pushes, whilst embroidered to appear like victories, were in reality little other than drastic defeats; all hopes of a speedy termination to the disastrous conflict were dying; and the idea of it being over in a year was forgotten—Lord Kitchener's three years' estimate promising to come much nearer the mark. But, taking it by and large, the passage was not a bad one; for a spice of danger varies the easy monotony of sea-travel, as all travellers know. The carefree atmosphere of peacetime sea-voyaging was tensed somewhat, that was all, and passengers began to take a more than academic interest in lifeboats and life-saving jackets in the use of which they were drilled. Day by day the *Lusitania* snorted her purposeful way to the East—towards the accepted danger-zone, where enemy underwater craft might work within their accepted radius. So she stormed into the 7th of May—a day of smooth water with trifling catspaws, of clear sky and general good times.

When questioned in the House of Commons after the event, the Rt. Hon. Winston Churchill, then Naval Secretary, stated without equivocation that two distinct warnings were wirelessed to the *Lusitania* by the British Admiralty as she approached the danger-zone; and that both of these messages were received and acknowledged. One warning commanded an alteration of course. The ship had ceased to be a free agent; and had come under Admiralty control. That Admiralty had a general idea that threats had been made and warnings issued by Germany, that ships would be attacked and sunk without warning. Maybe the assumption existed that this was just another example of Teutonic bluff, of which there had been much evidence since the outbreak of hostilities. Already the Central Powers had recognised that their one real hope of victory lay in starving Britain into submission; and their impression appears to have been that broadcast promises to sink without trace would deter mariners of England from approaching their native shores. They never made a greater mistake in their life; for one of the brightest gleams in the whole wartime era was the fact that not a single British merchant seaman held back from a voyage on threat of submarine activity; and the people of the *Lusitania* were the pick of that tough breed.

Why wasn't the *Lusitania* escorted to her port by armed ships? was an immediate question after the event. To this the First Lord of the Admiralty replied that warships were not available for convoying freighters or passenger craft; that the resources of the Navy were fully occupied in, first, keeping a bulldog watch on the High Seas Fleet, and, second, in escorting troopers and store- and munition-ships to and from the war-areas of the Continent. That is as may be. For what it was worth, a naval escort ought to have been available for the valuable *Lusitania*. It was this lack of an escort that gave rise to the canards that the *Lusitania* was *meant* to be sunk as a means of compelling America into an active hostility against the Central Powers. Similar sacrifices have been known in history, and will probably be known again, so long as secret diplomacy persists.

I say, for what it was worth, an escort should have been provided. It is extremely doubtful if an escort would have saved the *Lusitania*. The enemy submarine commanders had, even by this time, become extraordinarily crafty and expert in their ordained job. They had learnt the deft handling of their deadly tools; and they were determined men, as full of courage as any of the combatants; if they set out to perform a task they were not encouraged to return without completion of duty. It was not necessary to come out into the open to launch a torpedo; and a favourite method of U-boat attack, according to my own experience, was for the under-sea ship to take up a position directly ahead of the oncoming victim just at dawn, submerge until only the tip of the periscope was visible, wait until the oncoming prey was within safe striking distance, and then, submerging entirely, launch the levinbolt that spelt death and destruction; afterwards diving deep under the target ship and its escort; where depth-bombs could naturally not be employed for fear of damaging the convoy. I hold very decided opinions on the value of the convoy system under modern war-conditions; and I think that had merchant ships during the last war been permitted to go at full speed, in pairs, armed with depth-charges and guns forward, the loss of mercantile shipping would have been less heavy than it actually was. The speed of a convoy is that of its slowest unit; and I saw so many examples of ten-thousand-ton ships of twelve and fourteen-knot speed being eased down to a meagre seven or eight knots to suit the weakness of lesser ships in the flotilla, with disastrous results, as to convince me that convoying, as practised during the war, was not an unqualified success. A submarine commander, possibly unable to cope with big ships of fourteen-knot speed would have contented himself with sinking smaller fry. But by slowing down the fast ships, they became doubly vulnerable; and what man would waste a torpedo on a two-thousand-ton collier when the same missile would sink a ten-thousand-ton food-ship?

Although not immediately bearing on the regrettable *Lusitania* tragedy, an incident which came directly under my war-time notice might with advantage be mentioned here. My informant was the merchant master concerned.

His ship was torpedoed in the Mediterranean; and the majority of the crew contrived to get clear in the ship's boats. The U-boat responsible for the sinking, surfaced and, approaching the boats, demanded the master and chief engineers as prisoners of war. These two officers surrendered themselves, and were taken into captivity forthwith; and were treated with considerable humanity. Indeed, a quality approaching friendship struck up between prisoners and captors. On a morning, my friend was aroused from sleep by the U-boat commander and invited to the periscope table. The submarine was submerged; and the screen revealed a large and ponderous convoy steaming stately east to west, with its screens of sloops and destroyers. The whole thing looked like a picture; but so close was the submarine to this unsuspecting convoy, that the calibre of all ships and even their funnelmarkings were clearly distinguishable on the periscope table.

"Which two of them shall I sink?" the German commander asked, as if it were a joke. "I can only spare two 'mouldies' for this particular convoy." Naturally enough, the British shipmaster suggested that he should sink none; but let the entire convoy pursue its lawful occasions.

"My orders are to sink two ships of every sighted convoy. Two of them I must put down," said the German. "Choose two—it doesn't matter which." The shipmaster indicated two bottoms at a venture; did it half-jestingly, not convinced of his captor's earnestness, indeed. Two minutes later he saw them both hit by a right-and-left; singled out from the covey as neatly as two rabbits picked from a fieldful. Both ships sank; and long before the escort could concentrate on the menace, the U-boat was safely under the main convoy, and making for its usual resting-place on a sandbank.

Similarly, I am convinced that had the ill-fated *Lusitania* been surrounded by warships, she would have received her death-stroke at the appointed time. It was meant to sink her; and U-boat commanders took all risks in order to fulfil instructions; as we who are in the secret know.

The *Lusitania* entered the danger-zone; and Captain Turner increased his precautions; although he, like most shipmasters, believed that speed was the finest safeguard against submarine attack. He redoubled his lookouts; both forecastle, crow's nest and bridge. Under his capable instructions, all lifeboats under davits were got out of their holding-chocks and lowered to the rail-level in readiness for emergency, being already provisioned and watered and supplied with distress signals, in accordance with law. All watertight doors were secured, except for those urgently requiring to be left open; in fact, every precaution that could render the ship inviolable was taken—the long tiers of scuttles were screwed and screened with deadlights; extra officers were ordered to the navigating bridge, together with quartermasters; and all hands were warned to keep their eyes skinned for suspicious objects. Further than that, after the noon position was made, Captain Turner went into conference with his chief engineer, and instructed that, in view—presumably the warnings had been received—of the threat, a full head of steam must be maintained, so that quick manœuvring under helm would be possible. Many a threatened ship had dodged a hurrying torpedo simply by speed and adroit helmsmanship; and if given even a fighting chance, the *Lusitania* could repeat that performance. The moment the telephone rang in the engine-room, the throttle was to be thrown wide open and the steam-pressure raised by every effort in the engine-room's power.

Under these conditions the ship went ahead at twenty knots or thereabouts; tenseness pervading all aboard. One o'clock—two bells—sounded; and the passengers descended to lunch—the last meal for most. It was not exactly the elaborate peace-time luncheon served by the Cunard; but it was a good meal. By two p.m. it was practically over. The Old Head of Kinsale was distant about ten sea miles from the hurrying fabric; and the zigzag track which had been steered as an extra safeguard—a zigzag was about the most efficient counter-submarine device adopted during the war—was steadied whilst Captain Turner got a fourpoint bearing of the land, to adjust his position to the exact nicety required of skilful navigators. That steadied course was S 87 E. Through pellucid green water, as calm as a millpond, under a clear and smiling sky, the *Lusitania* rushed on. Submarine attack was usually carried out either under a grey sky with a pobble on the water to hide the periscope; or at dawn and sunset, when the low sun blinded watching eyes. A favourite trick of the U-boats was to lie directly under the low sun, and in that position they were practically invisible.

At two-fifteen, the second officer sang out: "Torpedo coming, sir!" This was the first indication of peril. Presumably the U-boat had camouflaged her periscope in some trifle of flotsam; a wisp of weed, anything was sufficient to hide so insignificant an object. Captain Turner looked to the starboard side and saw what he saw—the feathery track of a "tinfish". Almost before he had grasped the fact, whilst the second officer's shout was still echoing, the *Lusitania* was struck her death-blow, fairly amidships, between the third and the fourth funnels. There was a sudden upfling of dirty water crowned with foam; it climbed as high as the mastheads; and fragments of steel mingled with the soaring pillar of water—bits of the torpedo itself, bits of the *Lusitania's* tormented hide. This column broke in splashing spray over the decks; the steel splinters clanged and rasped; and No. 5 lifeboat was smashed to splinters. Immediately the stricken craft heeled heavily to the wounded side; her engines stopped with a horrid screech of mangled machinery; and havoc made itself manifest. Before the effect of shock was dispersed, a second torpedo came hurrying; to hit and explode whilst the low echoes of the first discharge were still rumbling away into silence.

Hit—hard hit! Nothing could stand against that attack; that scurrilous onset made without any hint of warning from the aggressor. Nothing had been seen until the torpedo-feather manifested itself. Here was a stab in the back, and a foul one at that! It was estimated that the attacking ship was less than 500 yards distant when she fired her bolts. Into the *Lusitania's* side were blown two gaping holes through which a railway train might have passed. Before the shocked mind had accepted the double detonation, a third torpedo was aimed at the ship's port side; but this missile missed its target and went away into the blue. Such a short time elapsed between the firing of number two and number three torpedoes as to give colour to the belief that two U-boats had been detailed to deal with the big Atlantic flyer; which proves that her finish was resolved upon without a shadow of a doubt.

One can imagine the scene on the *Lusitania's* decks when the reality became known. Here was no long-drawn uncertainty and suspense; the ship was doomed to sink from the moment the first torpedo struck her. From the bridge Captain Turner gave the curt order: "Lower out all boats!" He was obeyed; as the first one began to scream in its tackles: "Women and children first!" followed the first order. Captain Anderson was already by the boats, taking cool and competent charge of an operation that had speed as its first consideration. The boat-decks crowded with affrighted humanity; though panic was absent; for here were trained men in control of an impossible situation. Without a second's delay the women and children were passed into the readied boats; there was a haste toward.

A great haste; for the time remaining was so scant that it was impossible to deal adequately with the distress. As they were, unwrapped, children were lifted and their mothers hurried after them. But tragedy marked the lowering of the boats. A ship like the *Lusitania,* proceeding at twenty knots, cannot be brought to a standstill in a breath; she carries her own way for at least a mile, and probably much more, unless her engines can be reversed. The *Lusitania's* engines were shattered by the first explosion; were simply mangled scrap; and so were useless to check her onrush. The boats rattled down in the tackles as they were filled; competent men were in charge of their quick-release gear which was designed to allow the tackles to be let go as soon as a boat was water-borne; but that element of speed through the water caused disaster. At least two lifeboats were smashed or capsized in the emergency; they spilled their pitiful contents into the sea. It was probably the death-cries of such as drowned that fetched terror and panic to those remaining. A desperate rush, uncontrollable, instantly set in for the serried boats. Instead of aiding, the untutored laymen hindered the work of the trained crew; they blundered in their way; they pushed them aside. There was much confusion now—a terrible spectacle presented itself, as the claims of life surged uppermost; and men forgot manhood, and cowards became strong. Havoc stormed everywhere—it fed on itself and bred pandemonium.

Meantime, Leith, the chief wireless operator, realising what had happened, sent out an instant S O S to all stations: "Come at once, *Lusitania,* heavy list ten miles south of Old Head Kinsale!" This message he repeated insistently for as many minutes as his dynamo endured—only four or five. For the torrential inrush of water to the engine-room and stokeholds flooded out the furnaces almost at once; quenched the steam in the boilers; drowned the dynamos and put out every light; so that the horror of that prison below decks can better be imagined than described. Men fought for life in the blackness, with the terrible water invading, rising to chest, to neck, to mouth, pursuing them up the inadequate ladders—here was all the horror of a flooded mine without even the poor stability of the mine's foundations. Rumble of escaping steam, lash of devouring water, screech of tortured metals—the floor-plates lifted and slashing death-wounds; everywhere darkness, and only a couple of spidery ladders leading upwards to air and light and a chance for life! In the *Titanic* there were time and opportunity for calm reasoned thought; for strategic disposition, for attempt to deal with a catastrophe; here were none of these things; only the rush of imminent destruction, paralysing in its sudden completeness.

As the electric installation of the engine-room succumbed, so did the main wireless dynamos; Leith's signals weakened and died. The wireless cabin was equipped with a stand-by transmitting set; instantly the operator switched on to this; and continued his frantic appeals. S O S—Save our Souls! The startled world was told of this crowning act of warlike savagery—and it reacted into chilled horror and afterwards a strong resoluteness to die with backs to the wall rather than throw up the sponge. If Germany imagined that the dastardly destruction of the *Lusitania* would bluff the universe into the belief in Germany's indestructible will to win, it made its greatest mistake. It seemed to steel the waverers, and give fresh heart to such as trembled on the brink of despair.

Whilst Leith persisted with his failing spark, the work on the boat-decks was rushed on with every possible vigour and resource. Here amongst that weaving, panic-stricken mass of humanity, reduced to its rawer elements, notable acts of cool courage were performed. If men lost their heads and fought like beasts, so too did men discover a cool and thoughtful valour which more than atoned for the foibles of their fellows. Mr. Alfred Vanderbilt particularly distinguished himself by shouldering a way through the press with child after child in his arms, to be handed into the precarious safety of the lifeboats. He was still doing this to the best of his ability when the *Lusitania* rolled over and went down, and Alfred Vanderbilt went down with her—into a hero's tomb.

There is usually something to point to the insufficiency of human handiwork. The *Lusitania* had boat accommodation in abundance; means for saving every life, beyond those destroyed by the explosions of the torpedoes. But a lifeboat is put into a ship's davits on the assumption that it can be lowered down a perpendicular side. We have seen, in the case of the *Titanic,* how the list of a ship acts against safe launching. We have seen the same fact made plain when the ill-omened *Vestris* foundered. The *Lusitania,* having taken her death-blow, canted heavily to starboard; that brought her port side up and over, so that it became more horizontal than perpendicular; and across that expanse of rounded steel, no boat could be lifted. There was no apparatus for doing so. A ship's lifeboat is too heavy a craft to be manhandled even over a level deck; so the *Lusitania's* port boats were automatically put out of action when the first list to starboard happened. Nor were the starboard boats in much better case. The starboard side was like a concave cliff almost instantly and the boats swung in under the rail, so that those endeavouring to lower them could not see what happened. Nor were passengers able to obtain places in such as were lowered, all on account of this overhang. As a boat was lowered and the davit tackles ran free, efforts were made to bring the inboard, reserve boats under the tackles; but the deck sloped so steeply that these inner craft took charge before they could be checked, and so were lost.

Twenty minutes elapsed between the first striking and the ultimate sinking. Not a long time in which to evacuate two thousand people, even under the best conditions—in the worst, with the fear of instant sinking present in every mind, only a breath of time, considering the amount of work necessary to be done.

Through all the tumult and confusion the crew worked coolly and expertly, doing their job as British seamen usually do. They obeyed orders without an instant's hesitation; they handled such of the lifeboats as it was possible to handle with calm competence; but they were set a task beyond their capability. Demigods must have failed to succeed, indeed. The decks were tilted at that ungodly angle which made foothold difficult; and the mowing passengers burst in to interfere with the disciplined efforts; dragging men who knew their job away from their posts, and endeavouring, without skill, to do their work for them—and failing miserably.

When the *Lusitania* was struck there was nothing in sight afloat. The glassy sea offered no relief, no hope. Land was there—ten miles distant; and it was not land sheltering a port where were relief ships. The sky smiled down serenely on this tragedy.

It must be borne in mind that such panic as reigned aboard the stricken vessel was slow in breaking, and not altogether blameworthy when it did come. Once again it was the undisciplined element in the steerage that lost its head, and broke the calm of the others and obstructed the efforts of the trained men in the crew. Ingrained discipline is the finest asset in the face of calamity; always there is present some one individual or more who knows what is to be done and is prepared to do it if allowed a free hand, without obstruction. But, in the face of such dire calamity as this, when even the Divine Providence appears to have temporarily deserted His throne, it is not easy for weak mortality to hold trust in anything as human as itself. There were regrettable incidents in the sinking of the *Lusitania;* none may deny that; the only consolation is that there have been worse in mishaps of less significance.

Had the ship been fitted with rafts more must have been saved, since they could have been pitched overboard without ceremony or delay; and, being floatable, must have supported many until relief appeared. Had the boats been fitted to lower out from gangways in the hull nearer the waterline, maybe the port boats could have been got into action, and more of the starboard boats lowered without misadventure; but these possibilities do not affect the major tragedy.

Twenty minutes after being struck the *Lusitania* went down. She went down in a sea that still showed no hope. In a sea that was covered with struggling humans, men and women alike; for the end came suddenly. Fear destroyed many who might otherwise have survived—the shock of the explosion coupled with the shock of immersion stopped their heartbeats and left them to float lifeless as witnesses to man's inhumanity to man when the worst passions of humanity are aroused by the ravening passions of war.

The *Lusitania* went under; and a choked scream went up from hundreds of desperate throats. The wireless calls had been heard and obeyed; small craft were hurrying to the scene of tragedy; notable amongst these being the trawler *Blue Bell,* which arrived in time to succour many, though not in time to save all. Her crew worked resolutely and with splendid heroism to collect the drowning; in their heroism they were assisted by many other nameless small craft that came speeding; and when all who remained alive were collected, course was set for Queenstown where the hapless survivors, who had lost everything they owned, were landed, to tell their story to the staggered world.

Captain Turner, remaining on his bridge to the last, was pitched into the sea at the end, and, a stout swimmer, contrived to keep afloat until picked up; but his aide, Captain Anderson, lost his life along with 1,197 other human beings.

Eleven hundred and ninety-eight murdered people! Had they been male combatants the loss would have been deplorable enough; as it was, these were declared non-combatants, and subject to such mercy as war permits. Merchant seamen were considered immune from the penalties of war to a certain extent; it was assumed that as their lives were devoted to fighting the sea, they could not be saddled with any greater burdens. As for the civilian passengers—let a careful analysis be made; in order that such as read may add their voices to the prevailing outcry against the insensate savagery and folly of the war-idea.

Carrying as she did twelve hundred and eighty-seven passengers and a crew of seven hundred and two, the *Lusitania's* death-roll was eleven hundred and ninety-eight. Two hundred and seventy women passengers were drowned; and with them thirty-three boys, twenty-six girls; and—here is where war strikes its foulest blow—out of thirty-nine babies—tiny children, most of them in arms, surely the most helpless things in the world, thirty-five perished. War, said Sherman, is hell. He understated the case—such war is the seventh hell.

In addition to the passenger women, sixteen stewardesses and matrons and hospital attendants lost their lives. A bitter enough price exacted for daring to cross a hostile sea!

The memory of these piteous dead should cry aloud to high heaven against any further hint of war—which is the devil's holiday. The devouring sea is kindly as compared with such humans as avail themselves of its possibilities to darken the honour of the human race.

Even to-day, after a lapse of fifteen years, thought of this dastardly act arouses high indignation. It was so insensate, so ferocious, so unnecessary: bringing women and children into the firing line and mowing them down in hideous swathes; it set back the advance of civilisation by a century or more. Chivalry bowed its horrified head; here was the act of undisciplined savages, on whom the light of the Cross of the Prince of Peace had never rested.

At the time of the fatality, an indignation compared with which that of to-day is lukewarm possessed all Christendom. Not only were the Allies stirred to their deeps; neutral countries felt the same stifling emotion of detestation for inhumanity wrought. But what was done not all the horror of the world could undo. The Moving Finger had written and, having written, nothing could erase a word of that sentence of death. Particularly in America did the intensest detestation persist; such sympathy as might have existed there was blotted out by a vast wave of indignation; and there can be no doubt that the sinking of the *Lusitania* was a powerful instrument in forcing America's hand into an ultimate declaration of war. So Germany defeated her own purpose; instead of terrorising the universe she simply forged a weapon for her own undoing; for the entry of the United States into the conflict swung the balance into favour of the Allies, and the country responsible for this most inhuman tragedy of blue water was left with not much more than its eyes to weep with, that the word of God might be fulfilled: "Vengeance is Mine. I will repay!"

CHAPTER VIII

THE "KENT"—EAST INDIAMAN

THERE is a spaciousness, a breadth of romance about the action-
ful days of old John Company that even to-day, when India is
brought within a week's journey, when communication can be
effected with that amazing land in a matter of seconds, the old-
time glamour persists. And particularly does this effect of romantic adventure cling to the stately old East Indiamen; John
Company's navy which was the authorised connecting link between the fragrant East and the purposeful West. Commissions
in John Company's service were as eagerly sought as were the
King's commissions; almost an equal honour attached to such
service; most certainly a better prospect of fortune was the lot
of such as found favour with The Honourable the Directors of
the Company of Merchants Trading to the Indies.

Volumes have been written concerning the goings and com-
ings of these fine old ships. Some of them fought gallantly,
conquering the finest line of battleships of hostile nations. All
of them were armed, not so much for attack as for defence; but
John Company's sailors almost invariably held to Napoleon's
theory that the best defence is a vigorous attack; and seldom,
if ever, were they found guilty of neglecting an opportunity to
fight.

Amongst all that gallant navy, the *Kent* has attached to itself
one of the most tragic stories of the sea. The loss of the *Amazon*
was a grim and sinister event; made memorable by the sheer
hopelessness of the surrounding circumstances; but those attending the burning of the big East Indiaman do not fall far
short in sheer grotesqueness and horror.

Here, again, was a brand-new ship—a castle of her day. The evil fates of the ocean seem to have a special malignity towards new vessels, as if they were determined to drive home the lesson of man's temerity and the price that must be paid if any hope is to be got of ultimate conquest of the seven raging seas.

Thirteen hundred and fifty tons was the *Kent's* burthen— trifling according to our measurements of to-day; but in 1825, this ship was a giant; towering high from waterline to sheer, and riding the waters like a line-of-battleship. If anyone reading these pages should happen to pass the training ship *Worcester,* lying off Greenhithe, or the *Conway,* lying in the Mersey; or if he should hold in recollection an impression of the gallant old *Victory* down there at Portsmouth, he may satisfy himself that, for all practical purposes he has seen the unlucky *Kent,* whose dimensions approximated those of the three craft mentioned. So that whilst a thirteen-hundred-ton freighter of to-day looks insignificant enough to be negligible, thirteen hundred tons in 1825 was a considerable fabric enough; and when the *Kent* lay in the Downs prior to her maiden voyage on February 19th, 1825, she presented a picture that not only pleased the nautical eye but also impressed the layman with a sense of solid security and indomitable sea-fighting power. Her opened portholes grinned with her ordnance, calculated to beat off anything of a similar size; capable of smashing any piratical fleet that might venture within range; for the days of the East Indian pirates were at their height, and the Malay rovers were known to venture pretty far afield if a fat-paunched prize seemed to offer.

To see her at her moorings there in the Downs, bowing graciously to the whip of the whitecaps, ruffled by a stinging breeze; with the brisk Deal hovellers plying busily from ship to shore; and the laden bumboats clamouring around her towering hull was to see a picture of majesty. Her spars were trimmed squarely and her snow-white canvas had been stowed with a special harbour-stow, so that it looked as if snow had piled along the taut sparring. They went through ceremony about the tall ship of that day to make her a picture when she lay inert; and, since every ship was an advertisement for John Company, the *Kent,* be certain, had been trimmed and furbished until there was not a single ropeyarn out of place. For her captain, Henry Cobb, was a disciplinarian, more Navy than the Navy, as so many of John Company's servants were; and he stood for no nonsense. His ship was his pride; and he had her shining, from her coppered bends to her blackened trucks.

She was bound for China, with a call at Bengal; and she would conceivably be absent from home for a year, maybe two, maybe three. Being built more for roominess than speed, she would ply a leisurely way out round the Cape; not hurrying more than became her dignity; calling at Madeira to take aboard a few pipes of the island's wine, that improved by a voyage or two round the world; to deposit there such sun-seekers as did not intend to travel to the Orient; to embark fresh stores and replenish her water tanks; and generally go about her business with all the pomp and circumstance befitting a vessel belonging to the powerful, almost Imperial corporation that owned her and had dismissed her to sea with their dignified blessing.

You can picture old Henry Cobb's side-whiskers bristling with importance as he stood at the wind-swept gangway, gravely welcoming influential passengers aboard as they, having travelled overland by chaise or coach from London, climbed the rocking ladder, accompanied by their baggage and even their cabin furniture. The upper decks boiled with life and activity —here was a new crew to be sobered up and put through its facings, in order that the ship-work might proceed with the sharp click of perfect discipline. A few lately-arrived stores were being struck down into the peaks; and odd parcels of special cargo—the crafty captain's private ventures—were being bundled below into the holds—in which holds were carried something more ominous than "notions" or trade-goods or salt; since the *Kent* had on her manifest a considerable quantity of powder and shot for the use of the Honourable Company's troops in India.

Practically every East Indiaman was also a transport; since there was a constant coming and going of fighting men; time-expired returning, new recruits departing. For the most part, a man enlisting under the Company's flag, did so for life; and he went out and fought under a broiling sun, strapped up in leathern stock and padded tunic quite as gallantly as ever did his successors in easy khaki.

So the *Kent* on this maiden voyage of hers, carried a matter of 344 soldiers, together with twenty officers to keep them subordinate; and, in addition to the swarm in the troop-deck, bore 43 women and 66 children; dependents of the soldiers; together with twenty private cabin passengers and a crew of 148—making a total of 651. And amongst them all was not a single apprehension.

With the wind coming away fair, Captain Henry Cobb got his ground-tackle, and shook out his topsails; the hovellers and bumboats cleared from the gangway, and with a roaring rush the tall ship notched her bluff bow for the south. She pushed a pile of foam before her; and at the outset her forefoot started talking Spanish; and the vigorous wind kissed roses into the cheeks of the women who stared wistfully at the high white cliffs which so many of them expected never to see again. There's beauty and majesty in a great ship's sailing for the East; but there's more than a little pathos, too.

She ratched her way down-channel, with the canvas piling; the wind shifted, and she was compelled to begin a long, dreary beat to the westward. She wasn't crisp and lithe in stays; and, being new, she hadn't yet found herself; her chief officer was constantly planning some alteration in rig and trim to get the best out of her. But, beaten by the short steep Channel seas, she limbered herself, became elastic; her fastenings settled; strains were adjusted. There was no lack of hands to do such work as was necessitated; for all those soldiers were available to "hale and draw with the mariners", as Drake used to put it. So you may imagine an everlasting boil and flurry of labour along her busy decks and aloft on her wide-spread spars.

It took her nine days to ratch to Long. 10 West—so she must have made about forty-five miles a day or less; but she might have taken things even easier than that, considering what lay ahead of her. Storm struck her with increasing violence. It was the end of February, when the Atlantic usually gives its most venomous displays of spite; and an evil run of snarling combers piled up about her. Cobb head-reached as long as he could; but on March 1st he was compelled to submit, and hove his ship to under a three-reefed main topsail alone; which, as the *Kent* was a stiff ship, shows the gale to have reached the hundred-mile-an-hour mark or thereabouts. Carrying, as she did, a considerable freight of shot—chain, bar, round and lan-gridge, with some fusees or shells, this deadweight, naturally stowed on her floors, caused her to roll in an ugly fashion. She was, by this, like one of those toys of our childhood, where a half-bullet was glued to the base of a miniature bottle, which as a consequence never remained still for an instant. So the plight of her close-packed people became deplorable enough; and the promised warmth and luxury of the Orient became extremely remote. Soldiers were not cosseted in those days; and the lot of the troops was really miserable. The men who won our Empire for us were treated a little less shamefully than were felons under transportation for Botany Bay. Their women were required to make the best of cramped, exposed quarters, into which the boarding seas penetrated with remorseless insistence; and hot food was difficult to obtain. The select cabin passengers fared little better; and it might be as well if such voyagers to-day as complain querulously because they have to wait two minutes for a hot bath aboard a swagger P. & O. boat remembered the past.

Cabin-furniture was splintered and smashed; water penetrated and swilled uglily along the floors; because of being close-battened aft, the atmosphere became almost unbreathable. Shortly before noon on this day, a new sound added itself to the general pandemonium of elemental din.

"Something's fetched away below," was the decision reached. The wonder was, considering the violence of her jerky movements, the round shot hadn't already burst a way through the straining timbers. One of the ship's officers made his way below to ascertain the trouble; and, since the holds were inky dark, he carried a horn lantern with him. He discovered that a large spirit cask had carried away from its stowage; and being a man of promptness—John Company's officers were the best to be got—mustered a gang of men and set to work to secure it. This wasn't easy; a weighty cask in a seaway is a tricky proposition to handle. It can be even worse than a loose gun; and anyone who has read Victor Hugo's *Toilers of the Sea* knows what a frightful menace a loose carronade can become. They tried to scotch it with dunnage wood, and they tried to lassoo it with ropes as it rolled and thumped about on top of the other stores, but in the handling of it the cask was bilged; and the volatile spirit escaped. Some of the liquor touched the lantern held by the officer and took fire; the flame ran swiftly to the cask. Here was something inflammable and dangerous as gunpowder. The *Kent* was wood from truck to keel; and much of her cargo was highly combustible. Almost before a warning shout could be uttered, the entire lazarette was ablaze from end to end. Saturated by the spilt liquor, everything went up like so much tinder. An instant alarm was raised; the people were beaten to fire-stations; and an undercurrent of grim fear washed about the ship.

"Hands to the pumps and fire-buckets!" ordered Cobb. His chief officer took immediate charge of operations; Cobb left his autocratic poop and walked to the after hatch, glanced down and saw that matters were in train. "Wet sails to smother it!" he decided. So spare canvas was got up and drenched, and lugged below and spread; and it dried and took fire and added its volume to the general holocaust. All hands were busy—

soldiers and sailors alike; united in a brotherhood of fire-fighters. Flat-foots and leathernecks, old rivalries forgotten, were welded together in one dominant instinct to save the ship—incidentally themselves—from the threatened destruction. The fact of the gale quickened the threat. In still air a fire can be limited and confined; with eddies of wind whistling everywhere, flame-tongues leap and reach and catch and spread, and in a second a spark becomes a glow and a glow a raging furnace.

Bucket-chains formed from rails to hatches—no lack of willing helpers; but anon thick smoke was pouring up from all four hatches; driving in choking and obscene clouds along the wind-whipped decks; towering up among the stripped, gaunt rigging.

The captain of a ship so threatened must make quick irrevocable decisions. There is no place for argument; and if a decision be wrong, there is practically no time for amendment. Cobb was an experienced mariner.

"Open the sea-cocks and flood the orlop," he decreed. This was done; but the fire was not in the orlop; it raged mostly in the tweendecks. "Cut away the hatch-coamings!" was his next mandate. That was so the boarding seas would pour below without interruption; and to add to the inrushing volume of water, he ordered the lower-deck ports to be thrown open. This was a hazardous proceeding, the ship rolling in lively fashion, and the big seas running devouringly. But though the *Kent* threatened to be drowned, it was apparently preferable to being roasted; and of two evils choose the lesser.

There was a rush to obey—too hasty a rush; zeal outran discretion; and all the dangers of an uncalculated campaign made themselves evident. Without waiting for the lower decks to be cleared, the big ports were swung open from their fastenings; and torrential water invaded the body of the great ship in a Niagara. Sick soldiers, housed in sick-bay—which was deep down in the ship in order to be immune from aggressive shot and shell in the event of an engagement—were swept from their hammocks and drowned in the stifling dark. A woman, also below, and several children, were overtaken by the insweeping flood and perished miserably.   There was a scene of exquisite horror down there in the creaking darkness—and all the time the ship rolled and the loose shot pounded in a dismal requiem.   Imagine another horror.   Such people as were trapped below and were not actually drowned, were suffocated by the incessant smoke beating down from above and prisoned by the rising water.   If they reached and clung to keep their heads above the torrent, they choked and stifled and died, to drop back and swill about in the ugly flood.

The sea can excel anything the land may do in the quality of its bizarre horror!

Realising what had happened as a result of his impetuous command, Cobb immediately ordered the ports to be closed.   This was not easy; it meant desperate rushes through pouring brine; men had to swim, and a floating body lacks weight and force. But the swamping checked the flames; that was something; and the cure proved worse than the disease.   By the time the ports were shut the *Kent* was sodden and water-logged; and the word went round that she was sinking.   Instantly a panic-stricken mob broke for the upper deck, where was light, where was breathable air, and a prospect of escape.   Seven hundred people packed the upper decks—a milling, noisy mob, whose outcries were mocked by the clamour of the persisting gale.   Here was the *Amazon* on a magnified scale!

Young Mr. Thompson, the fourth mate, was a man of resource. He singled out the keenest-eyed man of the crew.   "Up aloft to the fore-top!" he directed, "and look out for a friendly sail." The man leaped over the sheerpole, and, spread-eagled by the weight of wind, tediously crawled aloft.   His progress was watched by many straining eyes.   They saw him cower before the drive of wind; they saw him straighten and peer around the horizon from under his hand: a stubby, bowlegged shape to be a harbinger of hope.   The tumult and confusion died down and the indraw of breath below was like a roar.   Nothing happened. Panic commenced afresh—to be quenched by a long-drawn hail:

"Sail on the lee bow, sir!" came down from aloft; and it was echoed by a wavering cheer. That was promise—they were not to die alone and unbefriended in the whirl and riot of that frenzied storm, with the smoke billowing in choking clouds about them.

"Hoist the distress signal—man the signal gun!" said Captain Cobb. Up went the bunting; whipping in the wind; fluttering itself to ribbons. A gun was loaded and run out, with a gunner's mate guarding the priming; his flint and steel at hand. Bang!

The gun leaped back to the extent of its breeching; but its roar was mocked by the elemental uproar; it sounded more like a croupy cough than a detonation. It was smartly reloaded; and the gunner watched the sand-glass until a minute had elapsed.

"Fire! Stop your vent!" Another cough—inaudible at a distance of half a mile and the watcher aloft marked no alteration in the sighted sail. But the minute gun—stark signal of woe—continued to fire; and the ribboned bunting was hauled down and replaced with fresh stuff, that in its turn fluttered to pitiful rags; and the people of the *Kent* waited; that being about all there was for them to do. But they were in hand again—the military officers had got mastery of their men—men, these, in many cases, drawn from agricultural areas in an England remote from the sea. Those women who had lost their children wrung their hands and moaned amid the sputtering sprays; but the men were calm and steadfast now. Their sufferings were great; the decks were exposed, lacking decent shelter. For the most part they were at least knee-deep in the chilly swill; and the spin-drift came with the sting of grapeshot. Drenched and frozen and almost hopeless—with a choking death awaiting them if they attempted to go below—they waited, the lines deepening in their wan faces.

"Make sail on the ship; get her away before the wind, we'll

run down to him!" instructed the valiant Cobb, very much master of the situation.

The yards were squared, and the *Kent* was given enough canvas to keep her ahead of the seas—forty or fifty feet from trough to crest by this time. That was a risky proceeding: setting sail in hard weather always is; and certain sails were carried clean out of the bolt-ropes. But the Indiaman got way on her and began to move through the water; with a pall of thick smoke all about her; and it was this curious sea-phenomenon, rather than minute-gun or bunting, that drew the stranger's attention to her. Having sighted the *Kent,* the stranger brig hoisted British colours in recognition, and, though herself under short canvas, set more sail and headed towards the big ship. Here was the courageous spirit of such as use the sea made manifest. There is every evidence—tragic evidence—that the gale was at hurricane force; the strange craft was only a brig, and consequently small and liable to be overwhelmed by the combers; but without hesitation she began to take steps to lend aid to those in worse plight than herself.

The *Kent* was not seaworthy; she was slugging sullenly in the troughs, always rolling, dipping her yardarms at every swing; with her trucks tracing giddy arcs across the screaming sky; so that all that was possible, with this succour in view, was to think of salving her people, not the ship. Whilst the *Cambria,* as the brig was named, was standing down to meet her course, discussions took place as to the best means of ferrying that large complement across from one ship to the other in a sea running mountains high. Captain Cobb knew how he intended to do it; but the colonel commanding the troops was a landsman and not versed in maritime practice; he knew his men were raw, unhandy in boats; and, so far as the vast majority were concerned, utterly unable to swim a stroke. Also, there were the women—soldiers' wives—and their helpless children. Transportation required thought. He handled the situation like a soldier and a man.

"Give instructions to the rank and file," he ordered, "that any man who attempts to desert his post until all women and children are safely rescued will be cut down where he stands." The officers carried their swords; they were ordered to use them without hesitation in case of need.

As it happened the precautionary order was not necessary of fulfilment: the troops behaved with fortitude in the face of a far more trying ordeal than that of battle on land.

Satisfied that no disorderly rush would take place, the colonel communicated the position to old Henry Cobb, who was watching from his poop-break, straddled on rounded shanks—always capable, and, though moved to his deeps by the quality of the catastrophe, betraying no outward evidences of the fact.

"Good enough, sir," he rasped. And to his chief officer: "Make ready the cutter." The cutter was stowed bottom upwards on top of the forward house. She was promptly righted; and men were set to work to keep her baled, as water was boarding with a greater determination than before. Men went aloft to rig the purchases necessary to lift her to the rail and lower her out without risk of bilging her—that meant fitting a yardarm tackle, with strong guys; for the swing of the ship threatened to make the cumbersome boat take charge.

"All ready, the cutter," announced the chief officer, after certain feverish activities.

"Let the ladies and little ones be put on board the boat," commanded Cobb. It was done. The cutter was the biggest, most seaworthy boat carried by the Indiaman; a capable craft in her way, but never designed for facing such seas as were at present boiling. The women shrank back from the menace of those curling combers; the infants wailed; all was misery and distress.

"I will give you a lee," instructed Cobb. "Watch a smooth and lower her handsomely at the right time." He would be somewhat pursy and pedantic in his manner, this heart of oak; always autocratic and precise; but behind his buttoned up martinetship was a mighty warm and kindly heart—now wrung by woe at the dire calamity befalling him. So he let the *Kent* run off a little, watched the ninth wave swing by, and then: "Lower away—lowered of all!" he brayed through his copper trumpet; and the cutter was dropped into the sea; a wave licking up to snatch her greedily from the tackles.

Incredible that so frail a craft could endure an instant in such a savage sea! Twice the cutter was all but swamped; and the cries and wails from her passengers rose up to combat with the scream and wail of storm. White water surged in and was rocked out as the boat careened. Then she was cast clear of the ship and, existing by a succession of miracles, began to pull across the mighty waves to where the *Cambria* awaited her, incapable of doing aught else but cheer the rowers as they laboured. Whoever had charge of that cutter knew his job. She was loaded pretty nearly to her gunwales; and although the Indiaman sheltered her to some extent, the big swing of the seas was very menacing, as foamy monster after foamy monster rolled up, and swung, and, swinging, grew into the father and mother of all waves, and impended and fell—in time to miss the squatting stern, where an officer laboured with a steering oar and performed a fresh miracle of helmsmanship with every new breath he drew.

The *Cambria* hove herself to some distance from the *Kent*. Captain Cook, commanding her, had a duty to his own ship's people and the 30 Cornish miners he was carrying on passage to Vera Cruz, as well as to the people of the Indiaman. That canopy of smoke was a threat—the big towering ship was armed; consequently she carried a considerable magazine; and fire in a ship of this kind almost always eventuated in a shattering explosion. A spar, torn from place, hurled in air, descending aboard a standing-by ship, might reasonably hole her fatally. And although the major conflagration aboard the *Kent* was drowned out, a fire still burnt below. So Captain Cook held off at a fair distance; and the cutter's crew found that a long pull and a strong pull lay before them. But by dint of heroic effort

[175]

they managed it; and succeeded in running alongside the *Cambria* to leeward; where their shivering, half-distracted passengers were tenderly got on board and looked after with kindness of the sea. Back went the cutter—and some idea of the conditions prevailing may be gathered when it is stated that to make the return journey occupied three-quarters of an hour.

The *Cambria* got out her long-boat, too; and some of the Cornish miners—stout fellows!—volunteered to help in its manning. Being Cornish they were naturally half-sailors already. But though the long-boat contrived to span the furious space between one ship and the other, it was found totally impossible to bring her alongside the menaced ship. To leeward was wreckage; to windward was death. Sailors being fundamentally opposed to acknowledging defeat, other steps were promptly taken. The long-boat, together with the returned cutter, could just live whilst lying off the *Kent's* stern. Ropes were cast into the boats, therefore, and the remaining women and children were lashed together to be lowered overside and hauled to that precarious safety. It was a well-meant project: a counsel of despair, indeed—it was that or nothing. But here tragedy stalked; for the roystering seas, greedy always, roared up and licked at the swinging bundles, as they passed down into the bight of the rope; and occasionally, the greybeards licked away the burdens from the bowlines in which they were slung, and roared triumphant over the pitiful spoil they snatched. So numbers of infant lives were lost; and not only infants perished, but also not a few strong men; for to watch little ones drown was beyond the phlegm of the soldiers. Several of them boldly leapt overboard to swim to the rescue—in a sea like that! They died —giving proof that though maybe they were coarse-mannered men, pagan according to certain constructions, they understood Christianity to the extent of laying down their lives for their friends.

A piteous sight, the poop of the *Kent* whilst this daring operation was in progress! Shivering, distraught women being held in shelter up to the last minute before they were taken against wind and sea to the exposed taffrail, there bound about with blankets that the hard rope might not tear their delicate bodies asunder; gingerly helped to the rail, lowered; men hanging grimly to the swinging, harping lines—until those in the boats took the weight and drew in; and other women peering fearfully to see the fashion of the frail bridge they must negotiate if they would live! Scared children hiding in their mothers' saturated skirts; fathers taking thick-throated leave of those they never hoped or expected to see again—and the shipmen going about their labours capably although their hearts were wrung by the tragedies happening overside. And every now and then a frail body whirled from that precarious thread and tossed to a wave-crest; and a red-jacketed man joining hands and leaping overboard to share in the inevitable death!

Darkness was closing in on the short, lurid winter's day. Down below the fire was still extending; eating its sinister way amongst the packages in the holds that were not yet flooded. Men still fought it; endeavouring to isolate the magazine; and the need for quicker evacuation grew imminent; since both Captain Cobb and Colonel Fearon were anxious to give their men every possible chance for salvation.

With women and children all away, Cobb devised a preventer transporter; he made fast a stout line to the end of the spanker-boom, which was cockbilled to act as a sort of crane; and down this flimsy line, when its other end was secured in a boat, the men were directed to slide. They did it, of course—it was that or die where they stood; but they did not all complete that hazardous journey. Unskilled hands failed to hold a secure grip of the rope; and the seas uproaring ever, licked them away. Some simply dropped and were no more; others fought frantically for the dear boon of life.

Now as only men remained aboard the sailors were given a fighting chance with the soldiers. Since a sailor is trained to such manœuvres, the percentage of mariners rescued by the boats exceeded that of the soldiers. When a soldier hesitated to essay the perilous descent, a sailor would invariably step forward to take his place and so make the most of the fast-passing time. When night had come, a large number of soldiers still remained aboard the Indiaman. In order that they might be seen when floating and so be given another chance for life, they were instructed to bind pieces of white linen round their heads, to be visible against the black-green background of the sea.

The work went on under these conditions. Below decks fire raged and water entered, above men laboured at the pumps whilst they awaited their turn to attempt the risky passage from poop to boat. The water inflowed so rapidly that the problem confronting Cobb was whether the ship would not sink before the flames reached the magazine. There was really nothing to be done beyond evacuate the people to the best of his ability. He began to bustle the soldiers about; endeavouring to nerve them to essay the drop; but darkness added to their landsman fears; and they became stubbornly resolved to die where they were. All the time the boats gallantly plied between the two ships, and miraculously continued to live, at cost of superb seamanship and much frenzied baling.

Dark though the stormy night was, there was light enough showing from the burning Indiaman to direct the boats one way; and the rigging of the game little *Cambria* was draped with storm lanterns; whilst each time the boats crossed flares were supplied; so that the wan gleams of these torches would show the hapless waiting ones high on the *Kent's* poop that efforts to save them still persisted.

Cobb first implored the remaining soldiers to bear a hand in saving themselves; when they stood hesitant, he threatened to heave them overboard to save their lives. Certain of the troops, regrettably—yet I doubt if they can honestly be blamed, for they had endured many hours of living hell—broke away off the poop and contrived to make their way down into the deserted cabins, where they found the means to forget their woes and laugh in death's gibbering face. They raided the store-rooms, and got gloriously drunk; just as people of a higher caste have been known to do in times of crisis; and they stayed below to drown or be blown to pieces—they didn't care which.

On the poop Captain Cobb decided that if the soldiers would not go, the remaining officers must. The majority of the officers, true to type, had hung back to give their men first chance, since they stood in the position of guardians to them; and it was the habit of an officer to set a good example to his subordinates.

"If the men will not save themselves, their blood must rest on their own heads!" was Cobb's dictum, which Colonel Fearon supported; but even so these two stout-hearts relaxed no effort to cajole and threaten the weaklings into making a bid for safety.

Whilst these efforts were in progress, the ominous sound of explosions was heard, shaking the sodden ship. The guns of the main-deck, reached by the advancing flames, exploded solemnly, one by one; as if firing a minute-signal of hopelessness on their own account. The time had come when every man, if he hoped to live longer, must look out for himself. The junior officers descended the ropes, hung there, were caught and dragged into the waiting boat—or dropped and struggled and drowned. Remained in the event only Cobb and Fearon apart from the huddled, paralysed men, who could not be lifted or coerced into making effort for self-preservation.

Captain Cobb placed the rope in Colonel Fearon's hands, and invited him to go, commending him to God. Black night, black as the hobs of the Pit itself; a screaming tornado blowing; the water leaping as high as the great stern-lantern and the small —very small—boat leaping and rioting like a delirious fury! Colonel Fearon made suitable acknowledgments of the courtesy shewn; wrapped his cloak about him and essayed the venture. He had a rougher passage than most of his men. The darkness confused; the boat was almost unmanageable; every time it roared near Fearon was crashed against its planking. He let go too soon in response to a call, and was dragged clean under the furious craft; and it was only when a hand reached out and gripped his hair that it was possible to get him into the boat at all. But he was salved; and, after a final effort to kick some sense of what was happening into the remaining men, old Cobb gripped the rope of safety and lowered himself overboard. Being wise in the ways of the sea, he was hauled aboard without mishap; and the boat then moved away to the *Cambria*.

As it did so, flames burst forth from the stern-windows of the Indiaman; as proof of her dire plight; and this wall of fire effectually cut off any further attempts at rescue. The stern, recently the only spot where a boat could lie, was now unapproachable. Some twenty-odd soldiers remained aboard, frozen with terror and unable to do anything to help themselves. They should not have been left. Cobb should have had them manhandled overboard, where at all events they had a fighting chance for life; but in the darkness and inevitable confusion it is possible this plan evaded his notice.

The *Kent* was nearing her end. She presented an awe-inspiring sight from the foamy distance as the flames, now untrammelled, gained rapid ground. The whole upper-deck was quickly alight; and the poop-deck crumpled away; the flames leaping higher after a temporary set-back. Wreathed in flame, palled in smoke, and the fire-glow lighting the underside of the smoke-cloud into the likeness of an Inferno, with lowering storm-clouds appearing to press the smoke down, the wild wind whipping the flames into contorted fury, she floated soddenly there in the yeasty waste, white-fingered combers leaping madly at her, anxious to claim credit for this new victory of the sea over man-made ship. Flame shot up and licked away the gaskets holding the foresail and the mizen; these great sails dropped, were scorched dry in a breath, took fire, and fluffed away like tinder. The tarred rigging caught; so did the well-greased masts; immediately the entire ship, from truck to waterways, was outlined in vivid fire: an amazing spectacle. By that ghastly light the final boats approached the gallant *Cambria;* by that light the rescue work continued.

It was not easy; the *Cambria,* a small brig of 200 tons, was lively as an intoxicated cork in the seaway. Her comparatively low freeboard afforded scant shelter for the boats; and so vicious was the 'scend of ship and smaller craft that not a few of the salved dropped between ship and boat and perished in the gloom, with the flames of the blazing *Kent* their last sight in this life. The sea showed them no mercy; it seemed, indeed, eager to wrest the poor boon of continued existence from such as had dared its anger. But it reckoned without those stalwart Cornish miners, who dared much by hanging by their knees from the chain-plates, reaching into the jolting, soaring boats, and dragging their fellowmen by sheer strength from thwart to rail, and so to another chance for life. Herculean labour, this; but effective.

Before it was completed, before the last man was out of the last boat, the flames reached the *Kent's* magazine; the night was torn asunder by a thunderous roar; the glowing masts shot upwards, the spars parted company; a roaring maelstrom of fire whirled high, then was suddenly quenched; and the *Kent* dived in her shattered fragments down to the bottom of the sea, her life ended before it had fairly begun.

Certain of those fear-paralysed soldiers remaining were not blown to pieces; they were merely blown overboard, where for a while they struggled among the wreckage that came snarling down from the sky. Some were lucky enough to waken from their coma of fear and snatch feebly at the charred spars and gratings, to cling frantically thereto, not with any hope of ultimate salvation, but merely in obedience to the primitive law of self-preservation, which is the strongest emotion known to mankind. And, so clinging through an indescribable night of stress and despair, they were miraculously found by the trading vessel *Caroline,* voyaging from Liverpool to Alexandria. Her master, Captain Bibby, chanced to see the vivid pyrotechnics of the final explosion, and promptly stood in that direction, arriving on the scene in time to snatch a few from the salty maw of old ocean, which can never be sufficiently satiated with human prey.

So, thanks to brave work and the sterling fellowship of the sea, which acts regardless of nationality or creed, the tragedy of the *Kent* was limited, insofar as loss of human life was concerned. The total lost and missing numbered ninety-six souls: comprising 55 soldiers, 1 seaman, 5 Marine boys; and, alas, fifteen women and twenty children—these latter either being torn from the lowering rope, or lost when it was attempted to pass them aboard the *Cambria*.

Still, that loss was big enough, and should have been lessened. The fact that only one sailor perished is sinister: no sailor should save himself whilst one entrusted to his charge is in peril. That is part of the duty he takes upon himself when signing into the service of the sea—and it is very seldom that he is found wanting. There are critics who would say that Captain Cobb failed in his duty by leaving a single man aboard his ship when he slid down the rope to safety. Personally, I think he had done everything in his power; and obviously he was not afraid to face the ensuing enquiry, so he was justified in making his escape when he could; because all the gallant and reckless dying in the world cannot advantage the world, whereas a living, competent shipmaster can.

Although torn from the sea, the plight of the survivors aboard the *Cambria* was not by any means enviable. She measured two hundred tons, and carried a cargo; in addition to her crew—fifteen men or thereabouts—she had these thirty hardy Cornishmen, who had distinguished themselves so notably by snatching the helpless from the leaping boats as they roared to the wave-crests. There were well over six hundred people aboard the brig when the muster was called; and the ship was provisioned for forty men alone. She was tempest-tossed and clean-washed by every sea; and she laboured several hundreds of miles from the nearest port of refuge. Since there was insufficient room in her small cabins, it was necessary to stow the human crowds on her exposed decks; and although effort was made to rig some sort of shelter, the force of wind and sea ratched all coverings away immediately they were rigged. Since the storm had wrought havoc to her bulwarks, tearing them clean away along one side of the hull, the *Cambria* was in pitiable plight enough. It was necessary to rig a netting of ropes across the breached bulwarks to prevent the huddled survivors from being washed incontinently overboard to the death they had so narrowly escaped. Under these conditions, she put about for the English coast.

The gale continuing, to set full sail was out of the question; those breached bulwarks gave Captain Cook much concern, naturally enough. But he shook out what canvas he considered it safe to carry; and let his brig snort along, her scuppers awash; and turned to the problem of stores. For six hundred people, even if narrowly won from the jaws of death, remain human enough to feel the urge of appetite. Captain Cook had disturbing visions of six hundred people insisting on food when food there was none. He doled out what he had sparingly. This was before a motherly Board of Trade insisted on a six months' reserve of salt provisions being carried; and his sea-stock would be enough for his forty-odd men and boys and no more for the short passage to Vera Cruz. It was a case of stretching supplies to breaking-point; of making bricks without straw; but the meat available was boiled, and hard tack crumbled in the broth; and sufficient soup to set the worst pangs of hunger at rest was contrived, whilst the game little ship creaked and rumbled her stolid way to Falmouth Harbour; which was reached without further mishap by the 3rd of March. She dropped her anchor at half an hour after midnight; and any sailor must give full marks to Captain Cook for making a good job of it. For within an hour of his making an anchorage— imagine the gladness of soul aboard the *Cambria* when the cable rumbled out through the hawsehole!—the wind backed suddenly and fiercely; and became a dead-muzzler for the Channel. It persisted from the east-north-east for a considerable time;

and if Cook hadn't rushed things, one fears to think of what must have happened to his brig. She could never have made port against a head-wind; she must inevitably have been driven back to open sea, and compelled to beat a weary track up and down across the Channel mouth, in sight of land, and incapable of reaching it—with six hundred starving people aboard; people still saturated and weak through suspense and suffering. The *Cambria* would have become a plague-ship in a week; a death-ship in ten days; and the true story of the *Kent* might never have been told.

As it was, England rang with the tragic-gallant story; and both the Government and the Honourable East India Company combined to present a sufficiently handsome reward to Captain Cook and the *Cambrian* men. Which anyone who has read this narrative must admit was honestly earned if ever reward was.

CHAPTER IX

ATLANTIC v. "ATLANTIC"

In 1873, on the 28th of March, Captain Williams took the S.S. *Atlantic,* one of the newest of the White Star Line cracks, to sea, bound for New York; and in his charge he had 931 persons; a large proportion of them being women and children—a type of prey of which the Atlantic never seems tired. The *Atlantic* was the *Majestic* of her day—a ship at which to wonder; speedy and safe. Comparatively safe, that is—but then, so was the unlucky *Titanic.* The White Star Line have had a good deal of misfortune with their ships, owing to no fault of construction or handling; simply because the fates have been against them.

The *Atlantic* took the sea just in time to meet up with the equinoctials of that early spring; which happened to blow with rather more than common fury; dead in the liner's teeth on her present course. Those sharp, screw steamers of sixty years ago were not the seaboats of to-day; they were wet ships; dirty ships; and the *Atlantic* was no exception. Bucking into this head gale became a monotony; and as the dead-muzzler persisted, Captain Williams resolved that it was tempting Providence too strongly to hold on for New York; and so altered course to run for Halifax, Nova Scotia. Three days out, at night, the alteration was made; and the ship proceeded.

Retiring one midnight, Captain Williams gave orders that he was to be called without fail at 3 a.m. because the ship was making for a more than commonly dangerous coast. It was his intention to lie offshore until daylight. But he appears to have been considerably out in his reckoning. Chronometers

of those days were not the reliable instruments they are now-
adays; and, too, the continuing storm would naturally obscure
the heavens sufficient to prevent reliable observations. In a
lively ship with a misted horizon, it can be extraordinarily difficult to get the sun's lower limb down to the skyline; and as a
second of error in altitude can mean two miles of distance wrong,
it will be realised that close navigation under such conditions
was not easy. Long-range sounding machines were practically
unknown; and the *Atlantic* was crossing deep water.

At three o'clock in the morning—the darkest hour of the
graveyard watch—a sudden strident cry of "Breakers ahead!"
beat through the yelp of the gale from the forward lookouts.
The *Atlantic* was driving at full power of her considerable engines, trying to make decent headway against the west-wind-
driven sea. Before the fact of danger penetrated the mind of her
watch-officer, she struck rock, was driven hard on incredible
fangs. She stuck there, immovable; the big water tearing at
her in fury. They tore at her exposed port side; and they ripped
away her boats; for this liner had nothing approaching the freeboard of her later sisters. The seas ripped every boat on the
port side to matchwood; and, striking battering blows at the
arrested hull, caused it to heel; thus bringing the starboard boats
within reach of the leeward running combers. These boats were
bilged and broken, rendered completely useless. The plight
of the *Atlantic,* within a very few minutes of the first report
being made, was pitiable beyond expression.

As she touched, Captain Williams leaped from his sea-cabin
to the bridge, to take control of an apparently hopeless situation. His officers joined him; immediate reports were made;
the situation in all its ugliness was envisaged. Already the wave-
lashed decks were crowding with scared passengers who had
been hurled from their sleeping-places by the impact.

No boats; scant chance of lowering them if there had been—
Captain Williams instructed these shivering souls to climb the
rigging as swiftly as might be, and there secure themselves.

Other protection there was none; an unbroken succession of breakers was roaring and snarling along the decks, casting people down into the choking scuppers, bearing them against the rails; and generally making endurance hard for the astonished folk, whose brains were still full of sleep. They simply could not realise what had happened; everything had occurred with such staggering suddenness. One moment they were asleep, the next they were hurled to the floor of their cabins; as they rushed for the deck they were overborne and swept recklessly this way and that. In the dark of the night, moreover—such an experience was stunning to a degree.

The *Atlantic* had struck bow on; gaping holes were in her forepart; as she listed to starboard, the rock-fangs tore her plates wider open; and the hungry sea rushed in, overtaking the unfortunate steerage passengers before they were even aroused. Hundreds of these miserable souls, who had looked forward with eager hope to a new life in a new world, where legend had it, the pavements were of gold, and fortune awaited every man around the next corner, were drowned without a chance to save themselves. Their first intimation of anything being wrong was that screeching crash, the sick stagger and shock; and then—the invading cascade of resistless sea.

Certain of these emigrants made for the deck, pursued by hungry water; only to gain it and find fresh horror mowing at them; for the white water, borne by the cyclone, swept the ship's forepart without intermission; and as a consequence, the majority of those who gained the open, were swept overboard before they had a chance to find their feet. Nor was this enough of a tragedy. When the sea is out to kill, she makes strategic moves to cripple her victims. The ship's foreboom carried away at its heel, and swung inboard, hanging by its rigging, the bobstay and boom-guys; and it swept the exposed forecastle like a Titanic flail; striking down all in its way, hurling them overboard or leaving them without strength to stand up against the ever-boarding seas. Imagine the horror of that threshing spar—

licking backwards and forwards over the deck at a height that cut down everyone who happened to be within range! A black, hideous thing, striking—striking! The situation appeared entirely hopeless. To climb the rigging was but a postponement of the inevitable end; but desperate men are apt to take desperate chances. One solitary, precarious means of rescue remained; a chancy one enough.

One hundred and fifty feet away from the hull, already like a half-tide rock washed by every racing wave, a solitary rock reared up above the foam-swirls. It was vulnerable; but it offered a means of handhold until further measures could be taken. There was no time to make elaborate plans—the darkness was confusing, and it magnified the horrors even beyond their actual proportions. By dint of Herculean effort, the seamen of the *Atlantic* contrived to carry five ropes to this elevation. It was anything but an easy task—it meant swimming and scrambling in among sharp-tongued rocks, all of them lashed by the seething waves; but since desperation recognises no obstacles, those five lines were carried ashore, and in some mysterious fashion made fast to protuberances. In this fashion the frailest of frail bridges was constructed; a solitary link between life and death. From this elevated rock to the shore was a distance of a hundred yards; and, incredibly, a further rope was carried through more breakers, so that another link with dry land was effected. Mr. Brady, the gallant third officer, accompanied by two quartermasters, did this part of the work by swimming and fighting valiantly and refusing to be deterred.

The way of escape opening out, evacuation of the ship's people began. Two hundred or so human beings hazarded that spidery bridge; and succeeded in gaining the rock; many were torn away in the passage and lost to sight and life for ever. Of these two hundred, about fifty essayed the further dizzy journey successfully. These owed their continued existence to the remarkable gallantry and endurance of the third officer and his assistants; for anyone who knows that bleak Nova Scotian coast

THE "LUSITANIA"

THE "ATLANTIC"

knows what its breakers are like as they fret and thunder among the iron-hard reefs. Only supermen could have managed the feat; but Brady and his helpers did it; and so these fifty won to safety, precariously enough. The ferocious Atlantic called Arctic cold to its aid now, as if its own ferocity were not enough; it numbed the fingers of those who scrabbled for life; it broke their grip, and the sea clamoured along and licked them away one by one, as they cried aloud to a God Who had apparently forsaken them. Even those who retained a grip of the salving line were torn at by the breakers until their strength left them and their resolve died; when they perished: battered to pulp by the snarling breakers among the rocks.

Through the remaining hours of an unspeakable night, this purgatory endured. The *Atlantic* was at war with its namesake, and all the odds were in the ocean's favour. They always are; but there is one strong weapon in man's favour when battle with any sea is at issue—human courage and stamina. The Atlantic Ocean asked nothing better than to make a clean sweep of the *Atlantic* steamer; and leave no single trace of its grim passing, beyond a few clean-picked bones; but as has occurred so often before and as will occur, please God, until there are no more ships, the human element won a partial victory. With the coming of a howling dawn—steel-grey and sinister—a small boat put off from the mainland, which proved to be Meagher's Island—and after superhuman struggles on the part of its crew, succeeded in gaining the rock, where Brady still controlled his impromptu life-saving device. Into the boat Brady leaped, and, going ashore, contrived to discover three larger boats and people to man them from among the limited ranks of the islanders. With these boats he inaugurated a hasty ferry service, which was probably as hectic a service as has ever been founded; for on each trip a race with death was run; the surf raging and leaping, and the big noisy breakers doing their utmost not only to capsize the boats, but also to beat them to pulp and splinters.

It was a breathless rally enough; but it had its successes. From the intermediate rock, washed constantly by waves, and the masts of the *Atlantic,* now lying over almost horizontal to the sea, the lifesaving craft collected large numbers of bemused, distressed, unconscious people, and ferried them ashore as nimbly as might be, where they were looked after as well as possible under difficult circumstances. Brady, the junior officer, appears to have been the principal hero of this adventure; his pluck and determination did marvels; but for his devotion, it seems reasonable that practically none of the *Atlantic's* people could have survived this frightful night.

Captain Williams' duty was to stay by his ship; and this he did; his coolness and initiative impressing all who witnessed it. Nothing shook him; he superintended the ferrying of the near-helpless folks across that frail and precarious rope-bridge which Brady was inspired to construct; he personally lifted people to the lines; he fetched the paralysed from their corners, he encouraged them; and gave a signal illustration of the fearlessness of an honest master-mariner. Not until both his hands and feet were frozen, and he was satisfied that everything possible had been done, did he allow himself to be taken away in one of the boats and transported to shore, with the bare gift of life as his portion.

The loss of life in this duel between man and the sea was regrettably high: assisted in its magnitude by that sensational inrush of water into the steerage when the ship first took the ground. Four hundred and eighty-one people perished in various ways—by drowning in the dark, torn from their holding, or licked off the decks by that evil, swinging boom; and of this total two hundred and ninety-five were women and children. The Atlantic had taken its savage toll, regardless of sex or quality. No wonder, hearing of such elemental ferocity, men of the true blue breed are inspired to wage incessant war with an element that never ceases in its surprises and never slackens in its relentless attacks!

A big total in the everlasting price of Admiralty: close on

five hundred decent lives! But when one bears in mind how many thousands—how many millions, indeed—are safely transported from continent to continent in the course of an average year, the ocean's occasional victory cannot be considered overwhelming.

When a shipmaster loses his ship, he is required to answer for a professional misdemeanour. Frost-bitten though he was, Captain Williams was no exception. He came up before his professional court—the British Board of Trade—which sets a high standard; and because he had neglected to stop and take soundings at regular intervals when knowing himself in the vicinity of an ultra-dangerous coast, he was severely censured. His gallantry after the crash and his sterling devotion to duty spoke in his favour, however; and instead of losing his certificate of competency for ever, it was merely suspended for two years. But his punishment lay in the knowledge that he had unwittingly thrown away five hundred precious lives. The man-inflicted penalties are not the bitterest man has to bear.

CHAPTER X

H.M.S. "EURYDICE"

CONSIDERING the length of its beat and the quality of its service, the British Navy in peacetime can claim a singularly clean sheet in regard to major disasters. True, disasters of staggering proportions there certainly have been: but weighed against the sea-miles traversed and the police-work done, the percentage is so small as almost to be negligible. The period of transition from sail to steam, from wood to steel, from muzzle-loaders to breech-loaders, was, however, fairly fruitful in catastrophe; although it was fruitful, too, in deeds of outstanding gallantry and in escapes from disaster that can only be considered miraculous; as witness the sturdy *Calliope* getting her ground-tackle and steaming away to sea in the teeth of the frantic Samoa hurricane, when representative ships of the world's finest navies were incontinently lost. Yes, bearing in mind the onerousness of its service, the fact that it is not kept to well-charted trails, and the exactions demanded, the British Navy shows a pretty clean sheet—especially where loss of life is concerned. We have seen how the sinking of H.M.S. *Victoria* cast a gloom over the country; and how even to-day the mystery of that mishap has never been clearly solved. There are many who remember the grounding of the *Montagu,* a brand-new battleship; but the total loss of that ship was not attended by loss of life; so that it may hardly be termed a disaster; and that the worth of the ship itself was negligible was afterwards proved by the Admiralty's action.

But the middle part of the nineteenth century was notable for the number of victories scored to the credit of the sea; and not least of these was the tragic foundering of H.M.S. *Eurydice:* one of the Navy's white-winged ships, employed in teaching the young idea of Britain not only how to shoot but also how to become worth-while sailormen, and a credit to the finest sea-faring service in the world.

Eurydice belonged to the spacious days of sail; and she was a beautiful ship of nine hundred and twenty-one tons; sloop-rigged, and built in 1843, when men put their hearts into the ships they turned out and so created things of loveliness as well as sea-fighting units. In her prime *Eurydice* was counted amongst the crack sailing vessels of the Navy; and I have met old sailors who have shaken sorrowful heads whilst admitting that her like would never be looked on again, who described her saucy beauty as she crowded on all plain sail and skimmed the Trade-crisped waters like a thing of pulsing life. They said there was nothing afloat to touch her, either for picturesqueness or for smartness; and these old veterans were critics who ought to have known. Maybe it was purely because of her perfections that the jealous sea ultimately claimed her; but to the account of manhood it must be said that the *Eurydice* licked the seas of the world handsomely for a period of thirty-five years; not a bad life for any ship; and a particularly long span for a sailing Navy craft. The average useful existence of a modern battle-ship, which might cost originally six million pounds or there-abouts, is twenty years, with luck; so the *Eurydice* might reason-ably be deemed a genuine veteran of the seas. When white water took its vengeance it did it thoroughly, as the record shows.

Built in 1843, she was converted in 1877 into a seagoing train-ing-ship for young boys of the ordinary seaman class, R.N. It was considered then, as it is considered now, that the best system of training for youngsters who wished to be handy, resourceful and courageous when waging war with the sea, was in ships carrying masts and yards. As a windjammer-trained man I contend that such schooling is invaluable; and by a coincidence, during the writing of this particular chapter, I was required to attend a meeting which had as its object the procuring of a square-rigged sailing-ship for the purpose of administering a final polish to the sea-education of the British lad. When the *Garthpool* laid her bones on the rocks of Boa Vista the other day, the last British square-rigger went; and this new dream-ship, the *Sea Lion,* may start a new chapter in the history of the sea.

For there can be no question as to the worth of this type of training. It not only teaches its pupils craftsmanship and handi-ness; it teaches him how to act in emergency and how to im-provise in distress. It does more—it acts as a fine filter; for the law of the windjammer was always the law of the survival of the fittest; whereas now a youngster might go to sea for forty years and never be required to jump smartly to save his own life or a shipmate's; and might never be required to fish his dinner from a swilling scupper; which, if it has nothing to do with naviga-tion or seamanship, still teaches a youngster to appreciate the food set down before him! And although to-day a steamer fares from port to port with much about the same regularity and monotony as a train going from Glasgow to London, there is always a risk of an emergency arising when a quality of handi-ness and pluck and dogged determination to make good would be a useful acquisition to such as serve aboard her.

Something of this idea was in the minds of the Admiralty, at all events, when they commissioned the *Eurydice* in 1877 as a seagoing training ship; where boys who would spend their future lives in steel-walled steam-driven leviathans, would be taught certain qualities which make for good service to Crown and country. Captain Marcus Hare had been specially selected by the Board to commission and command the ship, because he possessed qualities not always granted to men—even to men of senior rank and world-wide experience. Marcus Hare was not only an able seaman and officer; he had shewn particular apti-tude for dealing with youngsters—the raw material from which the solid seaman is made. He had a knack of winning their confidence and their admiration; and when a man has that quality, he stands confessed as an ordained teacher of youth.

The *Eurydice* left Portsmouth in November of 1877, sailing in company with the *Martin,* another training-ship; and bound for the delightful island of Madeira as her first port of call, where the policy of showing the world to the tyros would be fulfilled. The boys were light-hearted and happy as monkeys at prospect of a visit to foreign parts; and we may be sure they thoroughly enjoyed every minute of their shore-leave when Madeira was reached. You can see them cruising down the stony streets in those quaint toboggans, clamouring through the narrow thoroughfares overhung with gaudy poinsettias and hibiscus-bushes; wondering at the grave, stealthily-treading oxen in the sumptuous passenger-sledges: bathing in the crystal-clear sea under an unflecked sky. Lying at Funchal they gave smart exhibitions of sail-drill for the benefit of the leisurely pleasure-seekers who came a-visiting in nimble boats; and they vied with the native boys in diving deep down for shining coins carelessly tossed by the interested visitors; whilst hard-pulled and craftily-sailed boat-races were a matter of everyday occurrence. In duty-hours they were put properly through the mill; the decks of the *Eurydice* were a picture in their shining whiteness; with all ropes Flemish-coiled in perfect precision; and the much brass-work shining like burnished gold. For, to the old Navy com-manders, a ship was a ship: a precious thing to be groomed and trigged out like a beautiful woman. The *Eurydice* boys were required to work hard, from being piped at four-thirty a.m. to midday and beyond; but they were also encouraged to play hard when off-duty, as that is the Navy's way. Their young laughter resounded through the tortuous by-ways of Madeira; their voices were hushed when the conducted parties stood in awe to contemplate the grim grandeur of the Gorge of the Wolf; that vast fissure that splits the island in twain as if by the stroke of a Jovean axe.

At Madeira, the training-ship *Liberty,* of a similar type, joined

company with the *Eurydice,* and course was shaped eventually
for the West Indies; which were safely reached after a brisk run
down the North-east Trades. From island to jewelled island the
little squadron passed—showing the Flag in accepted fashion;
and showing to the eager eyes of the boys the wonders of worlds
incredible. But since these good times were not fated to endure
everlastingly, and orders being orders the world over, in youth or
age, on March 6th, 1878, the ship weighed anchor at Bermuda
and shaped a course for home.

She must have picked up a useful sailing breeze; and the
quality of her going is proved by the fact that, although not
sighted in between, she was spoken off Bonchurch, Isle of Wight,
on March 22nd; and at 3.30 p.m. she reported herself as heading
for Spithead. It was noticed by the receiving station that she was
going briskly under all plain sail, with saucy studding-sails set
on foremast and main; and a few bonnets and skyscrapers and
heaven's disturbers to pile the snowy "bone in her teeth" at her
impetuous bow a little higher and broader. Obviously she was
hurrying to find an anchorage before night drew down. She
presented herself as an eyefilling picture of Naval completeness
and perfection—a tall ship, clothed tautly, sailing like a witch
along a sea that was comparatively becalmed under the lee of the
high land of Dunmore Head, between Shanklin and Ventnor.
During all the early part of that afternoon the weather was fine
and sparkling; with a useful sailing breeze blowing steadily;
but later on, towards sunset, a thick and sinister bank of clouds
came sweeping up from the north-west; and the barometer
dropped sharply—sure portent of bad times coming. But, the
wind remaining fair, the hurrying ship kept stoutly to her course;
her canvas roaring jubilantly in welcome to the English land;
her hammock-rails crowded with eager young faces to whom
the sight of the Motherland was as welcome as the smile of a
living friend; for to youth an absence of merely four months
can seem an eternity.

Just before eight bells in the afternoon watch, whilst the watch below was making ready to take the deck, the wind shifted in a biting snowsquall from north-west to north-east, in the tricky way Channel winds occasionally do. That squall reached gale-force; and was heavily laden with blinding snow. Instantly there was a hurry toward aboard the *Eurydice*. All hands were called; sail was reduced, the yards were braced. That snow-squall endured for only a short time and when it passed the sky showed comparatively clear and tranquil again. Only— something had happened in those pregnant minutes; something unspeakably tragic.

Standing on the shore were interested people who had been watching the stately up-channel progress of the beautiful ship and glorying in the perfect sea-picture she presented, with her snow-white canvas and air of purposeful striving. The English Channel of those good days was continuous frame to such vignettes; for if there were not a sailing warship in the offing there would, as likely as not, be some tea-clipper like the *Ariel* or the *Cutty Sark* crowding on every stitch of canvas in a headlong race for the London market. But the *Eurydice* was as beautiful a sight as any of those eagerly watching eyes had ever seen; and naturally, although driven under cover by the biting flurry, as soon as it eased, the interested watchers focussed their glasses afresh and asked one another if they still saw the fleeting ship.

"Why, she's gone!" exclaimed one observer, rubbing the object lenses. "She must have put on a fine turn of speed in that squall!" To all seeming the *Eurydice* had indeed sailed out of their ken. The sea lacked that lovely presence; and appeared lonely as a result.

The glasses raked the horizon afresh. "Clean gone—that's what I'd call sailing!" mentioned one watcher.

"Remarkable!" agreed another, and then—after a further search; "Wait! what is that?" Bearing E.N.E. from Dunmore Point, distant two and three-quarter miles from the tide-mark, the astounded onlookers saw the topmasts of the *Eurydice,* still clothed with their canvas, protruding from the white-flecked

surface of the sea! In the brief space of time taken for the
squall to blow past and clear, the *Eurydice,* well-found, her crew
at stations, all a-taunto and in no wise cranky, had foundered.
Foundered as cleanly as if writing had been wiped from a slate!
Incredible—she was; she was not, for the sea took her.

It is for us to examine precisely what transpired during those
calamitous minutes of howling wind and driving sleet and
snow. That a stout ship should perish thus instantly, with no
warning given, appears a nautical paradox; although we who
have had experience of the sea's vicious manner of striking need
feel no acute surprise.

No one had seen what actually happened; because the snow
formed an impenetrable screen, and, driven by the wind, had
effectively blinded all eyes that might have been on the lookout.

It came out that Captain Jenkins, master of the collier *Emma,*
trading from Newcastle-on-Tyne to Poole, had noticed the threat
of that fatal squall at 3.45 on the day in question; and that he,
too, had sighted and admired the flashing *Eurydice.* He lost
her in the flurry; and when it was over, he saw the projecting
masts as final trace of the ill-omened ship. Then, as he rubbed
his amazed eyes, and looked again, with the snow still drifting,
though more lightly now, he fancied he heard a shrill shout;
and, being a man well-trained to swift action and emergency, he
promptly ordered a hand into the rigging as an extra lookout.
This man kept his eyes well-skinned, and presently shouted
that he saw something floating; whereupon the *Emma* headed
in the indicated direction, and was able to grapple and salve a
survivor, who was afloat in a life-jacket.

Lowering her boats promptly to search that immediate vicinity, the collier began to beat up against the wind towards the
pitiful tokens of disaster; and cast around for such swimmers as
there might be. She found a total of five—and all of these
were so exhausted that only a hint of life remained in their
bodies. The *Emma* searched throughout what remained of the
day; and then, realising the completeness of this tragedy, headed

as quickly as she could for Ventnor, to obtain treatment for this
pitiful quintet. Yet even so, one of the unfortunates died as
he was lifted aboard the collier, from exhaustion. This was
March of 1878, remember—a particularly bitter winter; and the
Channel waters were almost at freezing point; so that a long
immersion was pretty drastic.

Captain Jenkins half-masted his flag in mourning for brave
souls sped, and kept on his course for Ventnor; and two other
men died *en route*. A collier-master is a handy man; he learns
many things; but he was, in those days, a better seaman than
surgeon; and although we may be satisfied that honest Jenkins
did his best, he couldn't keep life in those exhausted bodies. One
of these two casualties was Lieutenant Tabor, the *Eurydice's* first
lieutenant; probably the one man who could have told with
some verisimilitude exactly what happened during that ominous
squall.

So that, of the ship's full complement, only two survived; and
of these, one was so bemused and shocked that he could say
nothing coherent for a long time; and even then, his story was
fragmentary and lacking entirely in detail. Fletcher was one
of the boys under training, and had not the stamina to endure
the rigours; however, the other survivor, Cuddiford, an able
seaman, did better, and was soon able to make a worth-while
statement.

Fletcher said that things happened simultaneously, without
a breath of premonition or warning. He was below at the time
the squall struck; and feeling the ship heel savagely he rushed
on deck, snatched the first lifebelt that was handy, and went
overboard, without waiting for anything. He obeyed a purely
primitive instinct to save his life.

But Cuddiford had a much more interesting, as well as horrifying tale to relate. Captain Hare had been summoned to the
quarterdeck shortly before quarter to four on account of the
falling barometer and the approaching squall. Seeing what
portended he immediately gave orders for all hands to turn to

and take in the studding-sails. Hard on the heels of this order he added a supplement:

"Hand the upper sails—watches to masts—at the double!" He realised the venomous strength of the squall that was bearing down; and he saw that carrying a full press of sail as she was, the *Eurydice* stood the risk of losing her upper spars at least, and probably her topmasts.

Before the hands could turn-up from below, the squall struck; and struck mercilessly; a savage burst of terrific wind that took the ship and heeled her over at such a sick angle that her lee hammock-nettings dipped clean under water. That meant that her masts were canted at an angle of at least forty-five degrees from the vertical. Whole water raced inboard over the lee rail; and washed away the cutter, that had been got ready for lowering out as soon as the vessel came to her anchorage.

Ordering the quartermaster at the wheel to "Luff and shake it out of her!" Captain Hare shouted what was about his last command in life. The ship was capsizing; the studding-sails were coming in too slowly; the press of canvas was killing the ship. He ordered all halliards to be let go by the run, to spill the sails of their downbearing load of wind. And the cant of the masts prevented the yards from budging!

There was a wild chaos of confusion aloft; studding-sail booms snapping, the comparatively flimsy canvas splitting, tearing itself in rags, flying away down-wind like a flock of frightened seabirds. Some of the upper canvas was torn clean out of the boltropes; but not before it had held a fatal weight of wind. The hands, scurrying on deck as water poured below, had never a chance; here was disaster striking with lightning-like swiftness and viciousness.

The ship was unprepared for such an emergency. Why should she have been prepared? The weather was fair and promising, until that sudden drop in the mercury to give far too short warning of disaster. In our latitudes heavy weather is usually foretold by the barometer and the sky-signs some time in advance; it is in the tropics that the fierce, unheralded squalls, the Pampeiros and the Southerly Busters, the white squalls and the typhoons strike viperlike out of a clear sky without so much as a hiss of warning. English weather takes after the nature of the English character—it is customarily deliberate, issuing its warnings in advance. This was the unexpected occasion.

Ships of war go in for close stowage in regard to housing their crews. The lowerdeck of the *Eurydice* housed three hundred and fifty men and boys; and on account of the good weather conditions, the sleeping quarters were being aired prior to piping hammocks down; the gun-ports were triced open. The ship was peculiarly vulnerable in consequence.

To be sure, everything that occurred will never be known in full; because only one man's description is available, and he was not a trained observer; his brain was muddled by the ominous swiftness of what happened. If it be borne in mind that from the time of the first order to take in the studding-sails being given, to the capsizing, or rather the actual foundering of the vessel, only three or at the most four minutes elapsed, it will be seen how vivid was the rush and how tangled the confusion. Three minutes is not a long time in which to envisage a predicament, size it up, and take steps to counter it. Unquestionably, knowing Captain Hare's capabilities, it must be recognized that he did all that any man could have done. As he ordered the halliards to be let go, the topmen and forecastle men, together with the extra hands, started for aloft. When the yards stuck on the masts and the ship continued her evil heel Captain Hare ordered all hands down from aloft; he sensed the imminence of disaster. The squall was already at cyclone strength. It was blowing men and boys about the decks like chaff; it was whipping water over the high weather nettings; it was snatching words from the lips that uttered them and making them inaudible. Dark lowering sky, driving snow—a slanted deck, its leeside dipped clean under, the hungry sea tearing away the loose hamper about the bulwarks; objects swirling through the froth; the slam and crash and detonation of tearing canvas, clang of chain, buzz of parting cordage—pandemonium raged.

Over and over went the ship; until her mizen topsail was on the water; she was dead on her beam-ends; and practically doomed from that instant of the flurry breaking on her.

Yet she still carried her way, curiously enough; and it was that fact as much as any other that caused her finish; for she appears to have run clean under. The foretopmast studding-sail had held in its booms; full of wind it gave her headway; and her progress through the water simply scooped in the sea through her gaping bow ports and flooded her hopelessly.

Over she went; but she made a desperate struggle to right herself, as every ship does in her death-agony. It is this fact which leads men to think that a ship is something more than a conglomeration of wood and steel and rope. I for myself have witnessed how gallant a stricken ship can be. I have seen a windjammer, overborne, out of human control, with her people unable to stir a hand to assist her, fight clear of death on her own account when by all the laws of deep water she should have sunk out of hand. There is a weird element of life in such a fabric; it is as if all the splendour of her inherent rightness were harboured and conserved in readiness for just such a moment.

But the *Eurydice's* gameness availed her nothing; the blow was too treacherous and violent to give her even a fighting chance.

Realising by her tremors that she was dying, Captain Hare gave the order: "Every man for himself!" It was too late. Those who had been warned for aloft had not time to come up from below; if they attempted obedience, the inrush of water defeated them. Through a dozen ports the Channel sea came in with a roar, the boys were plunged into darkness and swirling brine that held the force of a torrent. They were washed up against the deck-beams, and pinned there, exits were barred; the ladders swept way. All happening with tragic suddenness, moreover—

no time for dispositions of any sort to be made. Three minutes of horror between a squall breaking and a proud ship sinking—the mind almost refuses to grasp the enormity of the catastrophe.

With that death-throe the *Eurydice* righted herself a little, swinging back against the wind; she lifted her sodden mizen-topsail up; but the squall increased its frenzy and drove her back. Her bows dipped as she capsized; she performed a sort of cork-screw roll. Most of her hands already on deck were forward, grappling with that fore topmast studding-sail, according to orders; as the bows dipped and drove under, they were swamped without a chance. Being at work they had not even an opportunity to snatch a lifejacket, these being stowed away below under the deck-beams above the hammock-hooks.

As these lads were washed away, the *Eurydice* turned further over and sank—and only five minutes elapsed before she was clean under; after diving, she turned again, and this brought her upper masts above water, since the Channel at that point is shallow.

The snowy blizzard continued, as if anxious to draw a pall over the scenes of horror that supervened, whilst close on four hundred men and boys fought for life and failed to find it. The bitter chill stopped their heart-beats; they were dragged down and under by the sails and cordage; and only that pitiful five emerged. There was nothing whatever could be done; the boats were secure in their gripes; the booms lashed in position, gratings screwed down. Catastrophe sweeping like a sudden scythe! Just another illustration of the mercilessness of the sea in that never-ending battle!

Britain had lost what was practically her finest sailing war-ship, and close on four hundred promising seamen; together with a captain whose record was as bright as burnished steel.

Admiral Foley, on being apprised of the disaster, hurried to the spot with all possible speed; although this was before the day of the lightning-like destroyer. He examined the decep-tive stage; and drew his conclusions: which were that the ship went down whilst her people were actually endeavouring to get the yards down and the sails under control. The mizen topsail yard was actually on the cap; thus proving that it had been lowered—though not in time; and all other halliards were let go. Since all the lower deck ports were open, the water had entered in colossal volumes by the starboard openings, and the weight of water added to the weight of wind had brought about the death of a proud and goodly ship.

There was no one on whom to hold a court-martial, so that the final details were not elicited; but when an inquest was held on such bodies as were washed ashore, Cuddiford gave his insufficient evidence; and it was enough to exonerate Captain Hare and his officers from all blame. Here, if ever, was the contingency which human courage and skill may not provide against: an Act of God.

CHAPTER XI

THE "COSPATRICK"

In dealing with sea-tragedies one finds a difficulty in selection. What makes a sea-tragedy interesting? The horror of sudden death swooping? The magnitude of the disaster? The heroism of the people involved? The quality of their sufferings? Its effect on the future? Its stark, lonely aloofness from a workaday world? If loss of life lends interest—and I think it does by driving home the immutability of a wreck, whether by gale, stranding or fire—the burning of the *Cospatrick* is worthy of a brief chapter in this volume.

The Atlantic might aptly be named an ocean graveyard; its toll of loss has been, I do not doubt, heavier than that of any other ocean; but to the seafarer, the southern latitudes hold more menace than do the northern parallels. Down the Easting and off Cape Horn are the sailors' most tragic battlefields. It was down the Easting where the *Cospatrick* met her tragic fate.

We are again in that middle nineteenth century so fraught with maritime disaster. It was at a time when overcrowded England was hearing the call from the distant colonies to send settlers who would people barren wastes. A regular emigrant service was running from English ports to Australia and New Zealand; and the *Cospatrick* was one of these—a well-found wooden ship of 1,200 tons. On Sept. 11th, 1874, she left London River for New Zealand. In addition to her crew of 44, all told, she bore under her decks 429 emigrants: young people of vigour and determination and hope, who scented fortune on the other side of the world. These emigrants were allotted special quarters in the tweendecks, where they packed close; for the conditions of such as ventured to the Antipodes in these sailing-ship days were not to be compared with those of to-day. There was a certain amount of privacy, and the sexes were separated; but apart from that, the tweendecks of the *Cospatrick* were pretty tightly stowed with humanity.

Under these circumstances—a wooden ship carrying five hundred souls—the risk of fire was one of the greatest hazards facing the ship's people. The ship was exceptionally well-found so far as ordinary seaworthiness was concerned; as an added precaution her fire-fighting equipment was put into a most satisfactory state. She carried a fixed fire-engine in her forecastle—not a usual part of a ship's fittings; and every hatch-way was illuminated at night by a locked battle-lantern, so that emigrants could not light their pipes at it and strew dangerous sparks around. All the gangway lanterns to illuminate the steer-age during the night were kindled by stewards at sunset and carefully locked; and to satisfy any apprehensions the emigrants might have, the captain instructed the intending settlers to select constables from their own ranks to maintain a constant and efficient fire-patrol. Many coils of new canvas hose were car-ried and maintained in good order; so that, on the face of it, the *Cospatrick* was as safe from the fire-demon as any ship well could be. Smoking below decks was sternly forbidden, also the use of naked lights; for landsfolk at sea are not always apt to recognise the awful potentialities of fire. Any casual roll of a ship's hull might cast down an open lantern, kindle a flame, and so bring about a horror of destruction.

The hatches communicating with the lower holds were close battened and the battens padlocked; so that no unauthorised per-son could secure entry to the general cargo carried there. Ship's master and ship's doctor made it their especial care to enforce the strict regulations.

For two months life aboard the *Cospatrick* offered little out of the usual. Her people suffered from seasickness in the Channel and the Bay, fretted at their close quarters in heavy weather, forgot their woes when flying-fish weather showed up; they basked in the genial warmth of the Tropics, adapted themselves to the limited life possible aboard a crowded ship of this size, did their love-making, dreamed their dreams, and in general behaved as tightly packed communities generally do behave. There were quarrels; there were fights and peacemakings; but nothing to give concern to disciplinarians or moralists; and when she reached a position about three hundred miles S.S.W. of Cape Agulhas—Lat. 37 15 S and Long. 12 25 E, to be precise— her state was satisfactory in every respect. Two months to the Cape is not by any means a good passage; but there have been worse; and the sixty-eight days so far occupied had not been too tedious. On this 17th of November, the ship was running free to the south and east, readying herself for the wild Easting run which was the most vigorous and entrancing portion of a windjammer's voyage in those days. What wind there was came away from the north-west; and was merely a light sailing breeze, just enough to give steerage way, and no more.

At one bell in the first watch—quarter to twelve, when the oncoming watch on deck had been roused, the second mate, who had kept the eight-to-twelve, began his customary patrol of the emigrants' quarters and the ship in general; a part of the ship's routine never neglected under any circumstances whatever. He paid particular attention to the poop and the forecastle —as being most vulnerable; and, satisfied that everything was Bristol fashion, he handed over the deck to his relief, and went below to turn in for a well-earned rest. He was just dropping off to sleep when he was startled by a thrilling cry of "Fire!" Being a man of action and a useful officer, he ran out of his berth instantly, and at the cuddy door met Captain Ellerslie, who had also turned in. Ellerslie ordered him to go forward instantly and find out what was wrong. He hurried along the deck in the woolly darkness, under the rustling canvas and the lightly-rapping ropes; and found out immediately that something was far wrong indeed; for he was met by a cloud of dense smoke pouring up from the forecastle.

The chief officer, who had relieved at midnight, was already in action: getting the forecastle fire-engine into working order; and the alarm spread rapidly. Too rapidly; for once again terror reared its ghoulish head above a tall ship. Crew and passengers heard and repeated the dread call; they made for the deck in a mass; and gave way to their feelings without restraint. So far as evidence went, the fire had broken out in the bosun's locker; where combustible stores of every description were stowed—as chancy a place for a fire to commence as could well be imagined. Stockholm and coal-tar, oil and paint, oakum and cotton waste—here was food for the greediest of fires.

Captain Ellerslie acted as a shipmaster should when fire breaks out forward—he attempted to get the *Cospatrick* clean before the wind; to confine the outbreak to the forepart. If smoke and flames swept her open deck, panic would increase and the potentialities of the tragedy become more imminent. But the wind was so light that the ship refused to answer her helm and pay off; and as a torrent of flame suddenly leapt up the forecastle scuttle it was necessary to brail up the fore-course, to prevent it taking fire.

There was a terrible confusion immediately; the sailors attempting to force a way through the frantic passengers; the passengers estimating this action as a selfish consideration for their own safety; so there were arguments and fighting and a growing dread. Captain Ellerslie lost control of a rapidly developing situation. He was taken by surprise, and he was only human—he failed to grasp immediately the possible developments.

Now, in a ship of the *Cospatrick's* type, everything worth mentioning devolves on the master. He is lord paramount, standing to all aboard as a god; his decree is unanswerable; his action must dictate the actions of all subordinate. Captain Ellerslie, tried, was found wanting. Instead of grappling the situation instantly and capably, he hesitated. Valuable—priceless—minutes were wasted before any battle-plan was arranged.

Taking matters into their own hands, the two officers endeavoured to organise bucket-passing gangs; and manned the fire-engine with stout relays. Hoses were fleeted along to the forecastle scuttle, and pumping commenced. But under a ship's forecastle head space is cramped; there was scant room for a ready coming and going of bucket-passers; and the tropical weather had doubtless dried up the pump-washers; for the quantity of water obtainable was insufficient to confine the ever-growing flames. They had rich food down below there in the forecastle peak; and they roared triumphantly. So rapidly did they gain ground that almost before the full reality had dawned on the *Cospatrick's* people, the ship was smothered in fire—flames were running up spars and rigging; and torrential clouds of thick white smoke floated everywhere about her. With the big foresail brailed, the weight of wind in the after canvas inevitably drove the ship's head right up into the wind's eye. Why the after canvas was not handed I do not know; the only explanation seems to be that the master had entirely lost his head. Had the after canvas been brailed or let go with a run, the vessel would have been balanced; and, as the weather was fair, there was nothing, so far as the record shows, to prevent a boat being lowered out and her head towed round away from the wind. As it was, the wind drove fairly along the decks from bow to stern, and on its crest it carried fire—fire and smoke in choking, blinding volume. Under this ominous pall the emigrants seem to have lost all self-restaint; so that the decks became a pandemonium of unloosed human passions.

Mr. Macdonald, second mate, urged on the captain the advisability of lowering out the boats. Apparently he had the idea of towing the ship's head away from the wind; also, he had the ultimate safety of the panic-stricken people in mind. The mere action of readying the boats would have restored a certain amount of calm and equanimity. I have been caught by fire in a sailing ship down the Easting—fortunately without the added encumbrance of some five hundred terrified men, women and children to hamper effort; and it is anything but a pleasant experience. The sense of remoteness, of complete isolation from the world is paralysing to effort. In my case, fire broke out in a gale of wind and the ship was carrying four hundred tons of explosives; but the flames were overcome and the ship brought safely to port. Under more favorable conditions the *Cospatrick* was lost; but then we do not know in detail what forces worked against her people.

Captain Ellerslie revealed himself as being an incompetent. Maybe he had never been tried out thoroughly before. Many a man can complete a lifetime at sea without being required to fight dire emergency; and we can only surmise that Ellerslie lacked the force of character and experience to tackle this dreadful episode in a seamanlike manner. When Macdonald advised the boats being lowered he was met by the stubbornness of a man reluctant to admit himself defeated or in the wrong. Ellerslie ordered the boats to be kept fast, as he hoped to save the ship. Obviously, being weak himself, he suspected weakness in others: if the boats were available, he fancied the people would bolt and relinquish their efforts. He held back; and the flames went on, eating through the bulkhead between forecastle and main hold, rushing aft with increasing violence, bursting open the main hatches; and roaring up triumphantly into the open. As soon as they appeared, they cast about for fresh fuel for their elemental ferocity, and fastened on the lifeboats—which ought to have been lowered clear, and which, instead, still hung in the davits. The boats were fine kindling—they snapped up in sparks and smoke, and were charred to nothingness in a breath.

The occupation of the forepart of the *Cospatrick* by this inferno of flame, limited the space for the milling passengers and crew. Frenzy was running riot amongst the human element. So many of them were women, drawn from the remote countryside of England, where emergencies of this type were never

H.M.S. "EURYDICE"

THE "COSPATRICK"

encountered. So few of them had been educated to crisis. They had been brought up in the faith that when trouble stirred they must look to their menfolk for succour and advice. Feminism —the ability of a woman to steer her own course—was un- dreamed-of.

The closer the situation is analysed, the clearer the defection of the captain becomes. It was the mate of the *Cospatrick* who saw the swift menace of the situation, not Captain Ellerslie. It was the mate who gave orders for the boats to be got out and lowered—such boats as the fire had so far spared. He sent forward to summon the crew to the davit-falls; and a mob of undisciplined men tackled the starboard quarter-boat forthwith; the mate's attention was attracted to another point; and, no officer immediately supervising the operation, chaos ensued. As the quarter-boat swung out, an enormous crowd of screaming, hys- terical women charged it, fighting like furies; they crowded in, trampling a way on the bodies and faces of their fellows; they filled it to the gunwales; and some idiots let go the falls. The boat roared down to the water and—capsized.

Of course it capsized. To lower a ship's boat in safety is a highly technical operation; and there was no technician avail- able. Eighty people, mostly women, crowded that quarter- boat; eighty people drowned when it overturned; and their death-gurgles met and were overcome by the strong roaring of the leaping flames. Here was another of those appallingly fre- quent holocausts of the sea, which linger in memory when tales of heroic deeds are forgotten. No wonder the sea holds terror for the layman, when his imagination is fed on such pitiable records! Too late, mate and master saw what had been done; impossible to save these sufferers; they took instant steps to avert a possible recurrence. Men were posted by the port boat.

"No one touches her, unless myself or the captain," instructed the chief officer. "Shoot anyone who tries—smash 'em!" And at once the officers began to get this boat clear. They worked under conditions of extreme difficulty: for with the disaster to the starboard boat harrowing their memory, the men panicked afresh; and failed to bear a hand. Whilst these staunch officers laboured the roaring flames took seizin on the boat's forepart, charred it into tinder; and rendered it worthless.

"No use here—try the lifeboats!" was the cry; and the mates headed that way—with the mob ahead of them; a wilder mob now; a mob that was fighting against the awful paralysis of fear. These got to the lifeboat first; shouts of protest were unavailing; the boat was flung from its chocks. Before she could be lowered, a crowd filled her to overflowing—thirty or forty people cramming in regardless of all the laws of decency. She roared down to the water, the tackles were unhooked; before she could be shoved off from the already hot side, three people —the chief mate, Macdonald, and a woman—either leaped or were thrust overboard. In Macdonald's case, at least, the latter explanation is much the more likely, in view of his subsequent conduct. Anyhow, however they left the ship, they were picked up.

The fire, during these regrettable scenes and immediately afterwards, made incredible progress; for the cargo below was highly inflammable: cotton goods and the like. Very shortly the mainmast took fire, and crashed to the deck, crushing an immense crowd of people to death in its fall. Over all the reddened hell of the spouting deck, the black pall of the Easting night was spread indifferently; under it the placid sea swung in the long, silky swell that had run clean round the world.

Crashing to the deck, the blazing mainmast burst the planking, and admitted more air to the furnace below, which quickened its efforts. People were engulfed in the breaking decks, and precipitated below to be cremated without a chance to save themselves. Outboard was the one boat, crammed to capacity and beyond. It seems strange to me, a practical seaman, that, since the poop was least affected by the conflagration, those on her did not make some attempt to lash spars and gratings together to make a considerable raft, capable of holding a full hundred people. There were enough men available to tear up the entire poop-deck as a raft; or to build a pinnace out of the timber on the boat skids. Nothing of this nature was done; and the fire, leaping, caught the mizenmast, which in its turn crashed down, breaching decks and bulwarks, and falling into the sea. With fresh torrents of air feeding the flames, there was an expansive explosion; and the entire stern-part of the *Cospatrick* was blown out bodily. So that the interior of the ship was now simply a shaft, along which the flames could race unchecked.

The night crept past; morning came—early, for this was the southern summer and it would be daylight by four o'clock or thereabouts. It brought scant hope to such as still survived. Very many of the people had been engulfed; more followed. The ship was simply a shell by now—gutted by fire; but one or two isolated parts still offered havenage for the desperate remnant. The one boat that had been got away remained in the immediate vicinity—incapable of offering assistance of any worth. Another entrant must have sunk it. But, along towards noon, cruising around that volcanic hull, it was seen that in some manner impossible to analyse, the charred starboard boat had been got afloat; probably it was blown overboard in the explosion that opened the stern-works.

It floated, damaged as it was; and it drifted against the wreckage of the mainmast, still held to the ship by the shrouds. On that wreckage some thirty people clung, still tenacious of life, defiant of death even in such a dire extremity; for the will to live is the strongest characteristic in human nature. These miserable souls contrived to scramble from mast to boat; since to them a boat was a floatable thing, offering succour. Macdonald appears to have been the dominant strong man of this crisis—emergency usually moulds some individual into heroic shape. He transferred himself from the still undamaged boat to the damaged craft, and took charge of her, leaving Romanic, the mate, to control the destinies of those in the port boat. So two boats, packed with shuddering, frantic people, were now afloat; and the

Cospatrick still burned horribly. Beyond these three objects, the face of the waters was deserted; not a single sail flecked the horizons; only the soaring albatrosses circling round the doomed ship broke the still monotony of the affrighting seascape.

It was now that the most ghastly discovery of all that ghastly episode made itself apparent. There had been disorder of the gravest character aboard the ship. The one mad idea uppermost in men's minds had been to get clear from the volcano, that might sink beneath their feet without an instant's warning. To lower out the boats was of first import—the future lay in Time's womb; who'd think of the future, indeed, with the present so alive with peril? The bare fact of continued life was all that mattered; and so the boats had gone away without a scrap of food or a drop of drinkable water aboard them! Immediate safety, potential death in its most prolonged and horrifying form —by thirst and starvation! That was what lay ahead of the survivors of the *Cospatrick*.

Further than this, although one boat was moderately equipped, the starboard lifeboat contained only one sound oar, and one broken oar-loom; of mast or sail there was none. Here, then, is a stage set for drama of the first magnitude—two boats, empty of life-sustaining supplies, adrift on a hopeless sea. In the two of them, between seventy and eighty soul-wracked people, many of them scorched; many otherwise injured, all of them subject to human weaknesses so far as hunger, thirst and love of life were concerned. Real life can supply greater tragedy than ever the mind of fictionist devised.

Like King Charles of blessed memory, the *Cospatrick* took an unconscionable time a-dying. There was to be no swift, merciful curtain; every detail of human agony and despair was to be protracted to the ultimate limit. Throughout the 18th and until the afternoon of the 19th, these two forlorn boats lingered in the blazing ship's neighbourhood. Close on forty-eight hours of fire, you will notice—not just a swift breath and then merciful darkness. During this period people were suffocated where they clung to the remaining habitable fragments of the charred and smoking hull, and dropped down into the incandescent interior. Or they took desperate course and forced themselves to leap overboard—where was no abiding-place for them; so they drowned incontinently, the awe-struck people still living in the packed boats unable to lift a hand in their aid. Still a few remained alive on the hull—with these were the captain, who had failed, and his wife, whom he had no business to be carrying on voyage; for, human nature being what it is, a man will usually devote his closest attention to one immediately dear to him than to hundreds who are merely of indirect interest. It appears to me, as a disinterested observer, that the fact of Mrs. Ellerslie's presence aboard the *Cospatrick* probably accounts for the colossal quality of the catastrophe. A man in control of such a situation needs to have a clear brain; if the best of that brain is occupied with apprehension for a dear one, he cannot do justice either to himself or to the situation.

Those watchers in the boats saw the *Cospatrick* lurch preparatory to engulfing her glowing hull in the Easting sea. They saw Captain Ellerslie throw his wife overboard and leap after her—an heroic gesture, but so pitiably futile. If he had only tied her to a wheel-grating, say, some useful purpose might have been served. As it was, they both sank, drawn down in the vortex caused by the hull sliding under. There was a long-drawn hiss as water met flame; a great and growing cloud of steam; a few shrill cries of scalded, drowning people; and this tragedy of deep water was consummated—or almost consummated. The *Cospatrick* went down.

There remain the two boats: one holding 39 souls, the other forty-two. If those in them had known what lay ahead, they would assuredly have committed themselves to the sea forthwith. Out of these eighty-one immediate survivors, only three found life: one of these was Macdonald, and it is his narrative to which we must turn for the harrowing details of those following days. Remaining in company for mutual protection, without a bite to eat or a mouthful to drink, the boats endured until the 21st, when, in the thick of the night, as men drowsed hopelessly, they somehow drifted apart. Someone wakened and shouted—no reply. Someone whistled—still no reply. There began a panic-stricken search; it was without result; the port lifeboat had drifted away, caught by some trifling current. With dawn, thanks to a limited horizon, the starboard boat was lonely on a vast and hostile sea. There were no navigating tools; and it seems reasonable to believe that Macdonald had only a vague idea of the position of the *Cospatrick* when she foundered. Judged by his actions, Ellerslie appears to me to be the sort of man who would keep his navigation a close secret, as so many shipmasters used to do; and in any case, lacking oars or sails, it made little difference to Macdonald where he actually was. He would naturally be desirous of doing something, being a man of stamina; and the only thing to do would be to head up for land—the nearest being at least four hundred miles away. But how to get there, with a single oar and a stump! I would not have cared to be in Macdonald's seaboots.

Thirst began to get in its full effects on them all very shortly. Lack of food was comparatively immaterial; the human stomach can go for long periods fasting; but water it must have or perish or suffer excruciating agonies. I fancy Macdonald, though he does not mention it, would be wise enough to do all in his power to assuage the thirst of those he was responsible for, by baling seawater over them, and keeping their clothing constantly drenched, so that the pores would absorb moisture whilst filtering it of its saltiness. That is the first resort in such a case—not by any means effective, but still ameliorating to a slight extent. A man fell overboard on the 22nd; he was drowned—I doubt if energy sufficient to save him existed amongst his boatmates; probably they thought his was the easier way.

Horror added to horror. Three men went mad with thirst, and horribly died. Their bodies were thrown overboard. There are sparse details; but three madmen in a cramped boat are an unimaginable menace; and no one could blame Macdonald if he took steps to quieten this trio. The survivors considered one another hopelessly, seeing their own fate prophesied by what had happened to these unfortunates. Macdonald saw something else—the threat of bad weather; for it is unusual for a calm to endure for long in those latitudes, where gales are the commonest feature. And the threat was fulfilled; for on the 24th a full gale broke; and with it came a high, furious sea. Misery was added to misery; four men died. Now we come to the most unspeakable horror of it all—cannibalism. The instinct to live can on occasion outbalance all laws human and divine. The remainder of the boat's people were frenzied for food and drink—especially drink. They acted as instinct dictated—and satisfied their cravings. We who have never been placed in similar predicament, may not condemn. We know —sitting at home at ease—that under no conditions, however grim and hopeless, could we so far forget our Christian manhood as to keep ourselves alive on human food. Let us pray we may never be put to the *Cospatrick* test!

The superstitious will declare that it was a judgment on the cannibals that they lost their only oar this day.

The 24th brought an increase in the storm; the sea ran high; and, lacking a sea-anchor or any means of riding the combers, the boat remained constantly full of water. Six men died on the 24th. They might have done better to die a little earlier; they'd have met their Maker with one sin the less on their tortured souls. During the ensuing night, the gale died away, so that the 25th dawned hot and lifeless; with only a lazy breeze. Heat on top of saltiness—a combination making for incalculable torment. By nightfall only eight people remained alive in the boat; and of these eight three were raving mad and under restraint. Macdonald had his hands overfull; it must have shaken even his Doric assurance to handle such a problem. He admitted that this day was the worst—a terrible period, impossible of description. But they endured, thanks to the remarkable tenaciousness of the human system.

During this ghastly night, with the maniacs howling and

struggling in their bonds, a ship appeared. Macdonald would be light-headed, of course—probably he thought it a figment of the imagination, though he was able to state that in her appearance she was a foreigner. Macdonald hailed, so did his spectral crew—hailing whisperingly out of constricted throats! Could anything be more pitiful—these ragged, gaunt scarecrows of flotsam, staggering to their scurvied legs in the boat of death, funnelling their clawlike hands about their skinless mouths, thinking they shouted heartily, whereas they only whispered wheezily from their inflamed throats; and the strange sail, dark against the darkness, passing ghostily by, indifferent to their agonies! For that is what the passing ship did—though Macdonald took oath and swore they were heard. But the mentality of a man in such plight might tend to fantasy. Maybe the whole vision was as spectral as Vanderdecken's ship, which is reputed restlessly to haunt those seas.

By dawn, another unfortunate was found to have died; and his fate was that of others—to preserve the breath of life in such as remained. The picture the surviving boat presented at this juncture is too horrible to contemplate—seven unshaven spectres, drabbled with their shipmates' blood, wolfish-eyed, mowing and gibbering, watching each other furtively, as if contemplating which would be next to go, next to kill. Their clothes were in rags; their bodies rotten with salt-water sores; and their swollen tongues lolled from their aching throats.

Around them the mocking sea swung in mighty swells, formless and implacable, and the sun rose and climbed and sneered and slanted down the western sky without one ray of hope in all its shining.

The 27th broke in hurrying squalls—the black clouds broke to pour the boon of fresh water on them. See them now, lifting their wan faces, their mouths agape, hunting the vagrant drops that fell on them, licking their lips, snarling at such as had presence of mind to wring the salt from their shirts and, saturating the rags, suck them feverishly. They had no vessel in which to catch and conserve this boon; they had to watch the rain cease, and know that help was impossible. Two more died that day—from disappointment as much as suffering. They cast one body into the sea; they essayed to rid themselves of the other; but these five remaining lacked collective strength enough to do it. They were weak as newborn infants. Human suffering can be prolonged to such an extent as to stagger the thoughtful.

Of the five still left: one passenger, two A.B.'s, an ordinary seaman and Macdonald; one, the passenger, was mad; the others hovering on madness' verge, for all had drunk salt-water; the surest, shortest route to insanity. All were dozing—the sleep that presages death, they were hopeless; desire for life had passed. The maniac aroused; and, inspired by an awful need, sank his teeth into Macdonald's naked foot; sting of added pain aroused the second mate; he leaped up—and saw a miracle. Bearing down on the boat of ghosts was a ship: a real ship, no figment of the imagination. She had sighted them; she approached—the castaways rubbed their doubting eyes—yes, she was truly a ship, her sails full breasted to a vigorous wind.

She lowered out a boat, since not one of the survivors could have caught a rope; and brought that miserable craft alongside. The wasted bodies were light to lift aboard; those who did it gasped and retched at sight of what the sea had rejected. So life came to the *Cospatrick's* wan survivors; to some, not to all. The insane passenger died; the others were so violently ill that all their lives were despaired of. One other died—the boy; but Macdonald and Lewis and Cutter lived—to be haunted by tragic memories through the ensuing years. Three men living; four hundred and sixty-seven men, women and children dead, dead terribly. The sea had wreaked vengeance on such as dared its dangers; three shrinking, fearful men had braved its mysteries.

During its eight bitter days of drifting, the *Cospatrick's* boat had covered a distance of approximately 540 miles. Speaking as a sailor, I do not know how it was done. Of the port boat, in charge of the unfortunate mate, no trace was ever found.

[219]

CHAPTER XII

H.M.S. "CAPTAIN," AND OTHERS

THAT tragic decade in our sea-history—1870–1880, held few
tragedies of more stunning completeness than the almost inex-
plicable loss of H.M.S. *Captain*—another new ship, fated from
the moment her keel was laid to carry disaster in her train.
She was an auxiliary ship of 4,472 tons; four-masted; and under
steam alone on her trials, she had satisfied her constructors and
testers as being unusually docile. That was on smooth water;
and some freak in her trial behaviour aroused a certain amount
—not much—of apprehension; certain who had witnessed her
performance insisting that she was not to be trusted in anything
rougher than a millpond. It was an experimental era, when
men did not really know what the new type of ship evolving
was capable of doing. Experience must be bought; it is a pity
it is so often bought at high cost of innocent life.

In September of 1870, commissioned by Captain Hugh Burgoyne, the *Captain* reported herself to Admiral Alexander Milne,
commanding the Mediterranean Fleet; the fleet then cruising
off the Spanish coast with an idea of testing the quality of these
new-fangled ironclads, which aroused much derision in the
minds of the old stick-and-string school, who yet could hardly
bring themselves to believe that iron could float.

On the afternoon of September 6th, Admiral Milne and his
staff made a visit aboard the latest-comer; the idea being to
watch her behaviour under sail; she being entered in competition with the *Monarch*, the *Inconstant*, and the *Bristol*. Milne
and his staff remained on board until the evening; when Captain

Burgoyne issued an invitation to the dignitaries to remain aboard for the night and return to the flagship next morning in daylight. This invitation was declined—apparently because the Admiral liked his comforts, and even the fact that a considerable gale was blowing and kicking up a heavy sea did not deter him from leaving at seven p.m. or thereabouts. Torrents of water were by this time washing down the *Captain's* decks; for the ironclad was not sea-kindly; preferring to plough through the waves rather than ride over them; and the Admiral's gallery, brought alongside, escaped swamping by narrow inches.

Weather conditions were ominous; a falling barometer and increasing wind presaged a wild night; by midnight this presage was amply fulfilled; for a full sou'-wester was bellowing; and the sea was enormous. Desirous of shepherding his flock wisely, the admiral signalled all ships, at midnight, to reef down for security, and was obeyed. At 1.20 a.m. all units of the fleet were comfortably riding the yelling gale; and making passable weather of it; and amongst them the *Captain*—the hoodoo ship of the Navy of that day. Under treble-reefed and fore- and main-topsails she was doing her best, her fore-topmast staysails helping to steady her.

Only a few minutes later a sudden, terrific squall struck down on the fleet—the sort of furious atmospheric phenomenon the seas off Finisterre specialise in exceptionally at that time of year. For the Western Ocean is a deceptive sea: her smiles, broad and sunny for the most part, can be as false as a harlot's; and she carries in her womb affrighting potentialities in the way of hard weather, as the ancients well knew, as we moderns also know. There off the Spanish coast the sudden upspring of a gale can be lamentably ominous. This squall was a father-squall, apparently. Even the line of battleships staggered wildly to its compelling fury. The Admiral, deprived of his comforts after all, gave the signal to wear round on the other tack for greater security; and for two hours the fleet laboured woundily in a colossal sea.

Laggard dawn broke, grey and steely—a high dawn, presaging more wind; and as the sea became visible, one question arose to the minds of the entire personnel of the fleet: "How has the *Captain* fared in this flurry?" She had fared uncommonly ill—she had, indeed, completely disappeared. Search the ruffled seascape as they might, no trace of the hoodoo ship was visible.

They quelled uneasiness with half-hearted sanguineness. "Stands to reason she never saw the general signal to tack; she's standing off on the old course to be sure," was the opinion. "She's away to hell and gone to the nor'-west; and she'll be in a hurry to rejoin as soon as she sees where she's got to."

This diagnosis satisfied some—not all. There were those who remembered earlier apprehensions; those who had seen her behaviour—that of a bogged cow in a trough—before the Admiral left her; and they began to fear disaster.

Full daylight grew—apprehension was stilled in certainty. Something tragic had happened to the *Captain*. The light showed the watchers a floating body; it was grappled and recovered; its cap ribbon bore the name: H.M.S. *Captain*. Also, there was ominous wreckage floating, tangled, shattered stuff—pitiful beyond the power of words to describe. One ship sighted a mass, another sighted a bilged and useless boat; a spar stuck up wanly here; broken lengths of her superstructure hove in sight there. Through a mournful day the ships of the Mediterranean Fleet were occupied in salving these piteous remnants of a new and powerful ship; were searching for some living survivor of the ill-happed *Captain*.

In all eighteen survivors were variously salved; and their conflicting statements were pieced together. This is the story of the *Captain's* ending.

At midnight, with gale freshening and sea running high, the watches were relieved; and Captain Burgoyne, keeping the deck on account of the ominous appearance of the weather and the pumping of the barometer, ordered an alteration in the trim of his roaring canvas. What time the men moved to sail-trimming stations, whilst the order still echoed, a tremendous sea struck the *Captain*. She was caught fairly on the weather-beam. She was a ship of low freeboard; built more as a gun platform than as a weatherly ship; the precursor of those later turret ships which were to break the Admiralty's heart. Her vulnerable decks were flooded and remained awash. Hit by that heavy squall, attacked simultaneously by wind and sea, she fell over on her beam-ends and made a valiant effort to right herself, being a ship, and, though clumsy, a sea-fighting entity.

Captain Burgoyne and all hands of the duty watch were up to their waists in swilling, tempestuous brine. The ship struggled gamely—but she failed. She was foredoomed to destruction. Another sea struck her, and she capsized, turning keel-uppermost, with dreadful suddenness. Those below died immediately, having no chance even to make a struggle; the water poured in through the companion hatches; the air escaped in a great rush; and even the stoutest swimmer could have had no time to draw a second breath.

As she turned over, the *Captain's* steam-pinnace, fitted as a lifeboat, was torn from its lashings on her deck, and floated away independently. The deck-watch—such as were not overcome instantly—were left struggling for bare life in the raging sea, aghast and stunned by this instant catastrophe; when they cleared their eyes and brains of the effect, they made out, by lightning flashes, the dim grey bulk of the overturned pinnace. Such as were able swam or floundered towards this glimmer of hope; and although many died on the way, in the result eight or ten of the men contrived to gain the precarious safety; and scrambling up her planking, took lion-like grip of the keel. Gasping, paralysed, they clung—a trifling remnant of a gallant crew; and when the stupor following on frantic effort cleared, and they were able to realise their immediate safety, they cast around for the other ships of that valiant fleet. They saw them quite clearly—headreaching in the gale; but of their own ship remained no visible trace. They shouted and made combined outcry, in hope of attracting attention of their fleetmates—their cries were unheard in the riot of howling wind and surging sea. They could do nothing but cling to that hazardous keel and pray for the day—which was long in dawning. Some failed to maintain their hold, and were torn away—they were rescued by their comrades, who obeyed the dictates of the sea admirably, in that they helped one another by every means in their power.

The pinnace was badly knocked about: as was inevitable. The men continued their shouting; although the disappearing fleet lacked ears; but after a period that seemed endless, the *Captain's* second launch, in which were ten survivors, showed up, and coming alongside the pinnace, took most of those clinging to it aboard. Captain Burgoyne and a seaman named Heard were amongst those who had gained the harbourage of the pinnace's keel; before they could be helped aboard the launch a squall set down and separated the two boats. Heard let go his grip and swam; Captain Burgoyne did the same. Heard was collected; Captain Burgoyne was never seen again—probably he was struck by the reeling pinnace, and stunned. He died, as so many of his men had already died.

From the time of the squall driving the *Captain* on her beam-ends to the time of her disappearance, was about ten minutes; no more. Here was an ending almost as swift, certainly as tragic, as the finish of the *Eurydice;* as dramatic, too. Such as were washed from her as she went down, reported a violent explosion from below; this would have helped to settle the fate of such as were trapped between decks when the ship capsized.

Thus, of all the crew, there now remained only eighteen men in the comparatively insignificant launch. An attempt was made to bring her head to sea; she was pretty full of men, and not intended for such heavy work; when this was attempted a sea roared over her and she filled to her gunwales. Two of the eighteen were washed out of her; they were lost to human ken forthwith, having paid another instalment of Britain's incalculable tribute to the sea.

H.M.S. "CAPTAIN"

H.M.S. "CAPTAIN" (Turret Deck)

Lacking tools, being handymen, the remaining sixteen set to work to rid the launch of water by baling with their caps—not useful balers. They did their best, however, and having ridded her of some part of the flooding water, made another and equally unsuccessful attempt to bring her head-to-sea.

A launch is a heavy, beamy boat; not meant for hard pulling; this one was equipped only with eight oars for pulling and one for steering. The men shipped the oars when it was realised that nothing else was to be done; and pulled aimlessly away before the wind, with that wind helping their drift. Through a tedious and stormful day she drifted; by evening she arrived at Corcubion; an insignificant port under the lee of Cape Finisterre.

As the rest of the fleet had seen no sign of the launch, it is no wonder that the story went the rounds that the *Captain* had perished with every soul on board. But these few men were all remaining of five hundred souls.

Mr. May, the ship's warrant gunner, sole surviving officer, who had taken command of the launch, was rendered liable to court-martial by his survival. He was acquitted of jeopardising his ship, since he was merely a junior officer and in no wise responsible for the heart-stopping tragedy; and he was further complimented and rewarded for his coolness and intrepidity in handling the boat under such unnerving conditions. The ultimate verdict of the court was that the *Captain* foundered on account of carrying too big a press of sail in heavy weather; but her sail-area was no greater than that of any other ship of the fleet after reduction—since units of a fleet must obey all signals. It was not too much sail that threw the *Captain* away; it was too low a freeboard and too little a margin of stability. She was an experimental ship; her design was faulty; and she proved her faults in distressing fashion. The loss of the ship as a ship was no great calamity—if she had not sunk when she did she must have gone under on some early future occasion; the loss of her four hundred and eighty-two men of all ranks was a deplorable calamity.

Though the Royal Navy continued to pay this distressing price of Admiralty year by tragic year, the merchant service, humbler but harder-working sister, added its quota of deplorable loss to the country's seafaring history. Twenty years or less before the *Captain* swamped herself and took half a thousand men with her to Davy Jones's locker, another drama of deep water shook England to its depths. The *Tayleur,* a colonial-bound ship of 1,800 tons, under command of Captain Noble, was lost in harrowing circumstances off the Irish coast in 1854. She carried a full muster of passengers bound for Melbourne, the El Dorado of that decade; and the most appalling feature of her loss was the large number of women and children who gave their lives in this pitiful tragedy of tidewater.

With a total of about 620 people aboard, she was as closely stowed as was the *Cospatrick;* but the fashion of her ending was different, though equally harrowing. Leaving the River Mersey on the nineteenth of January, she ran into rough weather almost as soon as she emerged into the Irish Sea; and this ill-omened start culminated in a raging gale very shortly afterwards. The causes of her loss have never been fully explained; and only intelligent surmise can be employed to account for it. The evidence goes to prove that the ill-adjusted compasses (held at the time to be the deciding factor) were indeed responsible for the casting away of a stout ship. But poorly adjusted compasses could not entirely account for her misfortune: there must have been something else. The evidence points as much to defective steering gear as to defective compasses; also, there is more than a hint of happy-go-lucky navigation, and an utter lack of seamanlike precautions in her handling; though where a sailing ship is concerned, too drastic a judgment may never be passed, as the state of the weather has often much more to do with the fate of a windjammer than her own condition and handling.

At all events, the *Tayleur* was driven out of her course towards the Irish coast, and by Saturday morning—she sailed on a Thursday—she was drifting, totally out of control, towards the dead lee-shore of Lambay; a few miles north of Malahide. After a night of unexampled discomfort and suspense, the passengers were allowed up from below, and crowded the decks in every state of abject terror, since here again, and surprisingly soon after sailing, were country-folks brought into contact with the perils of sea-voyaging. Mob-frenzy seized them: they became aware of the threatened finality of a menace; they did not understand, but they feared.

"Dead lee-shore!" was Captain Noble's summing-up. "Get the anchors ready for letting go—we'll bring her up on a short cable." Being in tidewaters the anchors were already catted. The mate went forward; the carpenter stood by the windlass; the anchors crashed down. For an instant, taking the weight of the ship, they held, the cables tautened like bars of steel; then —they snapped, one after another; and the luckless ship drove on to the rocks and snarling breakers. There was nothing humanly possible to be done. Without an anchor remaining in service, the ship could not be club-hauled—that last desperate resort; the spare bower was housed and chain-lashed in such a fashion that an hour was necessary to clear it. Had it been cleared, there was no cable left. The *Tayleur* took the ground with a tearing crash; a hopeless wreck; so near to the jutting rocks that several people, obeying the primary instinct for safety, instantly leaped overboard, with the intention of struggling through the breakers to solid land. They did not realise the savage treachery of the broken water. They were flung against the basalt, they were stunned, they were drowned as the surf swung them away. Regardless of the need of these untutored souls, the crew— Chinese and Lascars—caught the panic; and a general *sauve qui peut* resulted; these Orientals leaping for life in maniacal haste, regardless of the shouted order of the officers. Several of these poltroons contrived to scramble into safety; and satisfied themselves with their own miserable lives, without giving so much as a thought to those left behind. It was left to a stalwart passenger

to think of the general good; this man, when he made a bid
for life, took a rope's end with him; and so effected a rough communication with those remaining behind. By dint of rigging
a rough transporter he was instrumental in salving quite a
number of otherwise doomed people. As these felt firm ground
under their feet they lent their weight to the work of mercy,
formed a gang of life-savers, and toiled with the utmost heroism,
whipped by the bellowing sprays as they were, their feet torn
from under them by the backwash of the surf. They gave an
illustration of national courage at its best. The action of the
Tayleur's crew of coolies has tinctured seamen's outlook on the
Oriental races to this present day—although they are admitted
as sterling workers, their courage is everlastingly questioned.

Whilst this little company of stalwarts laboured faithfully for
the common cause, scenes of heartrending pathos and tragedy
were being enacted aboard the menaced ship. She was listed
badly, and swept by leaping water; the gale roared thunderously
in the tattered canvas; her rigging harped like a chorus of
exultant Valkyries. Men fought to the poop, flung arms aloft,
praying, threatening, cajoling—offering all they possessed for a
chance of life for themselves or those dear to them. They demanded what Noble could not give. The position of the ship,
wedged in among sharp-fanged rocks, forbade any attempt to
lower boats, which, if they had not been smashed to atoms, must
have capsized in the surf. Why the masts were not cut away
to form a bridge from ship to shore remains a mystery to this
present narrator. But only one actually present at the disaster
could realise the exact circumstances—and did one know the
truth the neglect of an ordinary seamanly measure might easily
be pardoned. But the ship being on a lee-shore, the drive of
the gale would certainly have carried the masts as a bridge
to the rocks; and hundreds of lives might thus have been saved.
As it was, the galloping surges, swinging in relentless sweep
from seaward, checked momentarily as they encountered the
obstacle of the ship, then leaped and swept it mercilessly, licking

[228]

away groups of screaming women at each attack. Since the threshing breakers overside were no greater threat than the white water that deluged the decks, scores of frenzied folks leaped overboard; but their desperate effort was foredoomed to failure. They were choked by spray, smashed to ruin against the rocks; they died; and yet others and others came, a piteous procession of the doomed.

The men tried to coax and threaten the hysterical women to attempt the precarious crossing by rope to the near-by rocks. Some did so essay this perilous venture; but midway between ship and shore their courage failed them; they let go their hold, and dropped—to die in the pounding backwash. Their choking death-screams unnerved such as attempted to follow; these also fell in clusters to be borne away to merciful oblivion. Women, their infants lashed to their backs with fragments of shakings and such oddments of cordage as could be discovered, set forth to cross that dizzy, treacherous bridge. As it sagged under their weight, their determination deserted them, fear paralysed them; they dared not advance; they could not retreat, because others and many others were on their heels, crowding them—blind to all order; and so the fear-palsied unfortunates were simply thrust off to make room for that terrible procession.

The sea charged the *Tayleur,* roaring its wrathful glee. It shifted her, it tugged at her stern, whilst these women dared and feared and died. Two hundred women the *Tayleur* carried when she left the Mersey; three alone lived to tell of the hell they had survived. Three out of two hundred—such is the price exacted by the hoary sea, that never forgets, that waits a long time, but never fails to strike.

So, whilst these pitiful souls perished in handfuls, the sea tore the *Tayleur* back from the rocks; her stern began to dip into deeper water. She staggered drunkenly, and that action snapped all the several ropes that had been carried to the rocks, snapped them like packthread. As they broke, the mangled hull slid back—further back, a wave roared in, pushed her up a little, tore her down still further; another wave surged in—and the *Tayleur* sank in the boiling maelstrom. The snowy surf was crowded with struggling bodies—only for a moment. Other waves galloped up gleefully; the great ninth wave came, and swept the battlefield clean. Two human beings clung paralysed in the scanty remaining rigging; the rest were dead. Those lashed to the shrouds remained as they were for a matter of fourteen hours, what time the solitary coastguard attempted their salvation. He worked notably, this shore-watcher, under a heavy handicap; the month, let it be remembered, was January, the stage was set in the bleak North Sea. For a matter of fourteen hours he toiled, and succeeded in rescuing both; what time Lord Talbot's steward—Lord Talbot owned the treacherous island— did the best in his limited power for the security and comfort of such as had survived. These were ill-clothed, dazed, many— very many of them injured, more or less seriously, from the savage battering they had received among the rocks.

After a bleak and bitter night, spent in such scanty shelter as was available, all survivors who could drag themselves forth went to quest along the shore; and they there saw the horror of the sea: bodies of their recent shipmates piled in stacks at tidemark, where the sea had flung them, most stripped nude by the tearing fingers of the surf. Such as were clothed were being looted by the ghoulish natives—who believed that a wreck was a blessing of the Almighty to their address. And that was the end of the *Tayleur,* and with her were lost three hundred souls, two-thirds of them women.

Almost before the staggering shock of the *Tayleur's* loss had been forgotten, before the sixth decade of the costly nineteenth century had drawn to a close, humanity was staggered afresh by a great disaster off the British coast: the loss of a noble ship within sound and sight of home. The *Royal Charter,* auxiliary ship, a big vessel of her day, registering 2,756 tons as she did, was lost off Point Lynas in the Mersey estuary, with a formidable death-roll. Her trading-route was between England and Australia; and she had effected some sensational passages; she was an extraordinarily popular ship; and ranked in the class to which our present swagger P. & O. and Cunard ships belong. What kind of a flyer she was can best be conveyed by saying that on her last voyage home she left Melbourne on the 26th of August, 1859, and sighted the Irish coast on the fifty-fifth day out; which was good travelling for a twelve-thousand mile run.

In sight of the Homeland, as testimony to Captain Taylor's seamanship and geniality and unfailing courtesy, the passengers combined to make a gift; and there were celebrations. On October 24th, the ship reached Queenstown to disembark a handful of Irish passengers returning from the Colonies—and from the Irish port Taylor telegraphed his owners to report almost a record passage and the welfare of the ship. All hands were in high glee and comfortable expectation of a satisfactory homecoming when the *Royal Charter* made her way up the Irish Sea Liverpool-bound. October the 25th broke with promise of hard weather, the advancing hours fulfilled the threat, for a full gale backed round to east-north-east, blew harder for the rest of the day; and by midnight had attained hurricane force. Battering her way stolidly into this snifter, the *Royal Charter* raised the Holyhead lights and, doggedly fighting every fathom of the way, came abreast of Point Lynas on the Isle of Anglesey; bringing the leading light abeam by six in the evening. It is under the lee of Point Lynas that the Liverpool pilots cruise in readiness for inward-bounders; and although a capable pilot, himself, Captain Taylor knew the Mersey for a treacherous river, especially in bad weather; and mistrusting his own capabilities, immediately sent up rockets and fired his signal guns to summon a pilot.

No pilot showed up; which is eloquent testimony to the severity of the evening; for Mersey pilots are amongst the hardiest and most daring in the whole world; and it was something more than the average that kept them snugged to leeward of their station. The *Royal Charter* had naturally ventured close in to the land to give the expected pilot every assistance. Off Anglesey the tides run fiercely; the Mersey tide often approaching a velocity of ten knots; there are innumerable eddies and shifting sandbanks caused by the scour. That estuary is, even for a full-powered ship, a difficult stretch of water; how difficult the *Royal Charter* proved immediately; for already her situation was becoming critical—with the E.N.E. hurricane blowing Point Lynas had become a dead lee-shore; the currents ran with the wind, battled with the tide, and created a terrible flurry. Captain Taylor felt trepidation, as was inevitable: he was responsible for the safety of the ship and all her people, numbering five hundred or thereabouts: not needy emigrants but prosperous returning Colonials. Among the passengers were two master-mariners of experience; and Taylor called them to conference in the general interest. You can see these three rugged veterans pooling their sea-lore and debating a situation that increased in peril with every fresh gust snorting down out of the hard north-east sky!

"Best get the ground-tackle down and steam to anchors!" appears to have been the conclusion reached; for at ten o'clock both bowers were let go. Presenting the wind-surface that she did, the *Royal Charter* promptly strained frantically at the leash of the cables; and in order to ensure a safe mooring, the engines were put to full speed ahead. Such wind-velocity may appear incredible to the layman; but it is not uncommon around the British Isles, though at that season of the year it was certainly violent. The Equinoctials can blow hard; but my own experience is that the December–February gales are the stiffest; and I have been placed in the same predicament as was the master of the *Royal Charter* by being compelled to anchor with both bowers and steam full speed ahead under the so-called lee of Cape Wrath. In my case the anchors held; but it was only by dint of using an open throttle throughout an exceptional night.

The suspense and fear aboard the great ship may well be

THE "TAYLEUR"

THE "ROYAL CHARTER"

imagined. A ship steaming to anchors is about the most uncomfortable thing in the world; she has lost her elasticity; and
the seas riot wildly over her bow, held down by the ground-
tackles; she jars throughout her length, and is afflicted with
tempestuous shudders.

The passengers' apprehensions increased with the tedious
passing of time; Taylor advised them to seek their berths and
rest, since nothing was to be gained by wakefulness, the ship
being in skilled hands, and the matter in the supreme care of
God; but the voyagers could not bring themselves to retire. As
they showed a disconcerting favour for the open deck, Taylor
put it out of bounds; and they were therefore compelled to
crowd into the saloons below. Wan-faced women affected an
air of unconcern, shuddering at every thick tremor; men endeavoured to assuage the quickening fear. Card-playing was
indulged in—but half-heartedly. The piano was brought into
action; hymns were chorused in defiance of the hammering
seas and the shaking quivers of the engines. As often as he could
spare himself from his vigilance on the bridge, Taylor went
below to reassure those committed to his charge, and to assert
to them that all was well despite the obvious discomfort.

He had just reassured them at four bells in the middle watch
when both anchor chains parted with the crack of a gun. The
ship was dependent on her indifferent engines at once—200
horse-power to keep a three-thousand-ton ship moving into the
teeth of a hundred-mile-an-hour hurricane! Withers and
Adams, the two veteran captains, were sharing the watch with
Taylor.

"The only thing to do is to cut away the masts—with their
wind surface she *must* drive ashore," was the verdict; and the
mainmast was promptly cut away. To the imprisoned passengers below the crash of axes and the harsh splintering of wood
must have presaged the end of everything. Almost as the mainmast thundered overboard, the carpenter's crew got busy with
the foremast; they hewed the rigging lanyards through with

adept strokes of the axes, and as they laid steel to the mighty spar, it fell away from them and overboard. They might have spared themselves the trouble; very shortly after the foremast was over the side, the ship, her steam notwithstanding, was picked up by a frantic squall and hurled on to the treacherous sands. As she touched bottom and canted, she immediately swung her broadside to wind and sea.

"Instruct the engineers to thrust her deeper into the sand!" ordered Taylor; making the best of what was almost the worst that could have happened. Then he went below to the cabins, again to reassure the trembling people, who, feeling the gride and lurch of the beaching, were naturally more apprehensive than ever. By way of lending a suggestion of calmness to the scene he casually ordered coffee to be prepared for all hands; and as the bleached stewards hurried away to perform this service, Taylor—honest hero!—calmly visited the huddled groups of women, asserting that the ship's plight gave no cause for concern and that, by God's grace, all hands would find themselves snugly ashore before daylight broke. He did not say that the lash of the broken water precluded all possibility of launching out the ship's boats in safety; there are certain matters best not mentioned until there is no alternative. He feared a panic, did this stout mariner, much more than he feared the rigors of God Almighty's fiercest gale.

Dawn came, wan and steely; showing a high gale; a livid waste of storm-lashed water, no sign of succour. There was a seaman in the *Royal Charter's* forecastle whose name—Rogerson—deserves to be bracketed with the names of the finest heroes. He looked out of the ship, over the white-lipped fury of the Mersey estuary—and there are few more bloodcurdling sights—and volunteered to try to get a line through the surf to the shore, so that a hawser might be conveyed. This sounds simple in the telling; in the fact it is miraculous. Solid land was distant not more than thirty or forty feet; but between ship and land ran such a riot of angry water as can hardly be conceived by any who have not seen it with their own eyes—a short, steep welter of water, kicked up in the shallows by that frantic wind. None the less, Rogerson being that kind of a man, he knotted the deepsea leadline around his chest and dived overboard. He succeeded in gaining solid ground after a gigantic struggle; where he was assisted by some of the country people, who had assembled when the knowledge of a disaster was made known to them by the *Royal Charter's* minute guns being fired. Rogerson lost no time in mistaken courtesies. He bustled the country folk about until they had hauled from the *Royal Charter* a stout hawser; which they set up as tautly as might be to a rock that gave decent holding; and an endless tackle holding a boatswain's chair was rigged—after the fashion of the breeches buoy that can be seen in practice action at most of our seaside resorts during the season, when subscriptions are mostly needed and realised.

With the Welshmen helping ardently, Rogerson contrived to draw about a dozen of his shipmates ashore in the chair. Whether the passengers were too timorous to venture or whether Taylor's idea was to send a useful working-party ashore to expedite the landing, is not correctly known. Probably both causes worked together to send the seamen first. With such a useful working-party securely landed on the inhospitable shore, there should have been no real difficulty in salving the entire complement of the stranded vessel. But she was attacked by the venomous spite of that pile-driving sea; it hammered unmercifully; it pounded her against the sand, it tore away her upperworks. Nothing constructed of human hands could withstand that slogging attack. At seven o'clock she broke her back and parted in two halves.

The happening was instantaneous; at one moment all hands were inspired by hope of a speedy and complete rescue; at the next—over four hundred people were struggling for life in the short, steep chop. The surf was not buoyant enough to support the swimmers; the hurl of the breakers was more than enough to cast them in among the ragged wreckage and batter the life out of their tortured bodies. Out of the swirls and the hideous mêlée of death, about twenty people were cast by the surges on to the shelving rocks of the shore. These, thanks to the battering they had received in transit, were infinitely more dead than alive. The rest died with gaspings and screams to a shrieking, indifferent sky.

The forepart of the *Royal Charter* remained on the sands, where it had been driven by the screw. To this forepart the remaining hundred of the people continued to cling, expecting every new sea to sweep them to destruction. Appalled by the terror of the spectacle they were compelled to witness, some lost hold and slid to death; others, fear strengthening them, clung desperately. Whilst they so held on, the pounding waves continued to attack, lacking mercy as the sea always lacks mercy; and as a result, the remaining section of the stricken hull parted again— in the wake of the forehatch. Half a hundred of those pitiable souls were overwhelmed at once, without even a fighting chance for life. The surging whitecaps roared triumphantly and continued their work; and Captain Taylor and all his senior officers were taken by the sea they had fought so gallantly for so long a time. The odds were against Taylor, a brave and eminently trustworthy man; but I fancy he would be glad to die that way rather than live to blame himself for a happening for which he was in no wise to blame.

Every woman and every child perished; for the sea knows no chivalry. Taylor was seen in the last extremity endeavouring to encourage and aid the few poor survivors who still clung to the trifling fragments of what had recently been a gallant ship; he was also seen swimming, heading shorewards; but a useless boat, torn from its davits, hurtled down on him and smote him to death; and he was never seen again. The country folks acted up to the best traditions of a coastwise race. In the last emergency, when the hawser failed, they linked hands and fought a way towards the wreck, steadying and supporting one another —and they contrived to snatch here a one, here another, to haul

[236]

them ashore to continued life; but this wild gleaning was tragically small.

Four hundred and fifty-nine people perished when the *Royal Charter* was lost; and an enduring gloom was cast not only over England, whence she hailed, but also over Australia, since such a great part of her people were Colonials.

Lives lost can never be restored; solid treasure endures, for what it is worth. The Australian gold-diggings were in full blast when the *Royal Charter* sailed from Melbourne that year; and in her holds she carried the ransom of a king in washed gold. Divers recovered most part of this treasure; not all the divers in the world could recover a single lost life of a woman or a child.

CHAPTER XIII

THE LAST WINDJAMMER

FOR a matter of two thousand years and more, wind-propelled craft have assisted materially in the creation not only of the far-flung British Empire but also in the development of the Mother Isle itself. From the time when the first Ancient Briton, brave in woad and ornaments of tin, discovered that it was easier to travel across, say, the mouth of the Bristol Channel if he showed the tail of his shirt to the wind, and so allowed his cranky coracle to proceed without the fatigue of paddling, until comparatively recent days, wind-propulsion has proved a greater factor than any other known in the advancement and welfare of Britain. Through all vicissitudes, sailing ships persisted. Time was when the ports of the world were crowded with square-riggers flying the Red Ensign gallantly at their peaks; but the advance of steam and steel rang the death-knell of these stately Southerners; and in the result it was left to one solitary windjammer to carry on old traditions and remind the careless present of the hard-won glories of the fighting past.

Though brigs and schooners might persist in the coastwise trade for a little longer, the colourful romance of blue water may be deemed to have passed with the last square-rigged windjammer of deepsea proportions; when the *Garthpool,* last, saddest of them all, piled her bones on an Equatorial reef, the glorious book of romance under sail was closed—though not, the indications go to prove, for ever.

Maintained as a picturesque survival of the spacious days by her owner, Sir William Garthwaite, this last relic of the spectral

fleets of white-winged beauties in which had been trained generation after stalwart generation of indomitable sea-fighters, sailed
on her tragic final voyage from Hull on October the 24th, 1929.
Economic conditions resulted in the fine old ship being run at a
considerable loss; but her owner's then and present desire to
maintain a leaven of sail-trained officers in the British merchant
service altruistically allowed him to continue her afloat, with a
number of selected boys in her half-deck to learn the trade of the
sea.

She was a fourmasted, stump topgallantmast barque of 2,842
tons gross; and under sail she was beautiful. Quite a useful
sailer, too, although Clark Russell would have compared her to
her discredit with the sleeker ships of his generation: she managed to run from Ushant to Cape Verde Islands in nine days, a
passable passage for a steel windjammer. She had an honest
record to her credit: not of sensational passages or of dangers over
past; though every world-circling windjammer naturally takes
her life in her hand and carries it there during most part of her
existence: but she was a seaworthy, trusty craft enough, and in
her bulk she embodied all that was finest and most romantic
of sea-life at its best and at its worst.

She had collected a strong fair wind when she sighted the
island of Sal, on November 11th; and was bowling along at a
fair ten knots, wind abaft the beam, her best sailing point, and
every stitch of canvas that would draw, humming melody to the
tropic seas. On that eventful 11th of November, all hands
celebrated the sad ritual of Armistice Day with bared heads,
silent under a half-mast ensign. Those who did so were not
aware that that historic day was to mark the passing of this
veteran ship from the warfare of white water to the peace of her
ending. Shortly after eight bells had changed the last dog-
watch to the first night watch, a lookout on the forecastle reported "Land ho." It was a clear, moonlight night, although
there had been mist during the day. In that shimmering, spectral light that shivered over the heaving Atlantic, could be seen

distinctly the outline of stark peaks. Sight of land to a wind-jammer presages action; the ship's mate roused the watch along to the fore-braces to point the yards and ease her headway. Braced up on the port tack, the *Garthpool* altered course to avoid this new-seen land; and slogged along for twenty minutes or so, when the lookout's voice stabbed the even hum of progress with a wailing yell of "Breakers ahead!"

The captain was a man of action; he skipped at full speed from the poop to the forecastle-head to see for himself. As he reached it, he saw; and seeing, he yelled through funnelled hands: "Hard up your helm! For God's sake, hard up your helm!"

Misted moonlight can be deceptive. The captain of the *Garthpool* knew what he intended, however; his penetrating glance had shewn to him a smooth in the rolling surf that indicated deep water, and, consequently, safe if risky passage. To make this providential channel was his only hope if he wished to save the last windjammer from ignominious death. This smooth patch was almost ludicrously narrow; but it was better than certain reefs; and as the wind was fair it seemed likely that the channel would be navigated in safety. He got the bow accurately pointed and steadied the helm, keeping forward as pilot. The *Garthpool* made entry of the passage and gathering way, streaked on like a steamer.

As she passed a steamer's bulk hove in sight ten fathoms distant or so on the port hand. She presented the appearance, in the moonlight, of a seaworthy craft steaming safely forward, and her very soundness impressed the windjammer captain with an idea of safety. She seemed to be in clear water—where one ship had gone, another ship could go. The *Garthpool* kept on through the gut, satisfied that all was going well. She was not to know, although the steamer carried no steaming lights, that the stranger was hard and fast on the ground and had been for a considerable time. Down in the tropics even reputable steamers have been known to economise on lamp-fuel, especially where the stern-light is concerned. This Italian freighter

THE "GARTHPOOL" TOWING ROUND FROM QUEENSTOWN
TO HULL, JULY, 1929

"MODERNITY"

looked like a ship under way; no hint was given that she had lain there for a matter of eighteen months. The situation was actually ironical.

That narrow channel would never have been attempted had not the loom of the Italian promised safe voyaging. As it was, once past her, with no earthly hope of turning back, the *Garthpool* discovered herself perilously near a lee-shore, outlined by creaming breakers. Had she known it, these breakers were crooning a siren song to lure her to her decent death.

To enter into intricate details of her stranding is at the moment of writing impossible, since the whole matter is considerably *sub judice* in view of a Board of Trade enquiry still to be held. Suffice it, then, that, according to an authentic account, the ship neared the reefs, and all hands were called on deck, and a general shortening of sail commenced, to lessen the *Garthpool's* way. Fore-and-afters were let run; the main course and crojack were hauled up in their gear; and whilst the pully-hauly cries of the crew were still ringing stentorianly, the cry came again from the forecastle lookout: "Breakers ahead and on the port bow!"

It was evident the good ship was closely embayed; with ragged teeth watering to pick her bones. Since she was officially in full passage, and not within the limits in which it is decreed a ship's ground-tackle shall be available for instant use, her anchors were safely housed. Getting out a sailing ship's anchors is not the simple task involved in letting go a modern steamer's stockless mudhooks, which can be released by loosening a windlass brake. All hands and the cook would have been necessary to get those big anchors over the side; and there was no time for that.

The ship was flying light in ballast; like a big balloon in the water, with no grip for close manœuvring. To tack was indicated, considering the lack of sea-room about her; but it was quite certain that she would not stay, flying light as she was. Consequently, the only possible chance of pulling the bewil-

dered ship clear of her massing trouble, was to wear her round
on her heel; a bit of seamanship that calls for space. The helm
was gingerly put up and the *Garthpool* allowed to fall off from
the wind; her main-yards were squared; the men working
nimbly, alert to the danger. Not that there was any real savour
of disaster in the night—here was a bright moon and an honest
wind, none-too-stormy water alongside; and in the tropics, too
—where nothing very extraordinary ever happens. Flying-
fish weather is the weather when seamen earn a respite from
much strenuous battling and are entitled to relaxation. Here
was no whirl of storm as was no roar of advancing flames; the
decks were dry, the canvas rustled in its buntlines. The men
worked nippily because of the urge in the voices of the afterguard; but as to there being hazard—rubbish!

Rubbish? Hardly. The *Garthpool's* head paid off handsomely. She steadied, she leaped forward—she crashed on
harsh rock; and dealt herself a death-blow. A booming swell
rolled up, and lifted her further on to her final resting-place;
and the harsh gride of the mangled steel dominated the rumble
of the murderous surf. She was holed badly, plates were
wrenched away from the main fabric; every succeeding swell
added to her unrest. The scream of steel torn by rock is almost
human in its agonised intensity; it might well be imagined as
the death-wail of a sentient thing. "It was as if thousands of
tons of coal were being shot down a chute," a member of the
crew put it.

The wealth of two thousand years of history is commemorated
in that pitiful incident: an epoch died when the *Garthpool* took
the ground. Better so—infinitely better that she should die in
harness, not fighting the storms she had so consistently weath-
ered, maybe, but at least fighting surf and the threat of shoal
water. Decently, she did not even hazard her people. Yes,
far better so, than to undergo the ignominy of being "sold foreign" or consigned to the ship's knacker-yard where good bottoms are broken up and melted down for their metal-value,

and no sentiment remains to speak of their passing. Her slowly mouldering ribs stand there on the murderous reef near Boavista Island in the Cape Verdes as a memorial of the bygone spacious days of sail—as moving to the mind of a sailor as a more enduring monument in hewn marble. Like the decent old lady she was, she folded her hands and lay down to sleep her final sleep, having ensured that no harm should happen to those who manned her—to whom she owed her years of safer voyaging.

There was nothing could be done to save her. Sand, yes; a ship might be recovered from the sand; rock—there is a different problem. Even had she been salvable it is questionable whether her recovery would have repaid the effort required. There was nothing to be done save for her people to swing out her lifeboats and leave her to this cynical end. She was still a ship, but in a little while the scend of the surf and the bitter grinding of her plates on those implacable rocks would tear her into her component fragments. "Leave her, Johnny, leave her! Times are bad and wages low; it's time for us to leave her!" If her men sang that dismal chanty as they clambered into the readied boats, it is the last time for many a day that a sea-chanty will be sung in its proper setting—on the deck of a tall ship under a wide and windy sky.

Everything was done in a hushed, seemly fashion; men almost whispered as they went about their occasions. The captain collected his papers and instruments; his example quelled all hint of dread in those under him.

"Sound the wells, Carpenter!" he ordered; and, surprisingly, only a matter of a few inches of water was discoverable. Holed she was, but on the face of it, not too badly holed to forbid a glimmer of hope.

"We'll endeavour to save the ship," said the captain. They did what they could, by backing the yards; she started and reared and fretted; but she opened her plates in the effort; and the water streamed in now, threateningly fast.

"Right, belay all that—clew up everything!" It was done; the ship was decently trimmed and put into mourning for her vanished glories. The *Garthpool* ground and grated on the rock; she tilted—the time had come. A tilted ship is apt to lose her masts overboard; and in their fall they might wreak havoc amongst the personnel.

"All hands, abandon ship!" A sad cry. I've heard it, under very similar conditions. It rings like a funeral peal; there is grim finality about it; for seamen do not abandon ship so long as a flicker of hope remains. It was like leaving a much-loved home; like bidding farewell to a favourite hunter that has broken its back in attempting to leap a double-oxer. The men collected their most intimate effects, a change of clothing, such food as was handy.

"Leave her, Johnny, leave her!"

One by one, men and boys first, officers next, captain last. A slap of the hand on the staunch steel; a hearty: "Good-bye, old lass!" and that was all. The staunch old ship was grinding her soul out on those rocks; and the slow clang of a loose steel door banging and slamming to the heave and scend of the tormented hull sounded like the death-knell of an epoch whose like will never be known again.

The boats pulled away into the moonlit unknown. They pulled away into a bewildering maze of reefs and isolated rocks, whichever way they turned they encountered breakers. The *Garthpool* had chosen a veritable ocean graveyard for her final leave-taking. There was nothing remaining save to anchor and await the day; and after sending up flares to attract possible attention, this was done. In the morning natives swam out through the surf, and—the world now being a civilised place—instead of attacking the castaways, piloted them into safe harbour; where rough accommodation was provided; and donkeys secured for the captain and second mate to ride to Sal Rei; where a trifling sloop was secured to collect the rest of the crew and convey them to St. Vincent, capital of the Cape Verde group, where were ease and comfort and succour. The last of the ultimate windjammer was a group of homeless men, possessing little more than the garments in which they stood, shaking grave heads and muttering: "Well, well, she was a good ship— yes, a good ship!"

But it is conceivable that out of her ashes a great new tradition may arise. The fact of her loss has driven home to the world the worth of her long-lived breed. The men who learned the trade of the sea in square-rigged craft proved the value of that training in a thousand difficult situations. They developed a praiseworthy handiness; and they developed more—a fighting spirit that refused to admit defeat so long as even the faintest glimmer of hope remained. It was the windjammer that made our Empire what it is to-day; and there is a strongly supported movement afoot to-day to build and equip the last windjammer's notable successor—a training school for the young manhood of to-morrow where old traditions might be remembered and old triumphs re-enacted to the glory of our race.

CHAPTER XIV

THE GENESIS OF THE LIFEBOAT

SEVEN years after the *Royal George* went down and cast a black cloud of mourning over England, another maritime tragedy was enacted off the Northumberland coast whose repercussions were to result in the opening chapter of what has since proved to be the most astounding, creditable and chivalrous epic ever created of the sea and such as use it and profit and suffer by its constantly changing moods. In September, 1789, the ship *Adventure* went ashore at the mouth of the River Tyne. The northern part of the white-lipped North Sea is not least of the world's tragic battlefields of the sea, as the dreary coast-wise records tell; and that stretch of coast from the Wash to the Tyne carries a tragedy almost for every fathom of its length.

Records are scant concerning the *Adventure's* previous history: so far as the chronicles are concerned she was merely a ship; the number of her crew is unknown, the quality of her voyaging and the name of her master are lost in the fogs of the years. She was a merchantman; and the merchant service possesses no meticulous Admiralty to keep a faithful log of every ship launched, from her inception to her ultimate doom; privately-owned ships simply turned in their logs to their owners at the end of each voyage; these logs were kept in forgotten cellars accumulating dust and rottenness, until they were discovered and pulped; and not a word remains to tell of the resounding history of the stately fabrics that spread their wings on every sea.

What we do know is that the elements of the *Adventure's* loss were tragic, and that out of grim tragedy a glorious new Phœnix arose. For, unlike most maritime disasters, the loss of the *Adventure* occurred under the close-range gaze of thousands of awestruck spectators—landsfolk, who until this happening had never realised the potentialities of white water for savage destruction and merciless cruelty. When the *Adventure* took the ground, driven thither by an equinoctial gale of surpassing fury, she was only three hundred yards from dry land, and her minute guns wakened the population of the northern city and brought them in their thousands to behold what the sea could do.

In "David Copperfield", Charles Dickens wrote what I contend to be the finest description of a storm and a wreck ever penned. The schooner in which Steerforth was lost offered a minor spectacle to the Yarmouth longshoreman, as compared with what the luckless *Adventure* presented to the hardy Northumbrians. For when the ship ran ashore on the sands, and the ragged water snarled high above the stranded hull, the crew took to the rigging and there held on, until cold, exhaustion and the relentless battering of the waves caused them to let go and drop, one by one, into the seething cauldron of the gale-lashed sea. Undoubtedly they resisted gallantly; they died hard, after the fashion of their breed; and this prolongation of agony took place under the eyes of those helpless spectators, who could do nothing to help their fellow-mortals in their throes of death. No doubt attempts were made to effect communication with the wreck—you cannot picture stout men standing by without making some effort to beat the sea; but such efforts were unavailing—so far as the men of the *Adventure* were concerned. So far as the generality of seamen were affected, a different story has to be told; for when the last poor numbed body had been engulfed and the triumphant breakers played madly with the parting timbers of the wreck, the gentlemen of South Shields met together and asked each other why such a thing should be.

"What is needed," they said, "is some form of vessel that will float in the roughest water and stand up against the fiercest gale."

Up there the coast-wise men knew a good deal about hard-weather boat-work; they snatched a difficult existence from the narrow seas; and since hungry mouths must be filled, both in December and June, bad weather and they were on familiar terms. As a result of this impromptu indignation meeting—the indignation being directed at that crafty monster, white water—a subscription was collected in a public-spirited way, and a prize was offered generally for plans of a boat—a lifeboat—"calculated to brave the dangers of the sea, and particularly of broken water". And forthwith the constructive brains of England were set to work to devise something worth while. Suggestions and attempts poured in; the country was stirred by the challenge issued to an ancient enemy; and out of this peaceful crusade a plan presented by one Henry Gatehead or Greathead was finally selected for the prizewinner; with a design by William Wouldhave a close second. Those Northumbrian committeemen were as shrewd as they are made; hard-headed visionaries; and when the vision and the deed link hands something out of the ordinary is practically bound to happen. The committee which was the nucleus of the present Royal National Lifeboat Institution, instructed Greathead to construct a life-saving boat according to his own specifications, but embodying all that was best in Wouldhave's scheme.

This first lifeboat, *qua* lifeboat, was built with five thwarts, each capable of seating two men with a sweep apiece; thus ten oars became the propulsive power of the craft. Furthermore, since buoyancy is the prime essential in a boat designed to beat white water, Greathead's lifeboat was lined with cork; and fitted with sixteen-inch-deep cork fenders outside her gunwale. She was not beautiful, by any means; but she promised to be useful. Greathead made a sensational departure from convention in his design: the centuries had dictated that a boat's keel should be straight as a lance. He made his boat's keel curved at bow and stern—gave it, to apply the correct phrase—a considerable camber. In this way he made his creation easier of handling, not only afloat—a flick of the rudder would spin her in the hardest weather—but also when being launched and beached. These are primary factors in a vessel constructed for the purpose of sea-fighting: very often the greatest risk to such a boat is not her fight when afloat but the mere getting of her water-borne.

The simple ingenuity of this scheme proved a success; and as a result of exhaustive tests further boats of similar design were constructed and posted at various points on the British coast, where wrecks most frequently occurred. The practical value of the new type was swiftly and amply proved. Hundreds of valuable lives that must otherwise have been lost were plucked from the hungry maw of the ragged steep seas that lash our wintry coasts. Greathead, inspired by success—his art lay not in losing life, as great generals did, but in saving it—went on boat-building to his utmost capacity; and within four years had constructed thirty-one of his life-saving boats. So much were their water-fighting qualities appreciated that eight of these craft were sent abroad for service—at a time when war wrapped most of Europe in its mesh, and news travelled but slowly! But news of good sometimes travels faster than news of evil; and the sheer humanitarianism of these boats appealed to the world; so Greathead's craft were sprinkled along foreign shores—to continue their invaluable work. One at least went as far afield as Russia, where it had a remarkably good opportunity of doing service; for the Baltic is a devastating sea for such as do their business on it; and that the lifeboat justified itself is proved by the fact that the Tsar of that time presented Greathead with a diamond ring; which, when you come to consider it, was richly deserved.

Greathead was a hard-headed Northerner; and adulation alone failed to satisfy him. He put in an application to Parliament for a national reward; and although Parliaments are notoriously ungrateful and stingy, he profited to the extent of £1,200; not a great deal of money for such a national benefactor, when we

consider the size of the grants being made at that time to in-
ventors of destructive machines. Trinity House and Lloyd's
—then becoming powerful factors in maritime circles—each con-
tributed one hundred guineas as a separate testimonial; whilst
the Society of Arts—recognising, one presumes, that a practical
picture such as the daredevil rescue of hapless men from a greedy
sea was even more inspiring than something painted on canvas,
expressed appreciation by a present of its gold medal and fifty
guineas. Even so, considering what great results sprang from
comparatively small causes, no one can deem Greathead over-
paid.

Not that the creation of his brain and brawn was in any wise
perfect. It was certainly better than anything that had gone
before, not only for its own performance but also because of its
value in leading constructive minds along unique and valuable
channels; but a school of thought grew up which was openly
hostile to the buoyant lifeboat, because, although the general
record of work done was good, there were misfortunes. And
the critics always pick on the demerits of any performance whilst,
too often alas! ignoring the many merits. Among the more
serious of lifeboat disasters of this era was the loss of a Greathead boat off the Tyne in 1810. The boat, manned by eighteen
volunteers, put out to the assistance of some weather-menaced
fishermen. It was blowing hard at the time and a high sea was
running. The Greathead boat contrived to reach the perishing
and took them into the shelter of its buoyancy; but on returning
for the shore, where the breakers ran nastily, a vast and hasty
wave swept the boat on to a reef of rocks, notwithstanding all
efforts of her people; and she was pounded to slivers; rescuers
and rescued perishing in a common grave to the number of
thirty-four in all.

But despite these mischances, the lifeboat idea was sound and
it persisted, although the country's brain was directed more to
defeating Napoleon and ensuring peace throughout the war-
battered world. Greathead's boats did not increase very greatly

in number; but such as there were continued a faithful record
of service; and then, twelve years after the disaster to the Tyne-
mouth boat, Sir William Hillary, who had done a lot of heroic
work in lifeboats, acting as coxswain and oarsman, too, published
a striking appeal to the nation on behalf of all shipwrecked
mariners. So heartfelt was this appeal that it resulted in the
formation of the Royal National Institution for Preserving Life
from Shipwreck in 1824; and its original subscription list can
have been but little longer than its name, for it started operations with a capital of only £10,000. In those days, however,
when income tax was lower and cost of living much more moder-
ate, this ten thousand pounds sufficed to build and establish a
dozen lifeboats around the coast in the first year. So that the
work of the honest ship's carpenter, Greathead, and that of his
no less worthy competitor, Wouldhave, permitted by the broad-
minded attitude of those gentlemen of South Shields, was doing pretty well, considering everything. But it is extremely
doubtful if anything worthy of note would have been done at
all—at any rate for many a distressful year of shipwreck and
wholesale death, had it not been for the incident of the *Adventure* and the fact that she chose for her death-place a stretch
of sand that formed a peculiarly arresting stage for the horrified eyes of the thousands who assembled to see what the sea
could do.

To attempt to give full expression to the ultimate progress of
this Royal Society with the cumbersome name—its present title
of Royal National Lifeboat Institution (familiarly R.N.L.I.) is
better—would be beyond the scope of this present work. Whoever actually founded the lifeboat idea may be open to controversy: but no one can doubt that it was the impetus given
by the competition inaugurated by the gentlemen of South
Shields at Lawe House which first opened the eyes of inland
England to the dire need for some means of succouring her seafarers in their hour of tribulation. Whether Greathead's boat
was best or Wouldhave's, as so many claim, the fact remains

that a lifeboat *was*. And while Wouldhave and Greathead were experimenting—one a ship's carpenter and the other—of all things—a parish clerk, teacher of singing and house-painter—one Lukin, a coachbuilder of Long Acre, was also making tentative tests. But Lukin, having converted a Norroway yawl into his conception of an immergible boat, was not fortunate enough to see it utilised to practical value; he was victimised by some Ramsgate smuggler who took his boat out for tests and failed to reappear with it. This gentleman of the sea carted the boat away to the smuggling trade, where it was apparently very successful until it was run down and destroyed by the unsympathetic Revenue.

What had happened, as a result of the *Adventure's* loss, was that a link had been established—a sympathetic, understanding link—between England's land-dwellers, whose daily existence depended on the sea, and the men who fought that sea in the interests of their more sheltered brethren. That link persists to-day as that noble service: the R.N.L.I.

Not that the link was strongly forged during its first half-century of existence. It was constantly crippled by lack of funds, as most philanthropic institutions are; in fine weather the public forgot the ominous threat of the sea; and it was in fine weather that constructive work was needed. But such boats as could be built were built; and judging by a record that is inscribed in shining gold on the annals of the country, short though the boats were, there was never any lack of men to man them—for the gallant longshoremen were accustomed to fight for places at the oars when the call went forth; and this, not for the scant monetary recompense allowed them out of depleted funds, but from a far higher motive—the pressing brotherhood and humanity of those who have business with the sea.

Unquestionably the R.N.L.I. owes its origin and its fame to Sir William Hillary—man of the world, hero of many hairs-breadth adventures by flood and field. Here was a man who knew from his own experience what the sea could do if given a

THE FIRST LIFEBOAT.

THE LAUNCH

free hand. In one season he was himself instrumental in saving 84 lives from two of H.M.'s vessels wrecked in sight of Douglas, Isle of Man; and the inspiration of a practical hero of this type could not fail in its effect on the public mind.

How necessary his appeal to the nation was is shewn by the simple fact that in the first twenty-five years of his founding the Institution, 144 wrecks occurred within sight of his abiding-place in the Isle of Man. To one of these wrecks he went out— amongst many others—and a curt narration of the episode will prove better than volumes what the conditions were. The Royal Mail steamer *St. George* happened to be wrecked in Douglas Bay. She was riding out a hurricane when her cables parted and she was driven ashore, much as the *Royal Charter* was lost. The lifeboat supplied was new and not yet conditioned for service; but notwithstanding this, Sir William Hillary per-suaded sixteen men to essay the task of succouring those who were dying within plain view of the land. He reached the wreck, after a most strenuous adventure, and saved the entire crew of twenty-two. In his effort he was washed out of the boat along with other three boatmates. The Douglas Bay seas were violent in those days! He had every right to esteem him-self a beaten man; but instead of throwing up the sponge Hillary got back into the boat, with his chest badly crushed and six ribs snapped, and went on with his job as if nothing out of the ordinary had happened. Not bad for a veteran of sixty-three! At the age of sixty-five he did a little more gallant work: helping, under similar circumstances, to salve fifty-four men from the wrecked Liverpool ship *Parkfield*. Altogether he was person-ally instrumental in saving 305 lives from shipwreck. The num-ber saved as a direct result of his initial appeal can never be esti-mated. This, then, was the man who definitely forged that glorious link betwixt shore and sea, and brought ships and their hazards within the ken of the common folk.

But inspiration alone will not suffice to keep a movement afloat; hard cash is also necessary; and though the R.N.L.I. worried along to the best of its ability, saving life where possible, and fuming when lack of boats forbade further humane work, it fretted at its lack of capital. It was attempting to win a battle without adequate munitions. It was, of course, handicapped by the outstanding fact that during these formative years England had a plethora of internal troubles to occupy her mind and empty her purse—for the record of the following quarter-century is as black a page as could be written in a country's history. Strikes, threat of revolution, misery, battle; the tale is grim; but the spark of humanity persisted; and in 1850, Algernon, Duke of Northumberland, set in train a movement that not only reorganised the lifeboat service but also quickened public interest in its labours to a most gratifying degree.

He originated a competition for the best workable lifeboat, offering a prize of one hundred guineas for the most acceptable model. The conditions of the competition were given a world-wide broadcast; and as a result there were 280 entries, not alone from England, but also from America, Holland, France and Germany. These entries required six months for judgment; but in the event the honour was awarded to one James Beeching, of Great Yarmouth, for a self-righting lifeboat; since one of the objections taken to the older pattern craft, on the lines of the Greathead-Wouldhave designs, was the fact that it did not right itself after being capsized.

There is a story current—it deserves to be true—to the effect that a veteran coxswain of the Whitby lifeboat was summoned to give evidence before a commission inquiring into this matter of the self-righting boat; and on being asked if he were in favour of such a lifeboat he answered with a stubborn No; from which stand he refused to be moved. One of the commission asked him his objection; and the reply was: "What I wants is a booat 'at wean't *capsize.*"

But a self-righting lifeboat was a vast advancement on previous models; and when Mr. Beeching, having won the award, was instructed to build a fullsize craft, he gave proof of his ability in building the Ramsgate lifeboat; whose model is still on exhibition in the Museum of the Royal United Service Institution in London—a clinker-built boat made of wainscot oak and iron-fastened.

This first boat was a success beyond all expectations; and, plying chiefly to the Goodwin Sands—that Devil's Playground of white water *in excelsis*—she did remarkable service, actually wearing herself out in the labour of humanity. She was a 36-foot boat; nine and a half feet in the beam, and pulled twelve double-banked oars. In addition to her cork fender, six inches thick and eight inches deep running around her gunwale, she was equipped with air-tanks to enable her to right herself; and she had a carrying capacity of seventy. Good under oars, she was still better under sail; and, weighing two and a half tons as she did, her total cost was somewhere in the neighbourhood of £250. The Greathead-Wouldhave boat cost about £56 all-in. Lifesaving at sea was comparatively cheap in those days; to-day, an up-to-date boat, a Barnett twin-screw motor, 60 feet long, costs £18,000 originally, and a matter of a thousand a year for up-keep. *Autres temps, autres mœurs.*

It was from this Great Yarmouth boat that the idea of the ship's lifeboat as employed to-day evolved itself; consequently Beeching may be considered one of the greatest friends the sailorman has ever had.

No apology is necessary for touching on the matter of life-boats, whether private craft or those of the Lifeboat Institution, for a work devoted to shipwrecks would be incomplete without a record of certain anti-wreck devices. Every disease clamours for a remedy; and just as the scientists of to-day are probing deeply into human mystery in search of a counter to cancer and similar deadly diseases, so, at the middle of the nineteenth century, were practical men devoting their brains to valuable research work to combat the death-toll exacted by the sea. The oceans will never be safe beyond all chance of hazard; but it is men of the Beeching stamp, inspired by such stalwarts as Sir

William Hillary and the Duke of Northumberland, who have drawn the worst of white water's grinning teeth.

But in questing for the best means wherewith to succour such as the sea has afflicted, bitter toll has been exacted, as following chapters purpose to show. The most tragic wrecks are not necessarily those which involve the greatest number of lives; a comparatively small death-roll can carry more poignant agonies, maybe, than one that fills columns of a newspaper. In any case, lost lifeboats are as much of the price of Admiralty as are lost liners; and when news of such a loss is made known, the effect is even more staggering to the public mind, probably because the lifeboat is a picturesque institution, within the comprehension of the layman, familiar to every seaside tripper, and informed by a spirit of high courage and sheer humaneness which inevitably appeals to the human race.

The publicity aroused in 1851 by the Duke of Northumberland's appeal to the world resulted in great good being done to what might be called the defensive lines of the sea-fighters. But though Beeching's boat—his original attempt—did invaluable service, it still lacked that perfection of construction which must be aimed at if a service employing it is to consider itself invulnerable. Two other boats built by Beeching capsized and failed to right themselves, owing to defects in their construction; and consequently a somewhat acrid controversy arose as to the comparative merits of self-righting and non-self-righting boats, during which the Whitby coxswain is supposed to have delivered himself oracularly as explained above. The committee of the R.N.L.I. adopted an extremely wise measure in dealing with all these pros and cons; instead of giving too open an ear to the theorists, its members took counsel with the stalwarts whose job it was to take the boats to sea under the extremest conditions; and, bracketing their opinions with the most scientific theoretical ideas, evolved in course of time a standard boat which stands as second to none for its qualities. Consequently, Mr. James Peake, of H.M. Dockyard at Woolwich, was commissioned to build a lifeboat embodying the best of all available; and his boat was put into commission on the bleak Northumberland coast in 1852. It was subjected to extraordinarily severe tests in the heaviest of surfs; and so well did it acquit itself that the R.N.L.I. immediately proceeded to build others to its sealed pattern. And until quite recent times the gallant lifeboats of the Institution adhered more or less closely to the combined Beeching-Peake model, with R.N.L.I. modifications and embellishments; and the records of the Institution prove how well warranted her sponsors were in pinning their faith to her.

Whilst the perfect lifeboat was being evolved, public support flowed in in gratifyingly increasing quantity; thus lessening the burden of financing not only the experiments but also the actual establishment of stations at every point where experience proved shipwrecks were most frequent and harrowing. As time went on, the "Boat" became one of the chief objects of interest at every seaside resort; and this was good publicity. Exhibition launches were made and it was shown how romantic, picturesque and gallant the lifeboat service was. Until then the actual seaman had been regarded somewhat as an outcast by those ashore—a man who was more or less paid to risk the sea; and if he failed in the battle, that was no concern of those who profited by his labours. A sailor was a drunken wastrel—ran public comment—a fool of a fellow, who hadn't sufficient brains to keep himself clear of harpies and sharesharks; and who more or less deserved what he got. But when a few wrecks occurred under the actual gaze of the shorefolks; as newspapers improved in quality, and were able to report with increasing impressiveness and reality the onerous conditions of sea-fighting, the national conscience wakened; and the sailor's safety became a matter of paramount concern.

The R.N.L.I. grew like a well-nurtured child; and is still growing lustily; but the more it grows, the more does it become costly of maintenance—and it is only right that this should be so; for every year brings an added need for more up-to-date equipment, for extra boats, and for more regular service; and —what is more—a due recognition of the heroic services of such as man the life-saving craft.

This vigorous growth dates from the Duke of Northumberland's stirring appeal which quickened the national interest in its shores and their perils, and opened purse-strings with gratifying frequency. Whether this vital, national question of a life-saving service should be dependent on private generosity, rather than on national compulsion, it is not for the present writer to say. But that the R.N.L.I. manages its funds with unexampled competency no man can doubt; as no man can doubt its ever-insistent need for yet more funds to fulfil still more of its altruistic dreams.

How keenly this public interest is maintained is illustrated by the incredibly generous response made to the appeal for funds to benefit such as suffered by the tragic Rye disaster of comparatively recent date. We are a warm-hearted nation, peculiarly responsive to stirring tales of derring-do; and heroism of this particular self-sacrificing type can never leave us unmoved. But it should not be left for such a tragedy as this of Rye to sustain interest in the peaceful fighting service. There is no man, woman or child, living and breathing in the embrace of our seagirt coasts who does not owe much to the men who brave the sea. There is not a cigarette smoked nor a cup of tea drunk that has not involved some seafarers in danger; as there is hardly a newspaper printed that does not owe its origin to material brought from overseas. An island race cannot exist without sailors; and sailors cannot be succoured in their hour of bitter travail without lifeboats. But for our seamen England would have perished in the Great War: she could not have endured the starvation pangs that must have resulted on poltroonery or weak-spiritedness during the dreadful years. It would be as well for all who realise that fact—the fact of continued existence—to remember in whose debt they are, and show appreciation of that indebtedness on the next occasion when

Lifeboat Saturday comes round. For if the sailor's sheet-anchor is home, as the old sea-ditty went, the sailor's best earthly friend is the R.N.L.I. which is as fine an example of practical Christianity as the world affords.

By 1865, principally as a result of the Duke of Northumberland's reorganisation and appeal, the R.N.L.I. has assumed a healthy condition: it owned 144 lifeboats—thirty-four of which had been provided during that year—and it had been instrumental in saving 432 lives during those fourteen years. So sterling an impression did this performance make on the world's mind—for lifesaving is not a purely British characteristic—that the Committee reported that during the year under examination three fully-equipped lifeboats of standard pattern, complete with carriages and launching gear, had been provided to the order of the French Government, others for Lifeboat associations in Marseilles, Bremen and Holland, whilst the National Lifeboat stations were a Mecca for naval officers of various nationalities, intent on seeking wisdom, who, visiting to acquire knowledge stayed to admire.

In this year, 1865, the Duke of Northumberland died; and anyone who has ever watched a lifeboat leave its slip and fare out to help the distress on angry waters, must unhesitatingly admit that, if only on account of his lifeboat work alone, his was a full and useful and valuable life. From the time of his sponsorship of a weatherly, self-righting lifeboat to his regretted death, unnumbered thousands of lives were snatched from the sea; and the gratitude of all who benefited thereby is his finest memorial.

Private individuals began to take an added interest in the R.N.L.I. about this time. It was realised that more honest satisfaction could be got out of gifting a lifeboat complete to the Service than out of most more flamboyant pleasures. Societies were formed to adopt a lifeboat; magazines provided a boat out of subscriptions collected amongst their readers; and so the good work went on. At the annual meeting of the Institution held in 1867 H.R.H. the Prince of Wales presided, and was able to announce that another thirty-four boats had been added to the fleet; and that public interest was well maintained, whilst somewhere about 550 lives were saved and twenty vessels succoured and preserved from loss. All this is heartening reading. Lifeboat work is not merely a matter of momentary emergency; nor yet of patriotic emotion, kindled for a while, and allowed to expire after a flicker or a conflagration, according to the magnitude of the need. Lifeboat work is an abiding reality; a never-ceasing warfare in the interests of humanity; it saves, not destroys; and its best exhibitions do not take place under approving eyes of interested spectators; but in the clamorous darkness of the wintry nights at sea, when the big restless winds are out to slay.

In 1870 lifeboats of the Institution contrived to tear 1,231 lives from the sea—not a bad achievement. By this time there were 220 boats in commission; and not a single lifeboatman's life was lost in gleaning this excellent harvest. By 1876, the Committee reported: "Happily, there is now hardly a dangerous point of the coast where a lifeboat is not to be found; and, what is equally important, where stout hearts and strong arms are not also found ready to man it and work it, even in the fiercest storm."

The year 1880 brought with it a tale of continuous gallantry and arduous service by boats and men; it brought a record of an unprecedented loss: five lifeboats were capsized, and eighteen members of their crews were drowned. To show the spirit of the men and the sea-quality of the boats, the following year yielded a total of 966 lives saved; at a cost of four boats capsizing; which goes to show that disaster in no wise deterred the stout fellows from attempting and in most cases achieving the impossible.

Through all this period of thirty years' indomitable service there is no event which stands out in such crystal clarity for fortitude, heroism and disaster, as the pitiful loss of the Whitby Lifeboat in 1861; a tragedy deserving of a chapter to itself.

CHAPTER XV

WHITBY FASHION!

FRIDAY, February 8th, 1861, brought, towards evening, a full and freshening south-easterly gale, which, by Saturday morning, had risen to hurricane force—that is a velocity of 100 miles per hour at least—and was in consequence causing great anxiety and distress amongst the honest Yorkshire folk. This increasing apprehension was founded on knowledge of the fact that a very considerable fleet of sailing craft was at that time off the coast in that vicinity, and the past night had been in the main sleepless; the lifeboat crew standing by steadily for the calls they knew must come.

Dawn broke horribly—a lividly ferocious dawn that presaged ill for such as were at sea; that presaged, had they known it, tragedy of the direst for the honest folk of Whitby. Within an hour of the steeliness first showing in the screaming eastern sky, the brig *John and Ann,* a Sunderland-owned craft, mazed by the tempest, her canvas in ribbons, and her crew powerless to help her, was hurled ashore at the little village of Sandsend, hard by Whitby; though distant some two miles from the lifeboat station. Now, without meaning anything derogatory to the men of every part of the English coast, it must be admitted that the Whitby men were and are the very finest seamen bred along that extensive seaboard. They have their weaknesses, as they themselves are the first to admit. Their forebears used to pray: "God bless father, God bless mother, and God send a ship ashore before morning!" In expansive moments they have told me tales of wrecking that would best suit a book of fiction; and they have occasionally boarded flurried ships, and insisted on the bewildered skipper allowing them to take charge, after which they have claimed handsome salvage for services which were not really necessary; but these flaws simply serve to illuminate their particular virtue—their ironhard courage when things are at their worst. They were cavaliers of the sea—prone to enrich themselves if opportunity offered; and in their hard-fighting cobbles they learnt every trick of cunning and valour the sea could teach them.

There were at Sandsend at this particular time living seven members of the Whitby Boat; and they were two miles or so from their station. Realising the distressful condition of the *John and Ann,* these seven stalwarts did not waste time in hurrying to the station to raise an alarm and take their places in the boat; but, at great risk and labour, launched out their own cobble and started away to the rescue. Sandsend beach in a south-easter is a treacherous spot, being wide-open to the full run of the North Sea, where a lively pobble can be knocked up in an hour, and a devastation created in a night. A Yorkshire cobble is a pretty staunch craft, it is built not for pleasure-cruising but for sea-fighting; and although their task appeared impossible, these seven good men of Sandsend contrived to reach the stranded brig. They collected the crew of five from the rigging, where they had lashed themselves, got them safely ashore, hurried them into the shelter of their cottages, and then, after having done what might reasonably be considered a useful day's work, began to think about being busy. Consequently, they hurried along to Whitby to stand by the lifeboat.

Shortly after they arrived at the station, the hurricane brought them toil. The schooner *Gamma,* of Newcastle, coal-laden for London River, drove ashore on the sands; and so the Whitby lifeboat, including in its crew the seven men of Sandsend, promptly started out to see what it could do. It found work to its liking. The fight through the boiling surf was strenuous; but the Sandsend men were in excellent training; and they took the boat through or under whatever came along. It is not easy to pull a fifty-hundredweight boat in the teeth of a hurricane, when the oars are skied or dipped vertically, when the blades as often as not engage with filmy spray that offers no resistance, and when the looms rise up and strike their wielders shrewd blows under the chin. The work of strenuous minutes is apt to be undone in as many seconds, when a flurry seizes the boat and hurls it back whence it came. But such annoying resistance is a part of the daily work to the men of Whitby; so these stalwarts persevered, reached the *Gamma,* and after skilful manœuvring, when their craft was in imminent danger of being crushed like an eggshell a thousand times, they took down the bemused unfortunates of the *Gamma's* crew, happed them safely into the big boat; and setting a scrap of canvas to ease their aching muscles, ran before the wind back to the shore.

Every man was landed in safety; the lifeboat's crew stretched themselves; and—the Prussian barque *Clara,* bound from Newcastle to Madeira, chose that moment to drive ashore on those greedy sands.

Already the Whitby boat had two very gallant rescues to its credit, and the day, as a working day, was hardly started. They went out again—repeated the old noble programme, with added numbers—for twelve men were hauled through the smother this time, and succoured, and the boat cast adrift from the crumbling wreck just in the nick of time; for almost as the last man was hauled from death to life, the *Clara,* torn back from her temporary housing, sank in the ravening swirls. The lifeboat returned to shore, handed over its latest salvage to willing, sympathetic hands, and allowed itself a long breath—really the first since daylight, when you come to think of it.

The serial story of undaunted heroism was only opening its initial chapters however. But as in any well-written serial story, the interest and action were now beginning to quicken: new characters were introduced; and a vivid series of incidents flashed across the pages without pause, leaving in the mind even of the writer a sense of breathlessness and consternation.

In this way: The brig *Utility*—proving her inability to live up to her name—came raging shorewards, out of all control, her canvas in rags, helm shattered and whole water devastating her decks. She in her turn piled up, and, arrested in this way, careened and swung a broadside to very devastating water; her people taking to the rigging as their single remaining chance of life. They despaired; not knowing the calibre of the Whitby men, or the Whitby fashion of doing business.

To see distress was to answer its appeal. The Boat proceeded seaward again, still manned by the same tireless crew; and the tornado was increasing hourly in its violence. Those shallow waters kick up a short steep sea that is heartbreaking; but the Whitby heroes understood its whims and fancies, and negotiated a safe passage to the *Utility;* from her they plucked the terror-stricken people, bundled them under their feet, and—pulled ashore? No—not by any manner of means.

Whilst they were taking off the *Utility's* crew, the schooner *Roe,* Newcastle-bound from Dundee, blown badly out of her course, was piled up on the verge of that maritime graveyard. The sands here shelve steeply in sudden steps; and gale-hounded tide makes the sea-bottom peculiarly treacherous. The attention of the boatmen was drawn to this fifth in the chain of disasters; and, as the *Utility* foundered just as the last man was hauled into safety, they spat on their hands, settled their cork jackets a little more comfortably, and, settling down to make a real day of it, fought across to the rapidly dissolving *Roe,* which they were fortunate enough to reach before she settled down on the floor of the locker. From her they collected a little more worthy harvest, and found it no light task. However, Whitby fashion is to do the work that's nearest though it's hectic at whiles; and having satisfied themselves that the *Roe* was cleared out of humanity, the Boat started back for land, this time containing the crews of two vessels huddled on her bottom boards.

By this time the forenoon was well advanced; zero hour had been at dawn or thereabouts; and the shock troops might be pardoned for feeling a little borne down by the weight and rigour of the battle. They were allowed a breathing-space and time for a hasty meal—but the busy morning was merely a prelude to the afternoon. Two p.m.—when human effort is apt to slack ever so little, when the tendency is to look back complacently on a morning's accomplished something—came. With it came the brigantine *Flora,* scudding like a startled gull for the safety of Whitby Harbour—which, comfortable and safe inside, requires a considerable amount of reaching in any sort of a sea way. There is a shelf of rock south of the South Pier that is an absolute magnet to ships; and the sinister currents seem to be employed by the reef to play siren in order to attract honest ships to their doom on the murderous shelf.

The shore-watchers speculated on her luck as she loomed up through the horror of wind and high-thrown spray, under a black and lowering canopy of storm-cloud which seemed to droop down to mingle with the ravening breakers. Unearthly shafts of livid light struck down, to bring her storm-wrecked canvas into sudden relief; she showed like a cockleshell among the white-lipped seas. But she was running fairly for port—she had the wind behind her; she contrived to keep afloat; and the Whitby folk decided that she had a fighting chance; only—it was just as well to take cognisance of the other possibility. They knew their own waters; they knew the scour of that current sweeping from the sand-ledges and striking south. Like anything else in that cyclonic ferment, the *Flora,* instead of centring between the harbour piers, missed her target; and crashed horribly on the Collier Hope.

"Another poor devil's for it!" was the verdict; and the boatman made ready; jerking the stiffness from their rheumaticky bones. They manned the oars and went; obeying tirelessly that simple call of duty which is bred of the unfair sea, which demands all and gives so little—so very little—in return. They went out and picked off the *Flora's* crew. Half a dozen words suffice to state the fact, a dozen chapters might fall short of conveying the amazing quality of this work. For though it may seem a simple matter to rescue menaced men off a ship when once the wreck is reached, actually, in nine cases out of ten, the real work only commences when the boat's anchor is dropped to windward and she is veered down slowly on the cable to a workable distance from her salvage. To get a heaving-line aboard is never easy—even to-day with line-guns and a number of deft instruments devised to beat the worst of the storms. In 1861 man-power was the primary factor in lifeboat work. Having got a line aboard as a start, often and often the men of the wreck were too numbed by cold and exposure, too terrified by the roaring imminence of death, to attempt anything in their own salvation; they could not even send a line across to the boat by which they might be hauled into shelter; and some one or other of the lifeboat men must needs take his life still more closely in his hand, and worrying a way to the wreck, help the helpless to fend for themselves.

However, notwithstanding difficulties, the Whitby men got the crew of the *Flora* off; and returned along the well-travelled path to shelter.

Six ships' crews saved without loss so far! Good going, even for a breed that sets itself a high standard of efficient courage! But actually only the *hors-d'œuvre* before the real feast of gallantry. The men of the *Flora* were barely lifted from the staunch lifeboat when fresh work offered itself for consideration. Close to the spot where the *Roe* had met her sorry fate the schooner *Merchant* piled herself up; and, without pausing for so much as a bite of food or a pull at a much-needed pipe, the Whitby stalwarts resumed duty. They never hesitated; they never flinched, though by this time of day the storm was reaching its screaming culmination.

"Let's get at it, lads," was the word; and they got at it. Round backs bent amain to the oars that by now must have felt as if they weighed a ton apiece; hard hands gripped the poignant looms; the coxswain, weatherwise and canny as only, perhaps, a

[266]

THE RESCUE

The Rye Lifeboat washed ashore near Jury's Gap, 15th November, 1928.
(Two men were found dead beneath it)

Whitby coxswain can be, surveyed his battleground, made his swift and cunning dispositions; and off she went—labouring down to the harbour mouth, shooting the tempestuous bar in a whirl that threw her about like an unconsidered chip; and so out across the furrows and ridges of one of the worst seas ever observed in a district famous for its unholy surges.

The womenfolk, who could do nothing really active according to their way of looking at things, crowded to the pier-head to watch the lifeboat fight its dogged way, inch by inch, yard by toilsome yard, against the tide and wind. Not least amongst the heroes these silent, uncomplaining women who had been taught through the years to give their menfolk to the sea and its bitternesses without protest; who lived with their staunch hearts in their mouths whenever the winds were out to slay; and who accepted continued life as a gift from on High. Action stifles dismay; these noble souls could not act save by deputy, but they stood there on the gale-lashed pier and waved their work-roughened hands and wrapped their shawls closer about them, and stared with misted eyes at the closed-in horizon, whence came the terror that was everlasingly theirs.

Seventy yards from the pier went the lifeboat; and every yard a Purgatory of undiminished effort; men fighting—fighting —teeth clenched, muscles literally cracking. Seventy yards of incredible effort—and a lean, grim sea surged along. Only one of many, maybe a little higher, with a little added impetus. The boat staggered and reeled, swung about in a vortex of froth. The coxswain dragged her bow to face the flurry—and before she was really moving again came another sea—bigger than the first, more venomous.

"Watch her, lads! Oh—give her *beef!*" They tried—they failed. The boat was hit foully—she was flung up; the seas hammering at her broadside; and as she was only the work of mortal hands and not a god-made craft, she capsized. She capsized, and hurled the men in her overboard into the bitter sea. A moan, growing to a scream, was torn from those hard-trained

[267]

spectators. There was a futile movement forward—expressing a human instinct of help, even where help was impossible. The stage was set for tragedy after the heroic act had been completed —grim tragedy, as hardy men began to fight for lives that, even on the highest estimate, were well worth saving. One man was flung by a sea towards the overturned boat; floating there like a white whale in the surges—she had not acted up to expectations; she did not right herself. He scrabbled with his fingers on the strakes; fought a savage way to the keel; clung there; the ugly sea mocking him with slashing blows. The rest tried to swim, tried to live—fought tooth and nail for existence, under the eyes of their kin.

These did what they could—terribly little considering the wealth of their desire. They tore down the lifebuoys available and flung them—short. The life-saving rocket apparatus was torn from its shelter and rushed to the pier; rockets, carrying lines, were fired out over the struggling shapes; the wind tore the lines away to leeward in futile bights.

In vain. These men had already expended the strength of a cohort of Titans and they were already weary when the time of ordeal came to them. They continued to fight until the sea numbed them, paralysed their best efforts; choked them, swung them against the pier-piling and crushed and stunned them; so they died before the horrified gaze of those to whom they were very dear in the dour North-country fashion. Their own children moaned their requiem as they perished—gallant men of Whitby, who were attempting what they conceived to be their duty.

Nothing could be done; that was the culminating tragedy of this tragic hour. Yes—something could at least be attempted. Men—women, too—linked hands and formed a living chain; it threw its end out towards such as survived. One man was grasped and with supreme difficulty hauled back from that insatiable maw. Twelve others died. Conceivably more might have been saved, but for the fact that the majority had omitted to don the cork life-jackets which were a part of their recognised equipment. Nor is this omission to be wondered at. The then orthodox lifebelt was a cumbrous, ill-fitting thing—buoyant, maybe, but apt to get in the way of the active muscles when their best effort was most in demand. Remember the Herculean effort these heroes had subjected themselves to during the previous hours of that fatal day. They had salved the crews of six ships—which ships were now no more than mangled flotsam. They had fought an unbroken fight, straining every effort all the time, with no breathing-spells to animate them. When this other call to action came, their bodies were chafed with the cork-jackets; and they, being skilled watermen, realised that the hampering of the bulky protections might doom them to failure. They sacrificed their own chance of life to the urgency of their fellowmen's need out there in the foundering *Merchant*. Their action was like that of a V. C. hero flinging off a gas-mask to lift a wounded comrade from the track of an oncoming tank. So twelve men died—that others might be given a chance of life; and the Book declares that no man has greater love than this. Maybe these Whitby men failed to achieve the spiritual standards of the doctrinaires; but I do not think they need feel any apprehensions when Judgment Day comes round, and they have to stand at the final bar of arraignment, in company, say, with such as trample the faces of the poor, and bear the responsibility for making world-wide war!

Ten widows were made in that brief hopeless struggle; they watched their widowhood with their own blank, horrified eyes. Forty-four children were left fatherless, two other dependents were rendered destitute, that the tale might be truly told. Not much wastage judged by certain standards; but still—something to lament.

Having glutted itself with rarely valuable human life, the storm showed no sign of abatement; and, as is the way of storms, cast about for fresh fodder. That is the hell of the sea—it cannot be sated; it feeds on destruction and remains everlastingly hungry. The rigours in no wise damped the lifesaving ardour of the rest of the Whitby men—who now had a motive of revenge to actuate them in addition to their normal antagonism to white water. The boat being out of commission they recognised that the plight of the stranded *Merchant* was still distressing; so they began to busy themselves with such contrivances as they had available. There was the line-carrying mortar—and they fired a line over the schooner, as she was breaking up; and thanks to Fate the schooner-crew retained sufficient energy and wit to make the line fast and comply with the instructions— hauling in the hawser and the whip, with the breeches buoy; and so permitting themselves to be hauled through the surf one by one to continued existence—the ship parting into her elements as they were drawn ashore.

Not that this Whitby working day was over yet; for before the crew of the *Merchant* were fully recovered from their ordeal, still another distressed vessel came hounding shorewards— the *Urania;* out of hand, and scurrying like a hare before those serried combers that pursued her with cruel glee. She took the ground as all those other hapless ships had done, and at once became the focus of Whitby interest. Handicapped by the loss of the lifeboat, only the mortar apparatus was available as a life-saver; and this gear the men ashore used with cunning and skill. To fire a line to sea against a hurricane is a difficult task; but up there they were not only good boatmen; they were good marksmen as well. They got a line over the *Urania,* and stood by to bring in the people; but as by this time the tide was ebbing fast against the wind; although the steep seas kicked up were very steep they began to diminish in ferocity.

The crew of the *Urania* decided to remain aboard; since seamen are naturally reluctant to leave their ship until all hope of salving her was gone; and aboard her the *Uranians* remained, until the battered wreck showed high and dry on the sandy shelf that was a complete port of missing craft. This gave the people of Whitby time to wipe the caked salt from their faces and snatch a draw of a needed pipe; there was a lull in the rush of business—for an hour or two; when the ninth wreck of the day happened. It is very obvious that the eighth of February, 1861, was a wildish day along the Yorkshire coast. The gale may have lulled a little towards nightfall; but it was only falling back for a fresh leap forward; and by dark it was blowing bigger guns than ever; and so the brig *Tribune* came ashore to add herself to the tribute due the sea.

Darkness was intense; but her distress signals were seen, even if her ghostly actuality was not discerned in the lightning flashes and the phosphorescence of the mangled water. If Whitby had turned a blind eye to these appeals she could hardly be deemed blameworthy; she had already done quite a fair day's work; but these distress signals acted as spurs to a tired horse; and once more the fighting line was stiffened. Still lacking a lifeboat, the mortar apparatus was again unlimbered; but the gale now being at such frenzied height, the missiles fell short or were blown wide; and the unfortunate brig could not be reached.

They had done what they could? No, not by a great deal! Lifeboat out of commission; rockets unavailing—the spirit of the Whitby longshoremen still rode high and undaunted. It was only the sea that was challenging; the sea that had devoured their forebears for unnumbered generations; just the sea—friend to all in peaceful hours, enemy to all when the great winds blew. When the newer pattern lifeboat was established under the shade of St. Hilda's Abbey after the reorganisation of 1851, the old boat that had a long record of invaluable service to its credit, was honourably retired as an emergency boat. It was housed on the harbour's east side—an object of interest to tourists, who were not so plentiful then as they are now; and folks from the inland towns marvelled at its scarred honorability. It was still a floatable craft, however—maybe a bit clumsy, totally lacking all the gadgets devised by an improving science; but fit for such desperate service as was now indicated.

"Get out th'owd boat!" was the cry. This from men who had

[271]

watched their gallent comrades drown a little while before; men who knew that the night-bound sea held ever greater menace than the light-revealed monster! They possess a quality of indomitableness up there; they may bend but they seldom let themselves break. The sea had issued another challenge—very well, let that challenge be accepted. So they got the old battered boat into the comparatively smooth water of the harbour, and pulled it down to the pier. To work out through the piers was recognised as impossible—this boat was not a self-righter; and the pobble boiling there on the bar was fiercer than ever it had been and there was no light for a coxswain to study its whims. On the pier-head was a crane, put there for precisely this purpose; and so the boat was hooked on and bodily swung over the pier and lowered down on the seaward side; where a trifling lee presented itself. There was just sufficient smooth water to hold the boat.

"Well, who's coming?" was asked stolidly, without any melodramatic posturings.

Thirteen men were forthcoming—no, more than that, many more; but thirteen were chosen. They took their places in the old boat and were lowered down into the fret.

"All right, lads—let her go!" They went across the watery grave of their townmates. They were attacked by that pitiless sea; but they suppled their backs—these were the older men, in honourable retirement—and they made the ashen blades bend like whips. They swung and lifted and recovered; they swung and lifted and recovered; until they got the old fearless rhythm; and the boat stole out of its shelter to open water, as it had done in the misted years of the past. Foot by foot, yard by yard, it ate up the intervening distance, beyond which the wan flares burned with diminishing brilliance; and it crept its strenuous way to the *Tribune*.

She was in sorry case; darkness hampered their efforts. The operations were prolonged; and the men regretted that they were only able to save a proportion of the crew—they missed one. They felt they could never forgive themselves for such a failure—one man lost from the crews of nine ships! It seemed a reflection on their ability. They believed that Fate was working against them. It didn't seem right, somehow—to lose this solitary soul, when they'd set their dogged hearts on succouring everyone thrown on to their responsibility. Personally, I think they needn't have worried. The sea might have had the last word; but with whom remained the victory it is for history to tell.

And that is why the legend was current in Whitby, before the war—it may be so still—that, when it was blowing big guns, the longshoremen took out the new boat to salve such as came driving on to those treacherous sands; but when it was really blowing—blowing, mark you!—they let the new boat rest in its shed and put out in the old boat that they'd proved through the dauntless years!

And anyone who may think that this is an overcoloured story, with imagination trifling with cold, stark fact, need only visit the Whitby Parish Church next time he is in that vicinity, and there he will see, engraved enduringly, the record of a certain Whitby day; together with the names of the men who died that the honour of Whitby might shine bright through all the years to be.

What England thought of it all is evident. Perishing in the course of their simple duty, these men's dependents were automatically thrown on the care of the R. N. L. I. which safeguards such dependents as part of its wideflung activities. But the Vicar of Whitby, who saw the work, and comforted the afflicted and buried such dead as the sea relinquished, told the story in the Press; and England was moved to its deeps. It subscribed £5,-000 for the benefit of those who had been spectators of that great and inspiring tragedy; but the great reward of all lies in the fact that the folk of Whitby know that when the call came it was obeyed unflinchingly, tirelessly, to the death—for that is Whitby fashion.

CHAPTER XVI

TRAGEDY ON THE WEST COAST.... ....

NOT that indomitable courage is by any means a prerogative of the bleak East Coast, where sea-fighting is concerned. I have a time-dimmed recollection of being taken by my nurse as a tiny child to see a lifeboat about which seemed to cling, even in childish fancy, an aura of terror and mystical dread. I was lifted in jerseyed arms to touch the craft; and I heard the boathouse keeper talk slowly and without overmuch emphasis to my nurse for a long time; whilst I was given a model lifeboat to amuse myself with. Further, this veteran produced a much worn trifle of timber which was polished like stone; and I was given to understand that this was actually a fragment of a wreck that had spelt disaster to the boat and to many men. I am of the opinion that this old boat-keeper had been one of the crew of the St. Anne's boat during the tragedy of 1886, but am unable to verify my belief; for he must be dead long since, as it was only six months after the accident that I holidayed in St. Anne's-on-Sea; and that is forty-odd years ago.

If he were indeed a protagonist of that memorable occurrence, I must have been told the story as it happened. I know that landladies and such friends as my nurse hushed their voices when they mentioned "The Boat"—and I feel certain that had I been of age and intelligence sufficient to receive information, I might now have been in a position to tell the story as it well deserves to be told.

It was on the night of the 9th of December, 1886, when the watchman at the Southport lifeboat house observed signals of distress soaring cloudwards out of a noisy darkness. To see such signals is to precipitate action; he sounded the alarm; and the crew assembled without loss of time; the earmarked horses were brought clattering down and hooked in to the lifeboat carriage; and since the position of the wreck was three miles and more westward of the boat-station, the convoy set out across the hard, level sands; since it is easier to propel a boat in this fashion than against a rough sea. Half a mile or so to the westward of the wreck—that is, to windward, the horses were unlimbered; the boat-carriage was thrust into the sea; the boat floated off, the big ashen oars bit the water, and the Southport boat was off and away. She had been built in 1874; and had made eleven hard-weather rescues in her twelve years of existence. She had been instrumental in saving 55 lives; and had further aided a vessel, that otherwise must have perished, to safe anchorage. A good boat, manned by stalwarts; all of them, boat and men, with a record to be proud of.

The *Eliza Fernley*—such being the name of the boat, after its donor—made a stiff fight of it. The quality of the weather may best be estimated by the fact that it was not until one o'clock that the wreck was reached—the German barque *Mexico*—the fragment of which my young eyes saw.

So far, so good. Strenuous work enough, but nothing, perhaps, out of the ordinary—a mere ordinary lifeboatman's evening. Having reached the neighborhood of the wreck, preparations were promptly made to deal with the situation, for the *Mexico* was in evil case—hard-stranded, with big seas boiling over her and her hull crumbling away piecemeal to the sea's attacks, which were not less venomous than those of the East Coast. The lifeboat's anchor was readied. The old useful procedure was about to be adopted—the wreck was to be approached from the weather-side. There is always a fear of ragged wreckage to leeward on which a boat might easily come to grief; and the weather-side is the favourite line of attack. Anchor to windward, veer out cable, ease the boat down to within

[275]

touching distance—there you have the plan. As they were about to let the anchor go, a big sea came hurtling; broke under the boat's bow, and promptly capsized her. Twelve feet of anchor chain with the anchor had run out; and it formed a drag to prevent the *Eliza Fernley* righting herself. Consequently she floated bottom-up, with a number of her hardy crew under her, pinned by the thwarts. Exactly how many were there is doubtful; for the statements collected later were conflicting. Some said as many as nine men were imprisoned there; some said six—but at least six were caught.

The evidence went to show that the boat made several gallant attempts to right herself; but the odds were against her. That anchor and chain ballasted her the wrong way, and the swing that her capsizing gave her was checked. Further, certain of the crew, clinging to her lifelines, added their weight and leverage; and so the boat remained bottom upwards.

Realising that tragedy had happened to those who had done so nobly in the effort to save them, the people of the *Mexico* continued their appeals for help; and these repeated signals spurred on the crew of the St. Anne's lifeboat to added effort. This boat had got the warning at 9:15 p. m. and by the time the crew were summoned, horses procured, and the boat got down to the slip, it was after ten o'clock. Got into the water by dint of strenuous energy, she started away to answer the wan flares in the yelling gloom; as is the fashion of the lifeboat crew, whether east coast or west, north coast or south. The striking fact about lifeboat work is that the louder the challenge, the more onerous the conditions, the more readily these longshoremen respond. It is a very magnificent fighting spirit; and another aspect of its quality was evinced during the Great War, when this type of manhood manned our minesweeping trawlers and decoy ships, and helped to subjugate the enemy in his submarine activities.

It was a long, hard pull for the St. Anne's men; and after labouring gallantly at the oars for a matter of five hundred yards or so, they decided that canvas should do what ash could not.

They put three reefs in their mainsail, and set it; and, gunwale awash, tacked out across the Salt Horse Bank. Fifteen proved men were in her; men who knew boat-work from A to Z. Zealots all, they were. Let this be testimony of their quality.

The coxswain was a man inured to the sea-hazard through many bitter years. He understood the tricks and devices of those seas better than any man in the neighbourhood, it seems certain. But his health was in bad shape. Evidence was led later to prove that he was physically unfitted for this strenuous ordeal; he walked under the shadow of death. Riddled with consumption as he was, his doctor had given him only a matter of three months longer to live. Doubtless he preferred the risk of a man's death suddenly to the lingering torment of a death in bed. He did not hesitate when the call came; and he took out his boat as hardily as ever he had done. Blowing in thickening squalls as it was, with the December murk clinging terribly, he never hesitated. Two or three of the oarsmen also laboured under physical disability: and one at least of them deserves special mention, when heroism is under consideration. Times were bad along the West Coast that winter; a succession of gales kept the fishing fleet idle; and this man—Bonney, may his name be honoured where bravery is known—had been in the habit of starving himself in order to keep wife and children fed to repletion. During the day before the call came, Bonney had eaten nothing more sustaining than a single basin of gruel; and it was with an empty stomach and a hunger-weakened physique that he took his seat on the thwart of the St. Anne's boat that direful night.

So we see the boat, manned by an emaciated, half-spectral crew, ratching her way through the darkness, heading as steadily as wind and sea permitted for where the signal flares burned low. We see her people fighting to reach the unfortunate *Mexico* —fighting against odds; and—we see little more. Something terrible happened out there; something mysterious. A good boat, brave, tried men—and nothing of a tale ever to tell; for on the morning of December 10th the St. Anne's lifeboat was discovered on the beach, bottom up, with only her pitiful dead to man her.

Three limp bodies were there beneath her, their knees still gripping the thwarts; and the tale of what transpired could only be surmised; never accurately known. Maybe the enfeebled coxswain made an error of judgment; maybe the forces of Nature were too strong for him. That the weather was affrighting we have the evidence of the capsized Southport boat to prove. Conceivably a hard squall raced down and took her by the lee, before the men, trimming the boat by their weight to windward, had time to shift across. Anything might have happened—the boat was lost; or, at least, her full crew of fifteen men were dead—staunchly, at the post of duty, gilding the sad chapter with the glory of their courage.

Stark she lay there in the grey December noon: a memorial to coastwise determination and humanity. There were men perishing out in the wild night, the St. Anne's boat must do its best—and that its best fell short of completeness in no wise lessens the worth of the effort made.

Meantime, the Southport boat was enduring her own Gethsemane. Such of her crew as were not imprisoned under the overturned craft endeavoured to right her; since, in their estimation, the work required of them was still to do. They failed. They died whilst trying, most of them. Unable to do anything of value they found themselves compelled to cling to the capsized fabric, and so clinging were hammered into stupor by the endless procession of hurrying waves, each one more venomous than its precursor. They could see the distress flares burning from the wrecked *Mexico;* and they could lend no hand to succour the afflicted. All they could do was drift with the drifting boat—their cries unheeded in the hell-broth. So through the night they swung hither and thither; now lifted as if to crash down on the wreck's parting hull; now swept into deep troughs that stank of the sea's dead things. Up and down through the hours—and snow-squall driving on the heels of snow-squall; spindrift lashing—minutes dragging tediously; until the in-running tide, weary of its grim play, cast boat and men to rest upon the drenched and shining sands three miles west of its home-place at three o'clock in the morning of the 10th of December. News of its tragic arrival spread; the townsfolk hurried down to see for themselves what the sea had wrought them. An overturned boat, a stretch of chain, a futile anchor, that was all—save that under the boat were the bodies of three dead men: Wright, Rigby and Jackson; whilst another man, barely living, was discovered by the light of the torches, prone and suffering some distance away, bedded in the sands. He died shortly afterwards without being able to give any coherent account of what had transpired—the boat had capsized; that was all he knew.

Near the stranded boat another man was found, standing to his knees in a pool of water, dazed, helpless—paralysed by ordeal. He had clung to the boat until she took the ground, was torn from his holding, and simply remained as he was, unaware of being alive. They tended him with care; they muffled him in wrappings, because he was blue and stiff with the biting cold; and they hurried him to the hospital; but as they took him in he died—another victim to duty. Two other men, named John Jackson and Henry Robinson, were brought to shore by the boat, still alive. They knew shipmates still survived; but they were too stupefied to lend a hand in their behalf. So far as they could report those under the boat were entangled in the gear of the masts and sails, or mixed up with the oars; unable to win free of the capsized hull, and so were drowned like rats in a trap. Thirteen heroes lost in all; two were saved alive; thus so far the *Mexico* had cost twenty-eight brave lives. And still she was appealing to the merciless night for succour.

It remained for the Lytham boat to effect the rescue of her people. She had seen the signals; she, too, had put out, and the luck of the night was with her; she succeeded where her equally gallant fellows failed, and brought the people of the wreck ashore without so much as knowing that calamity had befallen the boats from Southport and St. Anne's. So the Lancashire coast was plunged into mourning; and that shadow still remained when I, a child, was lifted to inspect the boat of death, and the lifeboatman pointed with an unsteady finger seawards to the sandbank between Southport and Formby as the site of Lancashire's blackest coastwise tragedy.

CHAPTER XVII

PREY OF THE MANACLES

THIRTEEN years later this present writer scurried into Falmouth in a distressed windjammer, and found a cloud of gloom as thick as that which shadowed the Lancashire coast, hanging over the Cornish harbour. The *Mohegan* had been lost on the Manacles, and the pilot who came to take our wounded ship to welcome moorings had been one of the lifeboatmen who had gone out to help her in her death-throes.

Whether the loss of the *Mohegan* rightly belongs to the category of wrecks or that of lifeboats is a moot question; it belongs by rights to both, I imagine. In any event, lost the *Mohegan* was —under circumstances that are as curious and heartrending as any sea-tragedy known. The *Mohegan* was an intermediate boat; a four-masted steamer, on the New York run; and on October 13th, 1899, she left London for the United States, with a part cargo only—general, coal and the like; her ballast tanks filled to give her steadiness in the bad weather to be expected across the Western Ocean.

With a crew of ninety-seven, with an additional seven cattlemen taking return passage after bullwhacking their way eastward, she picked up at Gravesend fifty-three passengers for transit to the land of the free. She made good going down-channel, in fine weather notwithstanding the portent of her sailing-day, and on the 14th, at 2:40 p.m. she made her number off Prawle Point and reported herself "All well." She was then distant three miles from the land, steaming sedately; not a fast ship but a steady-going big ship, built for general utility.

By 5 p.m. she had reached Rame Head, and was seen from the

[281]

shore-station at that point, although she did not signal; but her funnel was characteristic. She was then six or seven miles away from the Eddystone; and still later, between six and seven p. m. certain watchers at Falmouth saw her vivid lights in plain view, together with red flares, which were simply her name-signals; so far as is known.

Shortly before seven o'clock on this night; as black, said our pilot, "as the hobs of hell"; the coxswain of the lifeboat stationed at Porthoustock discerned a steamer's white masthead light in such an unaccustomed position that it was evident to him that any ship, pursuing such a course as was indicated, was in considerable danger. This precarious situation had also been observed by other watchers near at hand; and a flare was burned to warn the *Mohegan* of her peril. But the coxswain of the Porthoustock boat was not satisfied with this sort of preventive action; he sent out the call and got his boat into the water without any loss of time; because a fresh gale had sprung up and the sea was running high—so that its roar as it hurled itself over the relentless Manacles, most dangerous of reefs off a dangerous stretch of coast, dominated the black and strenuous night. He was a wise, sea-suspicious man, this coxswain; one who understood that when the Manacles' teeth were bared troubles hung in the offing for somebody. As the lifeboat made in the direction of the Manacles, the coxswain burned a white flare, as warning and promise both; but he received no answer to this signal. The only response obtained was grim. Soon after burning the flare, an overturned ship's lifeboat was seen showing wanly; with two men clinging to its keel. Their weak cries had been unheard in the sea-thresh; but a white boat carries a curious kind of glimmer with it on the darkest of nights; and so keen eyes detected its presence in the lifeboat's track. These two men were saved. As this work was in progress, hollow, despairing cries became audible from underneath the boat. Being a man of action the coxswain swung a grapnel to the keel, and, putting a strain on the rope, ordered his crew to pull like heroes; in this way he righted the boat; and found in its water-filled bottom one infant —dead—and two women—alive.

A stout fellow, this lifeboat coxswain; a man of ready resource! One of these two women was assisted into the boat, where she presently died, having endured unspeakable agony and suspense. But the second woman was hopelessly jammed underneath a thwart. A word to his bowman, and the coxswain had solved this problem. The bowman tore an axe from its cleats and watching his chance, leaped from boat to boat, smashed the thwart to splinters and extricated the unfortunate woman. She was unable to make any helpful statement. The gloom persisted unbroken; there was the surge of breakers, the hum and drone of the gale; of the *Mohegan* that had belched forth these wan evidences of her tragedy, remained no sign. The lifeboat coxswain thereupon burned a flare as indication to Falmouth that more assistance was required in order to make a comprehensive search; for in darkness even a large ship can go a-missing without leaving any noticeable trace.

As the flares burnt out, those in the lifeboat heard more cries of distress and proceeded to discover their source, coming upon another ship's lifeboat, badly damaged by rocks, practically full to the gunwale with water, and containing twenty-four people, who seemed to know little about what had happened and were chiefly concerned with getting ashore—anywhere. Considering that wherever they turned were sharp-fanged rocks, their chances of escape would have been problematical; as it was, they were taken aboard the Porthoustock boat, which, being comfortably filled, proceeded back to its base, arriving there at about ten p. m., still mystified as to what had really occurred.

Meantime, the Falmouth, Polperro and Cadgwith lifeboats started out towards the signals burned by the Porthoustock boat; and with these boats went a couple of those sturdy tugs for which Falmouth in windjamming days was famous; stout craft capable of keeping the sea in the worst weather offering on that tormented coast.

"If only they'd shown a light, any sort of light," complained the pilot who told me the story, "we'd likely have got them all off; but there it was—black as the pit; us not knowing rightly where she was, couldn't see anything, couldn't hear anything above the breakers. If someone had just burnt a newspaper to give us a line—! If anyone'd struck so much as a match, we might have done a bit of good; but there you are—she was black-dark, invisible." The tugs and lifeboats cruised three times clean round the reef on which the *Mohegan* had impaled herself whilst men were drowning or being battered to pieces on the adamantine rocks. For what had happened was simple, grimly so. She was a modern ship, and fitted with electric lighting plant; with no alternative oil lamps available. These were stowed away below in the lamp-locker. The *Mohegan,* owing, it was supposed, to compass defects, or to over-confidence, was steering a wrong course from the Eddystone—that was what the signal station noticed when it tried to burn her off. Probably—real facts can never be known—the burning of those warnings ashore was the first intimation to the ship's navigating staff that anything was amiss. The course steered was west by north; from the Eddystone it should have been nearer west by south; which is a very different matter, but such an error could easily occur when the wheel was being relieved, by the one man making the slight mistake "North" and "South"; or by the relieving quartermaster taking the course wrongly from his opposite number's lips. When the officer of the watch realised that something was at fault, he would instinctively order the helmsman to starboard his helm—to get away from the warning lights. It was whilst the ship was so swinging that she struck the fearsome rocks; and sealed her doom, without possibility of salvation. As she struck, she listed wildly; the shock caused her dynamos to cease functioning; and as there were no storage batteries, no alternative supply of light, every lamp was instantly extinguished, and the recently gaily lighted ship plunged into profound gloom. Having listed so severely, and backed off the fangs, the *Mohegan* began to sink by the bow, going rapidly; and the lamp-lockers were in the forecastle, which was immediately swamped with water and rendered inaccessible. Hence the reason why no lights were shown at a time when light was of vital necessity. Survivor after survivor stated that an attempt was made to attract attention by firing the detonating socket signals with which every seagoing ship must be provided. Such signals are fired by being placed in an inclined socket which is clamped to the bridge; a firing-tube is inserted, and a lanyard pulled, whereupon there is a heavy explosion, succeeded by the upward soaring of a vivid ball of fire which bursts with an added detonation on reaching its height, and dissolves in sparks. Mark this: the socket tube of the *Mohegan* from which her signals only could be fired, was on the canted side; it was difficult to fit and discharge them; and when fired they simply dropped into the water or hit the adjacent rocks and lost their effect, being invisible from the side by which the lifeboat first approached. Those red flares seen by the watchers at Falmouth were the only visible communication with the outside world; for the rest the *Mohegan* drowned in the noisy darkness. For she sank within fifteen minutes of striking; though, as it was shoal water that took her, her masts and funnels remained in view—I saw them—for some considerable time. To these upstanding remnants of a recently proud ship, men and women clung distracted, stunned by the amazing swiftness of the calamity; blinded and rendered hysterical by the overwhelming blackness of that unillumined night.

The Porthoustock boat hurried ashore and landed her rescued; then put out again and pulled strenuously in the direction of the Manacles. Within hail of this ugly reef, shrieks and cries became audible; whereupon the coxswain anchored, having found his target. They searched the blackness and after much effort distinguished certain outlines; they lifted anchor and headed that way—but on account of the fierce tide and the crashing breakers, dared not adventure too closely. But they burnt a flare to hearten the many who clung to rigging and funnels; and a man, Quartermaster Juddery, let his name he exalted! realising the difficulty besetting the lifeboat, dived over and swam to the boat, returning with a lifeline, and thereby saved all the people clinging to what remained above water. After tricky manœuvring, the lifeboat contrived to succour all survivors—some hanging to the funnels, some to the upper-works; after which, gingerly, the rocks around were carefully searched ; but there was no abiding place amongst those black fangs laced with ugly surf; and the boat decided to return to port, having done a creditable night's work. Not satisfied with its actual haul, the crew burned flares the whole way home, in hope that some survivor might be clinging to loose wreckage, or washed into some cranny of the rocks. The whole neighbourhood was a graveyard—in that gale it was a living hell. But no other survivors were there; and the lifeboat's loads represented practically all the saved— forty-four in number, as against 106 drowned and broken on the rocks; though a tug towing the Falmouth boat contrived to collect one man, and the coastguards ashore picked two or three out of the surf when they were in their last extremity.

Captain and all officers perished; so the truth was never told of that fatal mistake. But the Porthoustock lifeboat had accounted for itself, come what might.

CHAPTER XVIII

A CAISTER CHAPTER

ELEVEN o'clock on a wild East Coast night in December, 1901 —a whole gale bellowing from the N. N. E.— a nasty quarter in the grim North Sea—a high broken sea racing landwards; with thick rain and mist obscuring the outlook—such was the stage set when the Cockle Lightship hard by Caister set off the signal denoting disaster. A ship had gone ashore in the flurry on the Barber Sands, which the lightship was set to guard. The signal was picked up by the Caister lifeboat station; and without delay —that being the lifeboat habit—the Caister No. 2 boat, *Beauchamp,* was got ready for launching. As she went down the slipway heavy seas came triumphantly roaring, not anxious to be robbed of promised spoil, and washed the boat off its launching skids, piling it ashore. As this sort of thing was all a part of an average night's work, the Caister men swore and tackled the capsized craft, running her up the beach in readiness for another attempt. Honest-to-goodness lifeboatmen don't lose heart after one setback; and these Caister heroes were of the same stamp as the veterans of Whitby, higher up the stark East Coast, where sea-fighting is more or less recreation. Dark as pitch it was, and piercingly cold, that November night on the verge of the North Sea; but the boat was needed, consequently the boat had to go. Difficulties presented themselves: a lifeboat of the modern type is no cockleshell to be lifted by hand and carried where one wills. These stout fellows got skids and warps and tackles, and pulley-hauled the *Beauchamp* back to the launching ways, and got her afloat after three hours of the kind of work men are required to do in nightmares.

Once afloat, things promised to improve. Such sail as could be carried was hoisted; and the watchers ashore saw her scudding swiftly into the sea-fog, apparently in perfect condition and control.

"She'm all right, be old boat," the watchers decided. They had all borne a hand in the strenuous struggle to get the boat away; all were drenched to the skin and chilled to the marrow. "We'll get home for a change—come back afore she returns!" They slipped away from the thunderous strand, yet reluctantly, for their hearts were with the absent boat rather than with their own comforts, but James Hazlett, seventy-eight years young, the boat's assistant coxswain of many years' standing, elected to remain. He had hostages in the boat—a son, a son-in-law, two grandsons. Since Hazlett had been in the forefront of the battle during the first and second launchings, he was rather wetter than most; but he was more accustomed to the rigours of a winter night, so he remained at his watchman's post.

He saw the boat shape away on the port tack, gunwale under because the gale was high. She disappeared from the ken of his wise old eyes, beating a dreary way towards the sandbank, where the distress signals occasionally showed in the clear dead to windward.

Drawing near to the goal, after much effort, the coxswain of the *Beauchamp* wore her round, to adjust his mizen; not yet set. Satisfied that all was well, he stood shorewards on the starboard tack, the wind screaming defiance and the surf very noisy, and went about again to lay another board out towards his destination. Hazlett saw this manœuvre. Not making much headway on this new tack the boat was again wore round on the shoreward tack; and, when in the backwash of the surf, tacked yet again—but this time she missed stays. That is to say, as she came roaring up into the wind's eye on a full lee helm, instead of running through the wind and falling off on the other tack, she refused to swing, and her canvas fell a-shiver. Promptly the coxswain laid his mizen aback and put up his helm, so that the boat would fall off on the old tack, and, gathering headway, be ready for another attempt. Up she came roaring into the roaring wind once more; and once again she missed stays. Probably the water was too shallow and broken to stand up against her keel; whatever the cause, miss stays she did, and on this second failure, drifted clean into the scurry of the surf.

Realising that it was clean out of the question now to avoid being driven ashore, the boat coxswain dropped his mizen with a run, and put his helm up, so that the boat's head would come round and she would run fairly up the beach as if returning ordinarily. Just as he was rightly headed for temporary safety, an incoming breaker caught the boat, pushed her bow on to the sand about fifty yards north of her launching slip; and another great monster, hurrying up to enquire, lashed the boat's quarter savagely, and capsized her in an instant.

With her masts snapped off short, the lifeboat crew were pinned beneath the overturned craft. It was a good boat, of the Norfolk and Suffolk non-self-righting type, tested under most rigorous conditions and esteemed safe from all danger. The men of the Norfolk coast preferred this type of non-self-righting boat, and the R. N. L. I. always give consideration to the desires of the local crews when stationing a boat. This *Beauchamp* had successfully survived her tests. She was of five tons' weight when empty; and when afloat with full crew and impedimenta it required the weights of thirty-six men to bring her gunwale down to a level with the water; so that her reserve of buoyancy was considerable. This even when her water-ballast tanks were full; when they were emptied, as they would be with a fuller load, she could carry many more people with comparative safety. But the sea had caught her treacherously; and she lay there on the washed sands very hopelessly at three o'clock on a winter's morning, when landfolk were unconscious of the hardships attending on sea-service.

At this time came a younger Hazlett—a fruitful family—to collogue with his veteran grandfather. Young Frederick Hazlett had gone home to change; having done so he joined his grandfather in his solitary watch, advised him to get under shelter, was scorned; and then checked in his argument.

"Sounds like I heard someone shouting—down there by water's edge," he declared. Both men instantly charged down in the direction of the cries, and, horrified, discovered the overturned boat washing aimlessly in the surf. The wind-hounded tide was running bitterly; not only were the inrushing waves leaping high and crashing down with a force enough to shake the land; but the backwash scour was a horror. In such a backwash a very strong man may easily lose his foothold and be swept out to deep water, where he stands not one chance in a hundred of saving his life; but, well knowing these facts, the older of the two Hazlett men instantly tore down to tide-mark; battled his way into the clamorous surf, and contrived to get a lionlike grip on his son-in-law: Charles Knight; who, pinned under the boat, was none the less struggling gamely to release himself. Inspired by such an example, young Frederick Hazlett also charged down, and after a bit of wild scrabbling was able to secure a hold on another of the distressed crew: John Hubbard.

Old Hazlett lugged his salvage clear with effort, and, hauling him upright or thereabouts, assisted him with his ancient strength through the swill and up the beach, establishing him in safety beyond the reach of the leaping surf. That was pretty good for a man almost an octogenarian; but old men are sometimes selfish in their habits; and old Hazlett was far from satisfied with a haul of one. He consequently hurried back to the boat and made another dive; this time securing a grandson, Walter Hazlett. With infinite difficulty, battered incessantly by the inrushing breakers, old Hazlett contrived to tear his grandson clear and tow and lift and aid him through the broth to firm standing ashore. The younger Hazlett endured just as much in salving his one man; but there was a quality of doggedness in this salt-water breed that refused to admit defeat. It was well this was so; otherwise there would not have been a single member of the *Beauchamp's* crew saved that night of mourning. As it was, nine men perished in their gallantry. The increasing rigour of that storm forbade further attempts to reach the capsized boat, lying there forlornly in the tumultuous surf; and the shore-watchers could only attempt the impossible and await the merciless mercy of the sea to give them back their dead. It was a night of horror presaging a pitiful dawn. Between the Hazletts' heroic efforts and the hour of eleven in the morning, eight bodies were washed out from under the drowned boat, and stranded here and there along the lonely sands—eight poor martyrs to duty and the savagery of the sea. By eleven-fifteen the sea allowed the people ashore to approach the boat, and working gallantly they righted her—securing from her the last victims. One man was washed to sea and never seen again. So nine Caister men died that dire night; and the youngest of them was a boy of nineteen only—young Harry Knight, who acted notably up to his name, as this was his first trip in the boat; and his service was more leal, I fancy, than that of any mailed knight who ever waited at a cross-roads to avow the inimitable fairness of his ladye in the face of all-comers. The youngest was taken by the sea; the oldest survived—after doing a task of work that, told of curtly, deserves to rank amongst the finest heroisms ever perpetrated by our coastwise folks.

This is the stamp of men from whose iron ranks the lifeboat crews of our bitter coasts are recruited. These are the men who, when wind and sea are doing their worst, face the onus of their duty without hesitation or tremor; eager to do battle with salt water so long as their hearts beat; and who, more often than not, die splendidly in harness, giving life that others might remain alive.

Old James Hazlett, Senr., had been doing this sort of thing for half a century when he was called on to succour his own kin; his service with the lifeboats was measured by fifty years, no less; and his bit of work with the *Beauchamp* seems to set a shining crown on his heroism. No wonder the R. N. L. I. gave him their gold medal—most treasured decoration in the sea-fighting service, together with a copy of the vote awarding it to him inscribed on vellum and framed, and a purse of twenty-five guineas; by way of appreciating the sinewy staunchness of a seventy-eight-year-old Trojan who could remain working furiously on an exposed beach for twelve hours, drenched and redrenched, and without so much as a bite of food to cheer him. But of such are the salt of the sea made. There are, thank God, thousands like old Hazlett, ready and anxious to answer the boom of the distress signal from the misted wastes beyond.

CHAPTER XIX

MEN OF ZETLAND AND MEN OF RYE

THEY will tell you that the stamina and courage of our British race are undergoing serious change; that the ancient spirit which steeled our people to refuse to admit defeat even though the odds are very great, is growing extinct; that we threaten to become a soft-handed, dilettante race content to dwell in the brightness of our forefathers' glory. It may be so—inland; but around our coasts, where men are trained in a never-ending war against the cruellest foe known to mankind—a foe that never allows mercy to enter into its schemes—the tale to be told is different.

In a record of sea-hazard, disaster and gallantry such as the foregoing chapters show, one is apt to gather the impression that the major part of our tribute to the greedy sea has been paid in the remoter past. That is not so. Although conditions alter, the sea remains ever the same: a dreaded enemy, unalterable in its greed. But by its own ferocity it has raised up a breed of men who, whilst respecting its savagery, laugh at its threats; and continue, as they will continue through the coming years, to brave its dangers without so much as a hint of faltering. Let the narrative of the Zetland lifeboat and the Rye lifeboat bridge the gulf between past and present day.

February 20th, 1914—year of omen for the world!—the Norwegian schooner *Mexico,* from South American ports to Liverpool, made a mistake in her bearings and contrived to run herself ashore off the south coast of Ireland. Taking the merciless ground in Bannon Bay, she began to bump heavily on the rocks. It was heavy weather at the time, with the usual big, destructive sea running high. Even before the schooner struck, her parlous plight was plainly evident to the watchers of the Zetland boat, *Helen Blake;* and, the crew of this boat being collected, she immediately set out to give assistance. Before the boat could approach the *Mexico,* she had piled herself up on the rocks and was tearing herself about in a destructive fashion. Seeing this, then men of the *Helen Blake* redoubled their efforts, but when they had gained a point within fifty yards of the wreck, the lifeboat was struck by a heavy breaker which instantly filled her to the thwarts. The coxswain of the boat ordered the anchor to be let go; before it could find holding on the bottom, and so bring up the *Helen Blake,* a serried phalanx of breakers piled up and over the boat; hurled her against the rocks nearby—sharp as dog's teeth, only a thousand times more formidable—and smashed it to fragments.

Carrying fourteen of a crew as she did, the *Helen Blake* was doomed to tragedy. As she was borne to destruction, nine of her men were torn from her and lost for ever; but the remaining five contrived to swim and fight a way to the island on which the *Mexico* had docked herself: South Keenagh Island. Being lifeboatmen, and consequently tutored to a keen sense of duty, instead of shaking themselves and calling it a day, they promptly set about assisting the men of the schooner. This was a difficult task; but these gallant Irishmen did it—they beat a way to the wreck, and literally compelled eight men of the schooner's crew to save themselves ashore by means of ropes. They got them on to the rocky, deserted island, they gave them life; but they were unable to give them much more. For, with the gale persisting and cutting off all communication with the mainland, it was impossible to secure food, water or other shelter than the lee of the insufficient rock-spurs. Until the 23rd of February, these men were compelled to make the best of it in these comfortless circumstances. During this period the drenched and harassed survivors had a total diet of two tins of preserved meat, very small; a few limpets torn from the rocks;

a drop of brandy and half a pint of wine, which the captain of the *Mexico* had found possible to bring ashore with him. Not an extensive menu for thirteen able-bodied men. The rock-spurs afforded practically no shelter; seas washed the haven of refuge without cessation. There was nothing to do but flatten themselves and wait for better times. This gale was the worst ever known in years on Ireland's South Coast. One member of the schooner's crew found it impossible to endure the awful rigours; he died of exhaustion; and his companions in distress buried him as best they could; spreading rags of canvas over his body and weighing them down with poor sods of earth torn from the interstices of the rocks.

Not that their sorry plight had gone unnoticed on the mainland. On February 20th and 21st, the Kilmore lifeboat made three gallant, if unsuccessful, attempts to get in touch with them, but on each occasion was beaten back by the ferocity of the seas. A heavy ground swell ran constantly; and this, coupled with the surface breakers, deterred even those stout-souled men. Similarly, the Wexford lifeboat made frantic efforts to reach the sufferers; no result was obtained; and the Dunmore East lifeboat threw herself into the fight on the 22nd, equally unsuccessfully.

On the morning of the 23rd the Wexford boat was summoned to the fighting-line again by telephone; and she and the Dunmore East boat set off in the darkness to bring succour to men who, it was felt, sorely needed it. The weather conditions were still terrible; the island was practically unapproachable; but after waiting, the sea subsided somewhat and the Dunmore East boat made another essay. She had to cruise clean round the island before it was possible to find a sufficiently sheltered nook to permit her to drop her anchor, 100 yards from shore; and a stick rocket was fired, with a line attached. Having got hold of this codline, the men of the Zetland boat hauled in and endeavoured to secure the skiff-buoy that was attached; a sea swept the skiff among the rocks and smashed it to splinters. But an

[295]

ordinary lifebuoy had been lashed to the skiff and this was secured. Forgetting their own need, the Zetland men endeavoured to coax and cajole the crew of the schooner into attempting a precarious journey and being drawn through the surf; but the dazed and battered men were reluctant to help themselves, and only two consented to undergo the ordeal by water.

Since matters were not improving, the Wexford boat now took a hand; and, anchoring, sent off two of her hardier men in a tiny punt, which effected communication with the rocks, and collected two survivors. Elated by this victory, they tried again, making four trips in all, and by dint of gathering in two at a time—the punt's capacity—the stranded sufferers were salved, after strenuous, heroic effort. On the second trip made by the punt—this shows the conditions—the waves caught her and slammed her cruelly on the rocks, staving her timbers; causing her to leak badly. The lifeboatmen were resourceful; they jammed a loaf of bread and some casual packing into the gap and carried on, thereby bringing all they had set out to save, safely ashore; though nine of the Zetland boat's men had "lost the number of their mess".

During the war-years our coastwise lifeboat heroes were kept busy, both at their lawful trade, and also otherwise; hunting life instead of saving it. But their work during this period is worthy an entire volume to itself, and may not even be touched on here in a final chapter which must sum up in one episode all the cumulative tragedy, woe and suffering that wait constantly on such as use the sea, whether the deeper waters of the distant oceans or the ragged fringes of the coastwise surf.

Come we then to a tragedy the details of which are still so present in the national mind that recapitulation of the facts seems hardly necessary. Yet it is well that we should remember all we owe to the sea and how we, by deputy, contrive to pay that century-long debt.

On November 15th, 1928, the coastguard station at Rye Harbour—whence long ago the cogs and galliasses, the hoys and

great ships of one of the principal of the Cinque Ports were apt
to convey great companies of mail-clad knights in search of er-
rantry, and men-at-arms in search of plunder, to the shores of
adventure-giving France—received a message stating that a
Latvian vessel, the *Alice,* was in grave danger, drifting helpless
on a south-west by westerly bearing some eight miles distant
from Dungeness. This was at about five o'clock on a tempestuous Channel morning. The message was conveyed to the lifeboat station; and the entire adult manhood of Rye Harbour—
all that were capable of manning an oar, at all events—set to
work to get the boat, *Mary Stanford,* along to the launching slip,
with their women and children to cheer them on and suffer the
apprehensions common to dependents on such strenuous occasions.

It was a savage morning, incredibly so. November of 1928
was notorious for the frequency and intensity of its storms; and
this, on the 15th of the month, was much about the worst of the
entire series. Nothing deterred, however, by the threat of wind
and sea, the *Mary Stanford* was successfully launched by 6.45
a.m., tide then being at full ebb; a thick, blinding rain driving
before the shrieking thrust of the south-west gale; and the sea
running large and threateningly. The men of Rye took no account of such trifles in their hard-working, devoted existence,
and got to their places in the big boat, each man equipped with
a life-belt of a pattern sanctioned and approved by the R.N.L.I.
They set about their work in Rye fashion—than which can be no
greater praise—for they were of a stock that had never been deterred by anything the elements could do through something
like a thousand years. Their remoter forebears had braved the
Channel hazards to rescue escaping Royalists from France; they
had set out in trifling craft to harass the lumbering flanks of the
great Spanish Armada; they had outwitted the Revenue men
and run rich cargoes of contraband; and the fine spirit that ani-
mated their ancestors was present in full measure in these, their
latterday descendants.

Grey-white over green the Channel seas ran steeply; massing in torrential might, leaping, striking, recoiling, launching viper blows; torn into blinding spume by the ravening tempest. England, unknowing, turned in its sleep and reviled the chatter of windows and the occasional crash of falling slates, what time the men of Rye Harbour went out to die.

Five minutes after the boat was launched and away, another message was received by the coastguard station to the effect that the crew of the Latvian ship had been picked off their foundering craft by another steamer which had sighted the *Alice* and bravely done its duty towards a hapless comrade of the sea. Immediately the recall signal was fired to the *Mary Stanford,* advising it that its gallantry was not immediately required; but so far as can be ascertained, that recall was not seen; it was certainly not acknowledged. The boat went on its mission; it vanished into the Channel smirr, and searched the steep seas closely for its quarry. It spent a matter of four hours in doing this, and then, obviously satisfied that it had done all it could, returned towards the shore, the men disappointed at non-success, but satisfied that they had quitted themselves like men. At 10.30 a.m. the boat was seen returning out of the mists, with blinding squalls harassing it. Fierce had been the gale when she went out, it was fiercer by far now—coming away in frantic flurries; working itself up to a yelling crescendo of spite. But the boat appeared to be shaping well for the harbour mouth; her coxswain was an accomplished pilot, and a staunch, well-tried hard-weather man. The men on duty at the coastguard lookout hut, a mile and a half distant, made her out plainly through the hurrying thickness; she seemed to be running at ease, with a high following sea, certainly; but behaving well. As the coastguard were congratulating her crew in fancy, a gasp of horror was torn from their throats—the boat suddenly swung high on a white-crested comber, and capsized—instantly, like a flash of lightning. Immediately her crew were hurled into the boiling cauldron of the sea. Two men were entangled under the boat —a Liverpool-type lifeboat, non-self-righting.

The drama was enacted under the gaze of many horror-stricken eyes. The alarm spread like lightning; and as quickly as might be a crowd of willing helpers collected on the beach; making every effort to aid the crew of the boat as the hurrying waves brought them in—since the tide was making, and, helped by the storm, setting towards the harbour. But these efforts were unavailing; no man of the Rye boat came to shore alive. Anon the unfortunate boat was cast ashore by the sea that had mocked its gallantry and made a plaything of it; and with its piteousness came six lifeless bodies; a tragic harvest of the Channel seas.

At once this little village, so tiny and yet so immense because of its history and the sterling courage of its people, was plunged into woe. Seventeen men had perished in a breath, almost— and though seventeen men may not represent more than a casual handful to the average township, these seventeen were to all intents and purposes the entire adult fishing population of Rye Harbour; there was hardly an able-bodied breadwinner left to maintain the dependents. At one sweep the Channel had robbed a community of all that was most worth while to its existence. The wail of woe that went up from the women and children of Rye was echoed through the length and breadth of Britain when that day's papers told the stark details of the story. Here was the old brand of glorious heroism made manifest in its most appealing, most striking form. Here was the age-old sorrow of womenkind and infancy revealed in all its poignancy. Here an epitome of our island story was written for all men to read and wonder over: a simple story, yet sublime in its stark grandeur—the breadwinners of a community destroyed in fulfilling their duty that was not to themselves but to unknown strangers.

Sad-eyed women, bent with agony and loss, commenced a

tireless search among the keening breakers that fringed the shore, praying that the pitiful flotsam they sought might be gifted to them by that insatiable sea. But not all at once did the Channel disgorge its prey. Nine drowned bodies came to harbour slowly, at long intervals; they dotted the beach as mementoes of such bravery as must still thrill the world. Not until three months later did another victim return to his home-place; and one man, John Hird, was never given up by the element to which he had unhesitatingly sacrificed himself.

Under a lowering sky, on November 20th, fifteen bodies were borne with seemly reverence to the weather-bitten little church of Rye Harbour; and there, in the presence of thousands of sad-dened mourners, drawn from all England by the narrative of sterling devotion, were interred in a great grave. So consider-able was the assemblage that the little churchyard could not con-tain one tithe of it; only the officiating clergy, the immediate relatives, and the official mourners could attend at the graveside; but the roads outside were packed densely; and the sorrow of England at brave men gone to their gallant rest was made mani-fest in the bent heads and the heavy sighs that were but the echoes of uncried cheers in adulation of a bravery that the cen-turies and the softnesses of civilisation have not destroyed. Un-der great masses of wreaths sent in admiring affection from the country over, under laurels and yew, the coffins were lowered to the silent home that welcomes the coward and the hero alike, that had never welcomed more gallant men than these of Rye Harbour.

How it all happened no man may rightly say. At one mo-ment the watchers on the cliff saw the *Mary Stanford* riding the short choppy seas defiantly; at another their astounded eyes saw her overturn; but the misted distance blinded them to detail.

Into the controversy that ensued it is not proposed to enter; this is merely a simple chronicle of simple bravery, such as stamps our island story through the years. The Rye boat went out in course of its duty; the Rye boat failed to return alive; but the memory of those men who lie there within sound of the rushing seas that destroyed them must endure for the centuries as a constant inspiration to all who deem themselves worthy to walk in their gallant footsteps and fling defiance into the face of the greedy, treacherous sea. That England could do more than mourn with sobs and flowers was proved when, in answer to the Mayor of Rye's appeal, a sum of over £35,000 was subscribed to benefit the dependents of these godlike men, in addition to the pensions awarded by the R.N.L.I., which, appreciating service, sees to it that no innocent soul may suffer by its daring performance. And as the men of Rye Harbour proved to the world that courage is the dominant feature in our national character; so it behoves us, whose duty to mankind they attempted to perform, to order our future years in a manner to be worthy of their unexampled sacrifice.